Life

With Full Attention

Maitreyabandhu

*W*indhorse Publications

Published by
Windhorse Publications Ltd.
169 Mill Road
Cambridge
CB1 3AN
United Kingdom
email: info@windhorsepublications.com
web: www.windhorsepublications.com

First edition 2009, reprinted with minor corrections 2011, 2013.

Cover image © Mahananda
Front cover design: Geoff Sheridan
Printed by Bell & Bain Ltd., Glasgow

British Library Cataloguing in Publication Data:
A catalogue record for this book is available from the British Library

ISBN: 9781 899579 98 3

About the Author

Maitreyabandhu is an experienced teacher and member of the Triratna Buddhist Order. Ordained in 1990, he has published articles on Buddhism and meditation in the UK and abroad. He is a published poet and has worked in such diverse fields as the visual arts, opera and alternative health. Maitreyabandhu has often presented Buddhism in the media, including television and radio. He is currently the director of Breathing Space, the London Buddhist Centre's health and well-being programme. He lives and works at the London Buddhist Centre in the East End of London. This is his second book.

Acknowledgements

This book grew out of a six-week mindfulness course I initiated at the London Buddhist Centre in 2004. The course, entitled 'Living Practice', was designed to guide people on the path of mindfulness. To support people's home practice, I developed a day-by-day diary, including specific guidance for a daily mindful walk, mindful moment and meditation. This book grew out of that diary.

This book would not have been possible had it not been for my teacher Urgyen Sangharakshita. It is primarily his inspiration, clarity, and rigour that has guided my Buddhist practice these last 24 years. My understanding of mindfulness, meditation, and Buddhism arises, in the most part, from his vision and insight. Likewise my preceptors Subhuti and Suvajra – I have gained tremendously from their exemplification and guidance. I hope they have influenced every page of this book.

I want to take this opportunity to thank my editors at Windhorse Publications – Jnanasiddhi, who encouraged me to write the book in the first place and read my initial drafts, and Caroline Jestaz. I particularly wanted to thank Caroline for her suggestions for revisions, changes and cuts. This book is a much tighter, more focused and useful book thanks to her. I want to thank Geoff Sheridan for the beautiful front cover design, as well as for his generosity, warmth and wit. And Peter Wenman for his wonderfully clear page layouts. My thanks also go to Sue Griffith for her hard work researching this book. I also want to thank my old friend Mahananda for his photographs. Unfortunately, Mahananda died suddenly not long before publication. Photography was one of his many passions, so I'm delighted to use some of his work on the cover of this book.

All my friends have supported me in writing this, especially Paramabandhu, Jnanavaca, Maitreyaraja and Manjusiha. I feel particularly fortunate to have such good friends. The book has benefitted enormously from the opportunity to teach at the London Buddhist Centre. I thank everyone who has contributed to the work of the Buddhist Centre over its 30 year history. I also want to thank Gary Henson for his kindness and support, as well as for providing me with a room to write in. And Jane Henson and Martyn Cook for letting me stay in their lovely sea-view home in New Zealand – an ideal place to write – as well as for whisking me off to wonderful cafes whenever I needed a break from the keyboard!

Contents

Introduction

Seeing the blossom

I REMEMBER AN INTERVIEW with the television dramatist Dennis Potter. It was conducted when the writer was dying of cancer, when he knew he only had a few weeks to live. It is a remarkable interview: Potter sitting in his grey suit, sipping champagne, smoking 10 to the dozen, taking swigs of liquid morphine now and then to ease the pain. He talked about plum blossom in his garden.

'Last week, looking at it through the window as I'm writing, I see it is the whitest, frothiest, blossomest blossom that there ever could be.' He continues, 'The nowness of everything is absolutely wondrous, and if only people could see that... there's no way of telling you, you have to experience it, but the glory of it...'[1]

The interview is a testimony to what life could be like if only we were aware of death, if only we knew how brief and transient life is. As Dennis Potter puts it, 'The fact is, if you see the present tense, boy, do you see it! And boy, can you celebrate it!' When we set out on the path of full attention we are trying to see the 'blossomest blossom', we are trying to live with the kind of present-tense vividness that Dennis Potter celebrates in his last TV interview. But it's difficult to do that with so many things competing for our attention. Modern life is extremely complicated, especially if you live in the city. Most people have to juggle full-time work, family, and social life all at the same time. There are always emails to catch up on, parking spaces to find, food shopping to buy, mobile calls to make, heating bills to pay, vacuuming to do. There's your daughter to take to the swings, the car to go to the garage, your suit to be dropped off at the dry-cleaner's. All this complexity forces us to the surface of ourselves. We don't have the time to experience things deeply. Our minds are set on rush, on multitask.

If we want to experience life more deeply – if we want to see the 'blossomest blossom' – we need to look at how we live. We want 'life satisfaction' but what we get, in the West at least, is choice. We have a strong tendency to believe that more choice leads to more happiness. When you travel business class, for instance, one of the main things the airline offers, apart from more leg room, is more choice. So we tend to want more money, so we can have more choice, so we can be happier. But this can have negative consequences. We easily become paralysed by too much choice, and we often choose badly. We choose things that don't in the long term (or even in the short term) make us happy – cigarettes, fizzy drinks, junk TV. And of course choosing which school to send our children to, what filling to have in our bagel, or which airline offers the cheapest deal takes time. The more choices we have the longer we have to spend making those choices. We don't get that time back. Worse still: the fact that there is so much choice undermines the satisfaction we feel with the choices we make. A crowd of choices presses in on our lives; one consequence of this is that it is more and more difficult to give any of those choices full attention.

Of course, one of the main reasons we find it hard to live in present-tense awareness is because we're in no fit state to do so. We can't enjoy things if we are hyped up, stressed out, exhausted, or in a bad temper. To enjoy something we need an enjoyable object – the sight of plum blossom, a walk in the country – and we need a subject capable of experiencing enjoyment. In other words, we need to be in a state of mind that is receptive enough, clear enough, calm enough, to enjoy things. Simply surrounding ourselves with pleasurable objects won't do it. We need to be in a good state of mind.

It's strange, when we come to think about it, that of all the things we learn – from algebra to circle dancing – so little is said about the mind and how we experience things. We miss the one thing that absolutely determines whether the holiday in Majorca is enjoyable or the new IT job rewarding. Our state of mind filters everything. We cannot make the most of life if we are distracted by trivialities, rehearsing arguments in our head, or getting irate about how long it takes to make an online booking. If we want to live well, we need to attend to the mind. Of course, we don't have to. We could just party, shop, watch daytime TV, or surf the internet. It's up to us. No one is going to make us live with full attention. But I believe that if we want to be happy, if we want to feel that life is going somewhere – rather than just going round and round in circles – we need to attend to the mind. If you agree, then it will be worth your while reading on.

I imagine that most people picking up this book will want to learn how to live more deeply and richly; they will want to develop present-tense awareness. But some will read this book because they want to solve the mysteries of life. The reader I have in mind might well be happy enough – at work, at home – and perhaps they don't have any particular childhood traumas to unearth; they just have this nagging 'Is this it?' feeling, the sense that life should add up to something more than career, family, and pension. And what I imagine this person wants, as they read, is not just advice about how to be happier and more relaxed (fundamental though that is); they will want to find out about reality, and about how to gain insight into reality. So I want to talk to that person as well. I want to talk about how Buddhism concerns itself with gaining insight into reality.

This book follows a journey of awareness, from remembering where you put your keys to transcendental insight into the nature of reality. It is a journey that I am currently undertaking. I encourage you to join me. Much of what I write arises from my years of practice, from my struggles and my successes. The guiding influence is my own teacher, Sangharakshita, without whose wisdom I would have nothing much to share. I hope that this book helps you to live with full attention. I hope it helps you to see the blossom.

Introducing the course

I have designed this book as an eight-week course in cultivating full attention. Mindfulness has many different facets. So we'll start relatively simply with 'day-to-day mindfulness': remembering to recharge your mobile or switch off the oven. After that we'll explore mindfulness of the body, mindfulness of sensations, inner narratives, spiritual teachings, the environment, other people, and, finally, reality itself. It is more effective to learn systematically, so we'll take it a step at a time, learning one aspect of full attention then adding another as we go along. By the end of the book, I'll be guiding you in a daily 'mindful walk', suggesting regular 'mindful moments' – an island of awareness in your busy day – and recommending particular approaches to daily meditation.

You don't have to be a Buddhist to read this. We're not going to rush into metaphysics; we're going to take it a step at a time. I've been practising mindfulness and meditation for over 20 years. I'm a member of the Triratna Buddhist Order – an international Buddhist movement devoted to communicating the practices, attitudes, and insights of Buddhism. So I'll be sharing my experience of all that with you. But you don't have to be a Buddhist to gain from this book; you don't have to be particularly spiritual. All you need is curiosity, a desire to learn, and a willingness to put what you learn into practice.

Planning

Developing present-tense awareness means doing whatever it is we are doing wholeheartedly, fully. It's not saying we shouldn't think about the future.

One of the challenges of mindfulness is making sure that we plan carefully and prepare sufficiently – whether we're going ice-skating or on retreat, whether we're planning a meeting or a journey. Things go better if they are well organized. The difference between a poorly prepared business meeting and one with a properly thought-through agenda can be very marked. The first often results in tetchiness and impatience, whereas the second can be quite satisfying and lead to good decisions being made on the basis of fruitful discussion. If we want things to run smoothly and time to be used effectively, we need to plan and prepare. Of course, much of our planning is to do with maximizing pleasure and minimizing pain. That's fine. We just need to get better at it. We need to notice what really brings satisfaction and happiness and what actually causes pain. Planning is only problematic if we forget to notice the future when we get there, if we're so hooked on preparing for pleasure that we forget to notice the pleasure we actually experience! Planning can be the expression of fear and anxiety – the attempt to organize things so that nothing ever goes wrong, which of course is impossible. But this doesn't mean that planning itself is wrong. We need to plan sensibly, and then attend fully to what we have planned for. So our eight-week course in full attention will include planning: preparation, thinking about the future, organizing our time, even making dates in our diaries or setting our computers to remind us of our next meeting. That's part of mindfulness as well.

What is mindfulness?

'What is?' questions have limited value. They're fine for practical purposes – what is a Victoria sponge cake, a motorbike, a gas bill? We can get useful answers to these kinds of questions, especially if we fancy something sweet, or want to get somewhere fast, or find ourselves short of cash. But if we ask 'What is?' questions about qualities we are trying to develop, the answers are far less illuminating. When you buy your first set of paints, you don't start by asking yourself 'What is art?'. You usually don't read about the history of art or about what various critics have said about its social, historical, or political value. You just splash some paint around and see what happens. You find out about art by doing it. Similarly, when you start to practise mindfulness you don't need to be completely clear about what mindfulness is and where it leads. You can just get on with it and find out as you go.

So let's do that now, just as we might with a new set of paints. As you sit and read these words, see if you can notice the weight of your body. Are you tightening your thigh muscles, or curling up your toes, or furrowing your brow? And can you feel the warmth of your clothes, the texture against your skin? Are there any sounds you can hear – your partner cooking something in the kitchen, the distant wail of a siren? What do you see around you? Stop reading for a moment and take things in: the colours, the shapes, and the direction of light. Can you smell anything? What about any taste in your mouth? Then pause for a moment, and notice your breath. You don't have to close your eyes; just feel the breath in your body. Where do you feel it most? Do you feel it in your belly or in your chest? Is your breath quick, or is it slow and heavy? Now notice the weight of your body again...

That's mindfulness, or at least that's one aspect of it. Of course, there's more, a lot more. This whole book is trying to answer the question 'What is mindfulness?'. If you have just tried the above, then you have already set out on life with full attention. It's as simple as that. The real answer to 'What is mindfulness?' is found in your experience.

Mindfulness is something you do, like volleyball or cooking; it's not an abstract theory. And it's not something that can be pinned down to a final definition – just as you can't pin down 'art' or 'beauty'. One description of mindfulness is 'paying attention in a particular way: on purpose, in the present moment, and non-judgementally'.[2] That's fine as far as it goes. It's enough to get us going. But it's only the beginning. You'll have to read this book, and put it into practice, to really discover what mindfulness is.

Approaching this book

Mindfulness is something you can practise on a plane, waiting at the post office, or eating a takeaway. It's not religious. It's about paying attention. This whole book is about paying attention.

In this book, I want to explore the different levels and dimensions of mindfulness. I want to address the issues a reader might face when they try to put mindfulness into practice. And I want to clear up some of the common misunderstandings that I encounter when I teach meditation and mindfulness at the London Buddhist Centre. I begin each chapter by exploring some broad themes for cultivating awareness. For instance, in the chapter on mindfulness of the body, I suggest that you eat a healthy diet and take regular exercise – obvious things perhaps, but no less important for that. Then I go on to recommend specific daily practices, such as particular ways of cultivating mindfulness of your body on your daily 'mindful walk'.

I recommend that you take up the book in the way that I intended: that you read it and try to put it into practice over the next eight weeks. Obviously, it may take you longer than eight weeks, which is fine. Have a look at your diary and see if you can find an eight-week slot that is fairly standard, fairly typical, and, if possible, fairly routine. It's best not to choose a period that includes a business trip to Berlin, or a move to a new home. Try to choose a time when you are not massively busy, or at least not much busier than usual. But don't put it off. If you think now is as good a time as any, then start. Don't wait for the ultimate peaceful, hassle-free eight weeks – for most of us, that's not going to happen.

And don't worry: I'm not assuming you have plenty of free time. I do assume, however, you have work to do, people to see, things to accomplish, children to get to school. The art of mindfulness will be learning to bring more attention to the sort of things you already do. I'm not trying to add another task to your jobs list. For instance, I'm going to be introducing a daily 'mindful walk'. But this walk should be one you are already in the habit of taking – to the bus stop, the gym, or the train station. I am not expecting you to put lots of extra time aside. Having said that, as the book progresses, I will be asking you to notice more and more aspects of your experience. I have designed the eight-week course so that it develops gradually. With each successive week, I'll introduce new exercises to cultivate full attention. The course is cumulative – teaching one aspect of mindfulness and then adding another as you go. I'll also be asking you, as we go along, to reflect on the issues that arise when you practise mindfulness, and to jot down these reflections in a notebook. And, at the end of each week, I'll be asking you to review how your week of practice has gone. Did you remember to cultivate mindfulness? How did it go? What issues were you presented with? How did it leave you feeling?

And remember, this book is not a wonder-cure – something that will change your life without you having to do anything. I will be expecting you to make an effort. I will be asking you to cultivate mindfulness and authentic happiness, and this will require energy, persistence, and perseverance. I'll be encouraging you to practise mindfulness every day, to cultivate your strengths and virtues, and to put aside 20 minutes each day to meditate. In other words, I will be assuming that you want to live with full attention. So you need to be prepared to put some time aside to cultivate mindfulness. The more committed you are to the course, the more you will get out of it.

Thought bubbles

As you read, you will notice that I have written some short pieces
indented into the page and marked with a small icon, a bodhi
leaf for instance. I think of these as 'thought bubbles'. They are
reflections, specific applications, and further explorations of the
path. You could read them as you read the book, or you could
skip them, or dip into them at any time you like. They are like
those short 'thought for the day' slots you sometimes hear on
the radio. I mostly limit myself to three in each chapter and
I've tried to keep them pithy. The thought bubbles have three
broad themes: 1. Reflection on this week's theme — such as on
the 'mind and body problem' (bodhi leaf icon) 2. Specific applications of the teaching — such as how to work with physical
pain (lotus leaf icon) and 3. The path of full attention — exploring how one stage of the path relates to another, or arises out of
another (dhamma wheel icon).

Cultivating the right spirit

It's important to approach all this in the right spirit. We need an
attitude of exploration. When we explore something, we don't have
a particular aim in mind. We're just exploring. We're bound to get
lost from time to time, or find ourselves in dead-ends. That's all part
of it. We'll need to keep our sense of humour and cultivate a lightness of touch. Having an overly goal-orientated approach will be
counterproductive, as will being too determinedly self-improving.
Try to follow the course as I have written it. At the same time, if
you find yourself getting tired of me suggesting yet another way to

cultivate mindfulness, just ignore it, or try it out later. You don't
have to do everything I suggest. You can pick and choose. I'll remind
you about this as we go along. But remember: you're in charge. If it
all feels a bit much, you can simply drop one aspect of practice – you
might decide not to write in your journal, or you might decide to
lie in bed with the Sunday papers instead of getting up to meditate.
What I suggest is that if you skip something – an approach to mindful walking, a particular exercise – you put a note next to it in the
margin, so you can come back to it later. Of course, you might find
yourself drawn to some of my suggestions but not to others. That's
ok too. Not everything I write will be useful for you.

At the same time, be wary of letting yourself off too easily, or giving
up at the first setback. The main thing is to stick with it. Don't worry
about what you don't (or won't) do. Just keep on paying attention. It
will have its effect. What we are trying to do is cultivate a thread of
awareness – a golden thread that, as we practise, becomes stronger
and stronger. Each time we notice the weight of our body on a chair,
or our chattering thoughts, or what it is we feel – we are cultivating
this thread of attention. Gradually we become the thread: we live
our life with full awareness. But at first the thread easily breaks. So 'a
little and often' is the key. Be gentle and patient, don't be too earnest,
and at the same time cultivate self-discipline. It's like going to the
gym: you just have to go – it's no use thinking about it!

And be conscious of the diet effect. It's well known that the best day of
a diet is the first day. It's the day you feel most motivated. But it usually wears off. Soon enough you're sneaking out for a jam doughnut.
You have to build that into your expectations. You might feel inspired
at first – but like as not, at some point you'll want to forget all about it
or resist. Part of the path of full attention is wandering away from the

path. It's important not to get disheartened about that: it really is part of the process. The issue is how far from the path you wander, and how quickly you can get back. I've tried to counteract the diet effect by gradually building up the level of mindfulness as we go along. It's best to start with realistic aims rather than grand ambitions.

Find your own way

As you flick through the ensuing chapters, you might think, 'I couldn't possibly read this and put it into practice in the next eight weeks, it's just too much!' So find your own approach. You might, for instance, just read it without doing any of the exercises I recommend. That would be fine – after all, that's what you normally do with a book! Recently I started reading something on poetic form, on how to write in iambic pentameter and how to compose a sonnet, but I stopped because I didn't have time to do the writing exercises. It would be a shame if that happened to you. Just reading this book will have a beneficial effect. One of the Buddhist teachings I'll be highlighting is 'what you dwell on, that you become'. So just reading about awareness, about full attention, will help you become more mindful. As I say, don't let yourself off too lightly; don't fall into the diet effect and give up after a fortnight – but at the same time, try not to be overly fastidious about how you go about putting this book into practice. Find your own way.

What is meditation?

For the moment, and without getting stuck in the 'What is?' question, let's just say that meditation is a period of intensified mindfulness. When we are mindful, we notice what is around us and inside us – the shadow of a poplar tree, the song of a sparrow, the thought we have just had about a problem at work. We notice these things consciously. We try to experience them fully. Meditation is an intensification of that kind of awareness. But, in meditation, the emphasis is on noticing your mind, understanding your mind, and changing your mind. In meditation, we are noticing our mind with our mind. It is possible to meditate while walking or sitting in a chair and looking at the garden, but usually we sit still and even close our eyes – we withdraw from the world of activity to explore an inner world of quality. And often we use an 'object' to meditate on: we observe our breathing or we try to cultivate calm, wellbeing, and loving-kindness.

As my intention is to introduce mindfulness gradually and systematically, I won't be expecting you to meditate in weeks 1 or 2. In week 3, I introduce various relaxation exercises and breath-work. It's only when we get to week 4 that I suggest you establish a daily meditation practice. After that, and as the weeks go by, I'll provide more and more detailed instruction. Of course, you might be meditating every day already, in which case you can take my suggestions as a part of your ongoing practice. Otherwise, simply follow the day-to-day instructions. I've written them so they can be stand-alone practices or serve as particular emphases in your daily meditation.

I'll be suggesting that you meditate for around 20 minutes each day and I'll be asking you, if you have time, to jot down a few notes about your meditation each day – it will help you be more objective about how the meditation has gone. If you don't meditate on a particular day, mark that missed day in the margin of the book. This will tell you how often you actually meditate. Crossing out the missed days will provide something of a reality check. It will also mean that you can go back to those particular meditations later on, should you wish to.

Finding a mindfulness buddy

If at all possible, team up with a 'mindfulness buddy'. One of the things I notice again and again when I teach mindfulness is how easily people assume they are the only one who's forgotten to do the mindful walk, or who hasn't managed to meditate. If you share your experience with others, you usually find that they are working with exactly the same issues. Talking about it helps. It helps you keep things in perspective. It helps refresh your enthusiasm. It supports your motivation. It will also, very likely, deepen your friendship.

Obviously, don't browbeat someone into doing the course with you. Just see if there is anyone around who would like to join you. Then try and get in touch with them at least once a week. You could make a phone date – say on a Sunday night after you've written your review about how the week has gone. Or you could set up an online chat room with others doing the course. Or you could be in email correspondence. You could even meet up and talk!

Buying a journal

I suggest that you go and buy yourself a new journal. Find one that you can carry with you all the time, one that can be slipped into your jacket pocket or put into your handbag. Make sure you have it at hand for the duration of the course. As the weeks go by I'll be asking you to note things down, so it will be handy to have a notebook on you at all times. If it helps, choose a notebook that feels special, one that makes you want to write in it.

Check your diary and start

So, having had a look in your diary, start the course. But first of all take some time to think about what you would like to get out of it. See if you can come up with three aims. Make sure they are realistic, achievable, and specific, nothing nebulous and grand such as, 'I want to be a source of love in the world'. Worthy though that might be, it will be difficult to know if you have achieved it, and it sets you up to fail. Keep your aims as down to earth and practical as possible. An aim might be, 'I want to do the whole course and not drop out' or, 'I want to find creative ways of cultivating mindfulness at work'. Take your notebook and take some time to fill in the table on the following page.

YOUR AIMS FOR FULL ATTENTION

1. Aims

Spend a bit of time being as clear about your three aims as possible. Then fill in the left-hand column. Leave the right-hand columns clear so that you can evaluate your aims at the end of the course.

My aims for Full Attention	Evaluation - Have I achieved what I'd hoped for?		
	Yes	Improving	No
1			
2			
3			

2. Obstacles

Then try to think of obstacles that might prevent you meeting your aims, such as, 'I often stay up late, so I would find it difficult to get up early to meditate', 'I fear my partner might think this is another one of my fads and not support me in doing the course', 'I am prone to thinking that I am not making progress and therefore give up easily.' Really try to imagine possible obstacles: 'My parents are visiting for a week!' Jot them down in your journal.

3. Supports

Then try to think of supports and strategies that will help you overcome obstacles that might arise – just being aware of potential obstacles will help you prepare to meet them. You might decide to meditate during your lunch break (you know a local church you can go and sit in). You might ask your partner to do the course with you, or you might explain what you are trying to do and enlist their support. You might ask a mindfulness buddy to help encourage you not to give up. Whatever your supports are, write them in your journal.

Mindfulness makes life vivid: you feel more deeply, think more clearly, act more fully. You appreciate the simple things – the sight of a moorhen, the sound of a football bouncing, the taste of blueberries. Full attention is a kind of relishing of things. But if we're late for work because we've forgotten our bus pass or left our power-lead at home, we'll be in no state to relish anything. So we need to start with the basics – remembering our PIN number, having a place where we keep our driving licence, sorting out the kitchen cupboard. It may not seem very exciting, it may not seem very spiritual, but it will make all the difference.

Day-to-Day Mindfulness

Mindfulness of small things

HAVE YOU EVER WALKED into the kitchen to get something, only to forget what it was you were looking for? Have you stood at a ticket barrier searching your pockets for train tickets? Have you forgotten an appointment; lost your car keys; forgotten your passport; mislaid a vital piece of paper and had to go through the contents of your wastepaper basket? You are not alone. Something like 130,000 items of lost property are left in public transport and taxis in Greater London every year. This includes around 10,000 mobile phones, 7,000 umbrellas, and 6,000 pairs of glasses. If we imagine multiplying that across all the cities of the UK and across Europe, it adds up to an awful lot of forgetfulness! Each lost item causes pain – a wince of realization, a pang of regret, a fit of accusation.

Week 1

Set up positive routines

Cultivate a sense of mastery

Complete your cycles

Reduce input

Notice the consequences of unmindfulness

The predominant feeling of contemporary life is of lots of bits – bits to be finished, started, filed, read, applied for, cancelled, organized, emailed, tidied, sent, remembered, checked, documented, or binned. It's a recipe for stress. But it is not going to go away. So we need to pay attention to this bitty aspect of life. We need to explore day-to-day mindfulness.

When we practise mindfulness, we are trying to learn that small things can have a big effect. This is true of our emotional life, our communication with others, and our day-to-day mindfulness. How much time do we waste looking for the remote control or trying to find our house keys? We have statistics for how much of our life we spend in the bathroom or surfing the internet, but how much time do we spend looking for our address book, our sunglasses, or our train tickets? And we can forget that, when we lose something, we often get in a bad mood, which in turn sets off a chain reaction: we get bad-tempered with a work colleague; they get tetchy with the receptionist; they take it out on the cleaner. We pass on our irritations like pass the parcel.

When we are unhappy, frustrated, or angry, we so often look to the big stories – childhood traumas, the state of the world. We would be better off looking to make small, practical changes to how we lead our lives. For most of us, life is not full of momentous events and overwhelming emotions but of small things: the car to be serviced, toys to put away, an online booking to be made. Life goes better, runs smoother, is happier, if we attend to the small things. So mindfulness needs to start here: remembering the baby-wipes, double-checking our flight-departure time, prioritizing our to-do list. This is day-to-day mindfulness.

Take day-to-day mindfulness seriously

For some reason it's difficult to take this aspect of mindfulness seriously. The things we forget are usually fairly trivial – a mislaid document, a forgotten appointment. We can usually make do. And after the panic, the rush, the searching, and the blaming, we usually forget about it. Being a 'scatterbrain' can even become part of our personal charm; it can even be another way of getting people to do things for us! Then there is the question of temperament – some people do seem to be more naturally organized than others.

One of the reasons we find it hard to take day-to-day mindfulness seriously is because we fail to understand that actions have consequences. This simple fact of life is central to our path of full attention. Again and again, as we explore each new dimension of awareness, we'll find ourselves trying to learn that actions have consequences – for ourselves, for others, and for the planet. As with so many other so-called 'small things' – from how we joke about other people to how we eat our supper – we can easily think, 'Oh well, it doesn't matter, it's not worth making a fuss about.' We forget to add up all those acts of unmindfulness. We don't notice their cumulative effect. We fail to realize how much happier we could be if our lives ran a bit more smoothly. And we often find it hard to see that our lack of day-to-day mindfulness affects other people – that we make their lives harder when we forget to call them, mislay books they've lent us, or turn up 20 minutes late.

Remembering things, finishing what you started, planning – they are all part of growing up. As children, our parents check we have our packed lunch, our mittens, and our schoolbooks. They remind us to go to the toilet before long journeys. They get us to put things

29

away. Parents are a child's mindfulness. So growing up means taking responsibility for all this – not waiting around for someone to tidy up after us or remind us to do our income tax returns. Mindfulness, spiritual life itself, is about growing up.

Fail better

Day-to-day mindfulness is surprisingly difficult to practise. There are so many things competing for our attention. We write to-do lists, scribble little reminders, but inevitably things get forgotten, mislaid, or overlooked. So right from day one we need to remember what Samuel Beckett, the Irish playwright, wrote: 'Try again. Fail again. Fail better.'[3] If we're afraid of failing, we'll fail to learn. This is as true for table tennis as it is for day-to-day mindfulness. We need the courage to fail, to persist with failure. This means not losing heart, not giving ourselves a hard time, not expecting perfection, and not condemning ourselves. It also means admitting failure, coming clean with it. Failure is a part of life. There's nothing wrong with it. Our failures are only negative if we try to wriggle out of responsibility for them. All we need to do is 'Try again. Fail again. Fail better'.

It has already happened

Day-to-day mindfulness needs to be practised with patience and a sense of humour. Getting into a terrible mood because we have lost something will only make matters worse. We need to re-mind ourselves that whatever it is that has just gone wrong, just been mislaid or broken, it has already happened. Mindfulness is what happens next. If we reverse our car into a post because we're not concentrating on what we're doing, that's our fault.

But going over and over it in our minds and berating ourselves won't improve matters. We need to accept responsibility, say sorry, and do the next thing: phone the garage. We need to accept the situation we're in. It has already happened. We cannot make it un-happen. We take full responsibility for what we've done (or not done) and admit it; we're even willing to say, 'It's my fault, I'm to blame.' We need to make reparation if needs be – pay for the bumper to be mended – but none of that is helped by self-condemnation. We need to accept the situation with kindness and patience, and say to ourselves, 'It has already happened.'

First practice week

Day-to-day mindfulness means attending to the small things so that we can concentrate on the big ones. We need to find strategies that help us get on with what's important in life and stop us having to think about what isn't. Take kitchen scissors, for example. You probably have a pair in your cutlery drawer. They are useful for opening vacuum-packed coffee bags or packets of pasta. If you try to open this kind of packaging with a kitchen knife or your bare hands, they tend to split or tear badly – spilling coffee grounds or pasta shells over your worktop. So it's handy to have a pair of scissors. But they often go walk-about – your daughter goes off with them to cut pictures out of a glossy magazine, your roommate takes them to his room. You end up searching the cutlery drawer and going through the drainer. You become irate. You start blaming someone. You tear the coffee bag open and spill the contents. You have to get the dustpan. It's a small thing, I know. But if the scissors were in the drawer where they're meant to be, then you wouldn't have to think about them at all: you would use them, have your breakfast, and then go off to work feeling happier and calmer.

Mindfulness is sometimes talked about in terms of doing everything very slowly and deliberately – noticing every movement of the body, every flicker of feeling. Whilst this can be useful, especially on re-treat, what is really needed is the kind of mindfulness that allows us not to have to think about the whereabouts of the kitchen scissors, or where we keep our passport.

So this first week of full attention is about sorting out the small things so we can attend to what's important. It's a week of setting up the conditions for mindfulness to arise, a week of looking at how we structure our life – how we pattern it, organize it and order it.

Set up positive routines

We could start by establishing positive habits. Routine is a way of building shape in our lives. It helps us to persevere when we feel under-motivated. It is a way of making time for activities – Spanish lessons or trumpet practice – that our hectic timetable could easily overwhelm. Routines are sustaining and have a morale-boosting effect. People who don't have them don't usually have much energy, are not very effective with their time, and tend to miss out on things. Of course, routines have dangers as well – it is tempting to pack too much into them, and they can become rigid and inflexible – but without them we usually don't develop the kind of spiritual stamina we need in order to make progress. There is a value in doing some-thing out of 'force of habit'. If our circuit-training class takes place every Sunday, the habit of going protects us from the whim of the moment – from whether we feel like going or not. In the same way, meditation needs to become a positive habit (as we will see). This is often a sticking point for people who come to the London Buddhist Centre: they value meditation, they see the benefit of it, but they struggle to make space for it. Regularly getting to the meditation cushions is the biggest challenge. Habit is the biggest helpmate. Once a positive habit is established, it helps us to meditate or go training without having to exert willpower.

Check your diary

So, this week, think about the place of sustaining routine in your life. Are there things you want to do that you somehow never find the time for – attending yoga classes, learning to swim, cooking a meal at home? Why don't you get around to them? Think about the shape of your week. Are you burning the candle at both ends? Would it be worth planning a quiet night in once a week so you can read, relax, or do nothing? Does your week have some kind of shape to it that sustains you, or is it all very ad hoc? Is it too full of self-improving activities? Are you out every night?

Try to set up some sustaining routines for the next week – or two, or eight! You could decide to get up every morning half an hour earlier, pencil in going to the gym twice a week, or take the longer walk home through the park every Friday. You might think about your work routines – are they productive? Do you have work routines?

Make two resolutions

Try and come up with two resolutions. It might be that you (1) go on a creative-writing course, and (2) go swimming twice a week. Then, see if you can think of something you could actually do – something that commits you to your intention, confirms that you mean it. For instance, you could book for that creative-writing course, or you could buy a pair of swimming goggles. Using the help of others – your mindfulness buddy for instance – could be invaluable in this. For instance, you might agree to meet a friend at the pool. Or you might talk to them about your habit of leaving 10 minutes late for work. You might promise that for the next week at least, you'll leave on time. Then make a date at the end of the week to talk to them about it. Write down your two resolutions and accompanying actions in the 'week review' below. But remember: positive habits can take a long time to establish, so you may well need to be patient. What will help you most is some action that confirms and strengthens your intention.

Motivation

There is a common misconception that we should want to do something before we actually do it. If we don't feel like it, we take that to mean that we don't want to do it. This is fine for chocolate or beach holidays, but it is not useful when it comes to many of the things we find sustaining and satisfying. Very often we only feel the motivation to do something when we are actually doing it. Take swimming. The idea of going for a swim, particularly if it's raining, is not very appealing: the changing rooms are drafty, the showers feeble, the tiles cold and slippery. Then there is the question of how to get into the water – the macho dive into the deep end, or the gradual, painful descent from the shallow? But once you've got your head under the water and are moving, you start to enjoy it. You start to feel you want to go swimming. By the time you leave – your skin tingling, your body glowing – you're convinced of the value of swimming. You know that you'll need to remember this feeling the next time you resist the idea of a cold changing room on a November morning. Waiting for motivation to arise before you do something is de-motivating. Just do it. You'll soon want to.

Cultivate a sense of mastery

We need a sense of 'mastery'. Mastery is that pleasant sense of achievement when a task is completed – when that chaotic pile of documents has been filed away, when you have made the phone call you had been putting off for days, when that annoying bit of DIY is finished. Mastery is a sense of being in charge of what you do – instead of being at the beck and call of whatever happens to happen to you. It is the satisfaction of accomplishment.

Starting and finishing

Routines for starting and finishing can help foster mastery. They help you become more in control (in the positive sense) and more organized, as well as less rushed. When you get to work, for instance, do you plunge straight into your inbox? Emails are easy work. You don't have to think about what you want to do in that day, or what you need to prioritize. So it might be better to start by writing a list of the things you want to achieve before you log on. It's often suggested, for instance, that you don't start your working day doing emails. Instead, get on with something you can complete, or make substantial progress with. Otherwise it's easy to end up feeling that even though you've done lots of work – made lots of phone calls, sent lots of emails – you haven't really achieved anything. And it's that sense of achievement we're after. And just as starting well is important, so is finishing well. I write two or three mornings a week. I usually have lunch with someone. If I am not mindful, I write all the way up to the time I'm supposed to meet them. I keep forgetting that there are always a few things to do before I leave the house – back up my work, gather up my keys, turn off the computer. All this takes time. And I feel much better if I give myself that time, if I finish things off properly. When I do that, I experience mastery: I have done what needs to be done, backed up what needs to be backed up. I have not left the room with papers scattered everywhere, I have not forgotten my keys. Feeling self-possessed and calm, I can give someone my full attention.

Do three things now

A sense of mastery is important for wellbeing. If you're feeling de-pressed or overwhelmed with work, you may well feel better if you make a quick to-do list, and then do three of the most straight-forward tasks – tasks that you can accomplish immediately. For example, (1) put laundry in the machine, (2) take bottles to recy-cling, and (3) top up your pay-as-you-go account. Any three things will do. It will help you to feel in charge, and this in turn will give you the energy to start looking at the more complicated jobs. Just doing three things will help you feel in touch with a confidence-building sense of mastery. Either that or you could think of two things you could do this week that will help create an atmosphere of mindfulness. You might decide to (1) clear out your in-tray and file stuff away, or (2) tidy your bedroom and throw out clutter. The positive effect of doing simple things like this can be very surprising – they help foster mastery.

Complete your cycles

Our awareness tends to last only as long as something is useful to us. We forget things – and often enough we forget people – once they no longer serve a purpose. Like a teenager who litters the pavements after unwrapping a chocolate bar, we have a strong tendency to forget things once we don't need them. As I have said, training in mindfulness is about maturing as a human being. We might not leave our bedrooms in quite the mess we once did, but for most of us, there is still quite a lot of growing up to do.

So mindfulness means finishing our cycles – washing up after we've had our breakfast, putting the milk away in the fridge, wiping the table. It means finishing the whole sequence, not just the part of it that concerns us. It's about remembering that other people exist, that our actions (and non-actions) have consequences for them. It's remembering to put back the kitchen scissors.

And if we think we already do that, it might be worth thinking about rubbish. Usually it's at that point that we forget all about it. It is no longer part of our lives; it has no value for us... it's rubbish. But it still has consequences: massive landfill sites full of stinking refuse, plastic supermarket bags, soft drink cans, takeaway cartons, and rotting vegetables. Part of mindfulness is extending our imagination beyond what is immediately useful to us – beyond the wastepaper basket – to what happens next. So see if you can create less waste by recycling instead of throwing away.

Finish what you started

Perhaps you habitually leave the washing-up until the next morning, or assume your partner will do it. Perhaps you leave your work desk littered with documents. Perhaps you are not very good at clearing up after yourself. Again, this might be something you could talk to your buddy about, or your friends. We are often hypersensitive about what other people don't do – not cleaning the shower after them, not putting the bread back in the breadbin, leaving their documents in the photocopier – but we find it much harder to notice the things we don't do. So ask your friend, your flat mate, your mindfulness buddy, to gently point it out to you if you have left things half completed. Again and again, we'll find over the next eight weeks that to really develop mindfulness, to see ourselves objectively, we'll need to enlist the help of others.

Think of the consequences

See if you can extend your awareness beyond the immediately useful. You might start composting, or recycling. You might get an old-fashioned cloth shopping bag so you don't have to use the plastic ones. You might decide to make a particular effort to turn off lights when you don't need them, or make sure that you don't leave your computer on sleep mode.

Reduce input

The Buddha lived in a pre-industrial society, unimaginably different from our own. His followers led simple lives conducive to mindfulness, meditation, and insight. Our lives are different; we are bombarded by advertising, packed into public transport, or stuck in traffic. We seem to be always on the phone, or on the computer, or rushing somewhere, or being late for something. We often don't realize how stressful all this has become.

Our attention is so divided. We often find ourselves split between what we are doing and what we are thinking. We talk to friends whilst keeping an eye on the time and trying to remember what we need from the supermarket. We read a book whilst waiting for a text message. We work on a complicated spreadsheet whilst checking our emails and looking at news sites. There's always the radio on in the background. Our attention is constantly being pulled in different directions at the same time – advertising demands our attention and exploits it; we flip from song to song on our mp3 player; we multi-task. We live in a time of information-glut.[4] This divided state has become our basic mindset – so much so that we don't really notice how chopped up and unstable our minds have become.

Many of us are suffering from a chronic inability to attend. Deep experiences, satisfying experiences, are characterized by absorption – reading a novel, listening to music, enjoying a conversation. We need to set up the conditions that allow us to get absorbed in things. Often, all we need to do in order to get ourselves into a better frame of mind is get absorbed in something positive – weeding a flower-bed, playing badminton, listening to Bach. We need to wean ourselves off over-stimulation and over-consumption if we are to make progress with mindfulness. We need to make an effort against the colossal force of consumerism – even if it only means restricting our television viewing hours, or the time we spend on the internet. So try and think of some specific things you could do (or not do) to help you become more concentrated and less divided. You might write some resolutions down or make a resolution with your flat mate or your partner. For instance, you could decide to have an evening a week where the house is silent – no radio, music, or television – so you can read a book in peace.

Here are some suggestions. You could:

- Choose not to eat and watch television at the same time.
- Resist channel-flipping.
- Limit the amount of time spent surfing the internet, or playing video games.
- Set some time aside in your working week when you concentrate on one task – without checking your incoming emails or answering the phone at the same time.
- Prepare a meal without having music on, or go for a walk without being plugged into your mp3 player.
- Decide to turn everything off – your phone, your computer – after 10pm.
- Decide not to go clothes shopping for the next month.
- Lock your TV in the cellar for a fortnight.
- Have one evening a week when you go technology-free – when you don't stare into a computer screen, send text messages, or watch TV.

Commit yourself to reducing input for a period of time. But remember to be realistic. If you decide not to have music on whilst you work, or not to watch reality TV shows, decide how long you intend to do that for – a week, two weeks, the whole eight-week course? Be specific and realistic. Enlist the help of friends if possible. Our friends can help us be more objective about what we can manage.

They might say, 'If I were you, I'd just try it out for a week and see how you get on with that.' So test yourself out a bit – go cold-turkey on shopping, on going to the pub, or on watching late-night DVDs. At the same time, be realistic – otherwise you're likely to react against it. And remember, reducing input is to do with increasing quality – so that you can give your full attention to other things, so you can become happily absorbed. Try and come up with three ways of reducing input this week and write them in the week review below.

Reminders

One of the first lessons to learn about mindfulness is that it is easy to be mindful but difficult to remember to be mindful. See if you can come up with things that remind you to be mindful, that reinforce your intentions for day-to-day mindfulness. You could put a note on your bathroom mirror reminding you to leave for work on time. You could set the alarm on your computer to go off every half-hour to remind yourself to take a short break. You could cross out an evening in your diary to remind yourself to have a quiet night in. Find creative ways of reminding yourself to be mindful.

Notice the consequences of unmindfulness

See if you can do some of the things I have suggested, and try to notice the effect. It might be that you just tidy your files on your computer, or do the first three things on your to-do list. If you do nothing else, use this week to take day-to-day mindfulness seriously.

It's easy to want to get on to the more esoteric aspects of spiritual life – insight, mystery, and meditation. But first we need to apply ourselves to the small things of everyday life. We need to take them much more seriously. The way we do that is by noticing the consequences of not being mindful. Notice every time you feel stressed, rushed, or bad-tempered, and try to see if day-to-day mindfulness (or rather the lack of it) has played a part in that. You might realize, for instance, that you habitually don't leave enough time to cycle to work. You jump red lights and arrive late, out of breath, stressed, and defensive. So note that down; try to see much more clearly how leaving 10 minutes late has all kinds of knock-on effects: try to be aware of the consequences – emotional and practical – including the consequences for other people.

Jot down which aspects of unmindfulness have what effects (remember you are doing this to understand yourself and learn how to change, not to reprimand yourself). You could do this at intervals during your day, or you could take time to reflect before you go to bed. You might notice that your unmindfulness runs along habitual lines – such as always leaving 10 minutes late for work. So you could ask yourself, 'What do I get from that? And where does being late for work start? Is it because I find it hard to get out of bed?' Try to get a sense of the cause and the consequences. For instance, being late for work results in a bad relationship with your boss, but it begins with your tendency to stay up late sending emails and logging onto YouTube.

Week 1 Practice Review

1. This week's resolutions

In the left-hand column below, write down your two commitments for the week. For instance: (1) you have decided to go jogging three times this week; (2) you've decided not to leave late for work. Write any actions that you have taken that reinforce your intention: you have set your watch alarm to go off when it's time to go to work; you've made an agreement with your mindfulness buddy. Then, at the end of the week, in the right-hand column, review how the week went. Were you able to stick to your decision? How did it leave you feeling? If you didn't stick to your intention, why not? What were the obstacles? Were you being unrealistic about the intention in the first place?

Your two commitments	Review how it went
1	
Any reinforcing action?	
2	
Any reinforcing action?	

2. Reducing input

In the left-hand column below, write down the three ways in which you have decided to reduce input this week. Review how that went in the right-hand column – did you feel better or worse? Was it a worthwhile thing to do? Did you manage to keep to your decision for the whole week? Are there other ways you could reduce input?

	I will reduce input this week by....	How did it go? What effect did it have?
1		
2		
3		

3. Mastery and completing cycles

Did you manage to cultivate a sense of mastery this week – at work and at home? Were you able to be aware of the degree to which you finish your cycles? What aspects of day-to-day mindfulness struck you as important and as something that you need to learn?

Write your thoughts here

We've been trying to learn the value of small things – organizing our lives so we're not always looking for our car keys, reading glasses, or umbrella. We've been trying to see how the conditions around us affect us. Part of a Buddhist life is going on retreat. When we go on a retreat, we give up all kinds of things – sex, shopping, cinema, newspapers, the internet. We give up those things so that we can concentrate on other things: mindfulness and meditation. Most people find that when they do this, even if only for a weekend, they feel happier, more alive, and more relaxed. Reducing input means making our lives a little more like being on retreat. It means concentrating on what really helps us become happy and live well. When we have a quiet evening in, when we turn off the TV and the radio, shut down the computer – we start to notice things. We notice our body and how our body feels, we notice how noisy our mind is, how speedy we have become. In other words, we start to notice the four spheres of mindfulness that the Buddha taught 2,500 years ago.

Body

Body awareness

I SOMETIMES WONDER what the Buddha would make of us. I imagine him noticing the information-glut I mentioned earlier, how our attention is dragged out of ourselves and manipulated by the mass media. He would notice how complicated and technological modern life is, how intellectually sophisticated we have become. He would think of us as having a dragon's head and a snake's body.

We have a dragon's head. It is full of thoughts and ideas, arguments and opinions, knowledge and shopping lists. It is a wonderful head in many ways, but it is overdeveloped. We have a snake's body. It is long and thin and without limbs: it is underdeveloped. The Buddha would experience us as being one-sidedly cerebral – with a marked tendency to rationalize, ruminate, abstract, and complicate. He would realize that, more than ever before, we need to cultivate the first of his four spheres of mindfulness: mindfulness of the body and its movements.

Week 2

Stress first-aid kit

The health audit

The mindful walk

The daily body scan

Alienation

Many of us are alienated from direct physical experience of our body. There are many reasons for this. We no longer have jobs that require us to use our body – apart from our fingertips and eyes. Our work requires brain power and admin-power but not physical exertion. If we don't use the body, we don't feel the body. Then there is our alienation from the natural world. We are nature. We have all the physical needs and instinctive drives of an animal. And yet many of us live in massive urban condominiums dominated by concrete pavements, steel-and-glass office blocks, neon lighting, electronic ring tones, and roaring traffic. Alienation from the natural world is alienation from nature in us, especially from our physical nature. Add to this our increasing reliance on computer technology. When it comes to alienation, there is nothing quite like staring into a computer screen. After a few hours of double-clicking, we emerge cyberspaced out, dehydrated, physically stiff, alienated from our emotions, and disconnected from our direct sense experience.

Another reason for our alienation from the body may be to do with literacy. As the ethnologist Ellen Dissanayake puts it, 'Literacy (even more than advanced technology) is the major possession that separates modernized from the unmodernized persons.'⁵ Without denying the enormous benefits of reading and writing, and without undermining the value of reason and critical thinking, it is worth remembering that literacy has its cost. The literate mind tends to favour abstractions, classifications into categories, analysis, and generalization. All this will be liable to distance us from direct experience – we will want to stand back from it all and examine it cognitively. Literacy favours thought and words over body and sensation. Just look at a toddler: sight, sound, touch, and sensation are a continual diet of fascination!

Negative views about the body, including religious strictures on sex and sexuality, coupled with the alienation from physical experience caused by urban life, the new demands of the workplace, and computer technology, mean that awareness of the body is especially important if we are to live healthy and productive lives.

The Buddha's four spheres of mindfulness are found in an ancient Buddhist text called the *Satipaṭṭhāna Sutta*. This *sutta* – or 'thread' of teachings – is a systematic guide to developing full attention. It teaches us how to cultivate mindfulness, what to be mindful of, and how mindfulness can lead to insight into the nature of reality. The first of the Buddha's four spheres is mindfulness of the body and its movements.

Awareness of the body has many benefits. It makes us calmer and more effective; our physical movements become more dignified and graceful; and it is an effective antidote to stress and anxiety. Body awareness makes us feel more truly alive. It is also a vital element in cultivating insight, as we shall see.

Mindfulness of the body means escaping from dragon's head and snake's body. It means noticing bodily sensations, staying with them, living from them. It means being embodied. It starts with noticing the stretch of our arm as we reach up to hold the hand-rail in a bus, and it deepens, as we practise, into a rich sense of physical aliveness and vitality. Eventually it becomes an exploration into the nature of experience itself. However, before we look at how to practise this first sphere of mindfulness, we need to look at our attitudes to our body – because how we think about our body determines how we experience it.

Seeing life whole

We tend to think of the body as being separate from the mind and from the 'self'. We often only pay attention to it when it aches or knocks into something. Our default position is to make the body into a 'thing', an attractive, well-groomed thing, perhaps, but a thing nevertheless. I remember a comic strip I saw as a boy, in which the brain was drawn as a control station busy with little men sending orders to the toes, giving instructions to the belly, screening pictures received from the eyes. I assumed that the relationship of mind to body was something like that – a 'ghost in the machine'. And even though we don't perhaps think about it very deeply, most of us have a similar kind of view: as if there are little men in our heads who say, 'OK, now lift the arm, now reach for the doughnut.' But it cannot be like that.

From one point of view, the body is like a complex machine. Like any machine, it needs fuel, cleaning, and maintenance. Like any machine, it breaks down, wears out; bits have to be mended. It is an object in space like any other object in space. We can hang a jacket on it or a pair of glasses, we can put it into a car along with golf clubs and the dog; it takes so much space, weighs so much, smells a bit. Looked at like this, the body is a material object just like any other material object – like chairs, wardrobes, houses, or planets. And yet we experience the body in a wholly different way: we experience it from the inside. We take this for granted, it is how we know ourselves, and yet it's worth considering just how remarkable this inner knowledge is. Of all the material objects in the universe – including other people's bodies – there is only one that we know from the inside. Everything else we only know indirectly, from the outside. If we want to understand the nature of experience, if we want to discover what life means, we need to pay attention to the part of the universe we know from the inside.

And our direct, inner experience of the body is mysterious. We experience life whole. When we walk in the park, we experience sights, sounds, thoughts, feelings, physical sensations, memories, associations, and so on, all at the same time. To think about something, we have to make it into a something that we can think about: a body, a mind. We have to break the whole into parts. But it is never really like that. We break up experience in order to think about it. We then forget that this is what we are doing, and start worrying about how it all fits together. We ask questions like 'What is the relationship of mind to body?' Of course, there is a value in examining distinct aspects of experience. We will be doing so throughout this book. We just need to keep reminding ourselves that that is what we are doing – creating distinctions for the purpose of exploration. They are not to be taken literally. There is a mystery at the heart of life. Part of that mystery is to do with the fact that experience is whole – that it cannot really be broken down into parts: into a 'body' and a 'mind'.

Consciousness and body always appear together. They are interlinked. Even in sleep, we dream with a dream body. And anyone who has meditated knows that the body has depth: our awareness starts with muscle and bone, weight and warmth, and then deepens into a kind of subtlety that is difficult to explain in words. As we go deeper in meditation, our body and mind seem to interfuse

51

more and more fully. We experience an emotional body; a subtle, mind-made body; a body that appears to contain and reveal memories, symbols, even teachings. This is the body we are setting out to explore.

The mind/body problem

The question of the mind's relationship to the body has always interested philosophers. It is one of the unsolved questions – 'the hard problem' as it has come to be called. Just how does a non-material mind interact with a material body? Or, to put the question the other way round: 'It is widely supposed that the world is made entirely of mere matter, but how could mere matter be conscious? How, in particular, could a couple of pounds of grey tissue have experience?'[6]

Arthur Schopenhauer, the great German philosopher, argued that the body was the physical manifestation of the mind – self-made flesh. He thought that mind and body were different sides of the same coin. He used the example of blushing. When we blush we do so at the exact moment that we feel embarrassed. We do not feel shy and then blush – both happen simultaneously: mind and body are twin aspects of a single reality. What that 'single reality' might be is very mysterious indeed.

One of the first things we need to learn is to become more aware of our inner physical sense. When I was a student, I was plagued by neck pains. They persisted so long and were so uncomfortable I was sent to see a specialist. He asked me if I tended to be an anxious person. 'Not at all', I said. I thought of myself as a fun-loving, arty type. Looking back, my shoulders must have been half-way up to my ears! I simply wasn't aware of it. It was only later through learning to meditate that I started to become meaningfully aware of my body.

One of my first discoveries was that I held tension automatically, and this made it more difficult for me to be aware of it. In our day-to-day lives, we often fail to notice habitual tension. Do we notice, for instance, that we instinctively clench our jaw or curl up our toes? How many of us rushing to work notice that we are frowning and leaning forward? Are we aware as we sit at our computer that our legs are twisted around each other?

Our sense of what is happening in the body is often extremely vague. Nowadays, when I lead meditation, I often remind my students to make subtle adjustments to their posture as they go along. What tends to happen is that they simply jolt themselves into the straight-backed, upright position that they think I want to see. This 'correct posture' lasts for a few seconds and then gradually collapses. What is needed, first of all, is to notice what is happening in the body and then to make subtle corrections. Being aware of our body in this way is more difficult than it sounds because what is happening in the body is mostly unconscious and automatic.

Many of us, for example, will tense our shoulders, neck, and belly as soon as our fingertips touch the keyboard of our computer. It happens involuntarily, without our noticing. Even when we do notice, and try to relax, we often find that our shoulders and belly become tense again as soon as we stop thinking about them. Our tendency to grip the body becomes automatic – a default position that the body goes back to once we have stopped being aware of it. But it was not always like this. When we were toddlers, our shoulder blades naturally dropped down the back, our head balanced beautifully on top of the spine, our belly was soft and round. We are probably not like that now. Our neck will tend to be habitually tense, our shoulders will often be pulled in and up towards our ears; we're likely to automatically suck our belly in. As we grow up, we unlearn the natural, healthy posture of an infant and learn to habitually hold the body in a dysfunctional and unhealthy way. This 'habitual holding' inhibits our breathing, reduces blood flow, increases toxic build-up in the cells, and interferes with our digestion.

So, first of all, we need to develop a much greater sensitivity to what the body is actually doing. With mindfulness, we learn to notice that we are subtly hunching the shoulders or constricting the throat – and then, by taking awareness into those areas, we begin to let them go. What we are doing here is relearning our natural posture, helping the body to find its way back to health. Over time, this new healthy attitude starts to become automatic. It is one of the reasons why the neck pain I experienced as a student gradually improved.

Cultivating sensitivity to the body

The key to cultivating awareness of the body is sensitivity. It is as though the body is tied up with knotted bits of string. Our task is to unpick the knots. At first it may feel as though we don't have the dexterity: we're too clumsy and ham-fisted. But as we go deeper with mindfulness, we'll find that gradually – without pulling too tight or getting impatient – we will begin to be able to allow the body to release and expand. We'll find ourselves working through layer upon layer of habitual tension, and letting go at ever-deeper levels.

But this is not merely a matter of 'relaxation', a simple loosening of tight muscles. The body is not a system of ropes and pulleys, wires and armatures needing adjusting and releasing. There is much more to it than that. Physical mindfulness is an exploration into the mysteries of embodiment. Letting go of habitual tension is as much to do with working with the mind as it is to do with releasing the body.

Stress first-aid kit

Notice when something is causing you stress. The fact you recognize that something is causing stress is the beginning of changing it. Look for symptoms, such as tensing in the belly and shoulders, frustration, irritability, compulsive thinking.

Catch it early. Stress reactions can speed up and fire off very quickly. The longer they go on, the more difficult they are to work with.

Do something! This may mean you need to stop doing something else – stop shouting, or working on your computer, or rushing. Bring your mind into your body; notice especially the lower part of the body (feet, legs, belly) and the weight of the body on the floor. This is an immediate antidote for anxiety and tension. Notice the weight of the body, soften the belly and shoulders, feel your feet.

Extend your out-breath. When we experience stress, we breathe shallowly and quickly and in the upper part of our body only. This makes stress worse. So a good antidote is to extend the out-breath. Here's how:

Blow the breath out slowly through the lips as if you were blowing through a straw. Try to blow the breath out as long as possible – a long, steady stream of out-breath. Do this without taking a particular in-breath beforehand. Then, when you can't breathe out any more, relax and let the in-breath flood in of its own accord. Try to extend the out-breath as long as you can (without collapsing or squeezing in the chest as you do so, and without forcing). Do this a few times, no more than five or six full breaths.

Extending the out-breath empties the lungs of the stale air lying at the bottom of the lungs. It is also the way of taking a full in-breath. The way to breathe more deeply is to extend the out-breath[7].

Whatever we feel, say, or do affects our bodies. Emotions are at one and the same time movements of the heart, narratives in the head, chemical and muscular changes in the body. And it works the other way round – changes in the body affect feelings in the heart and thoughts in the head. A sleepless night will leave us more vulnerable to irritability; a head-cold will make it more difficult to concentrate; monthly hormonal cycles cause mood changes. We can work on our minds by bringing attention to our bodies. Mind and body are interconnected.

A central idea in this book is that mind has depth, experience has depth. The body also has depth. Mind and body are not two separate 'things', as we tend to think in the West. Physical mindfulness is a journey into depth. As the mind deepens, so our experience of the body deepens: both become progressively subtler, richer, and more

integrated with one another. Any experience of depth has the taste
of integration. The immediate symptom of integration is the sense
of mind and body becoming one. This sense of oneness brings about
a release of energy. It's as though we are not a self but a collection
of selves, pulling in opposite directions, wanting different things,
competing for supremacy. This inner conflict, which we may hardly
be aware of, robs us of our energy. And this conflict is played out in
the tensions and holdings of our bodies.

What we are looking for is to gather up these conflicting selves into
one harmonious whole. Awareness of the body – returning the mind
into the body again and yet again – is an effective way of doing this.
Body awareness earths us, makes us more stable. All we need to do is
notice the mind going off into one of its little fantasies or diatribes,
and then come back to the feeling of the body – feet on the pavement, backside on the car seat.

As we develop physical mindfulness, we start to enter a subtler and
richer relationship with our bodies. We might start to notice, for
instance, how the body is the map and history of the mind. We
seem to store memories in different parts of the body. I have had
many experiences of this – or rather of unlocking this – especially
in meditation. I remember, in one practice, noticing pain in my
shoulders. I tried to feel it without wanting to push it away, without telling myself how painful it was, and then a memory seemed to
come out of it – a memory of hiding under a low bridge and feeling
scared. All the fear came flooding back, and in that moment my
shoulders completely let go. My experiences of memories 'coming
out' of the body fascinate me. They remind me of the mysterious
nature of experience: that 'matter' – the stuff the body is made up
of – is not mere matter.

The body has wisdom of its own

If we engage wholeheartedly with mindfulness, our bodies will begin to speak to us in an intimate, symbolic language. The best way to think about it is, once again, in terms of integration; the arbitrary and illusory distinction we make between body and mind – or, more poetically, 'body and soul' – softens and dissolves. We start to experience the body in a new way. Thoughts and emotions have a much more direct and immediate effect on the body. It is as though we become more connected up – thought with emotion with body. And because of this, the body starts to give us clues about what is blocking our awareness, what it is we need, how we feel, what our deeper motivations might be. We start to understand our lives through direct physical sense. Body and mind are experienced as two sides of the same mysterious coin.

As absorption deepens in meditation, we can experience strange physical symptoms. I remember my hands suddenly feeling like massive baseball gloves. A friend of mine felt he was meditating upside down, and was tempted to open his eyes just in case! These kinds of experiences have a Buddhist name. They are called *samāpattis*, which roughly translates as 'attainments'. They are signs that the mind is loosening up, that we are going in the right direction. Whilst they can feel unfamiliar and even a bit frightening at first, if we let go into them they are often very pleasurable.

Of course, the danger of reading about this kind of thing is that it can make us feel inadequate. Questions such as, 'Am I making progress?' or, 'Am I having deep experiences?' can be really unhelpful. I have known people who have psychic experiences – visions and the like – without seeming to become kinder or wiser as a result.

Any good meditation teacher knows that 'strong' experiences can be unhelpful, that people can 'get off' on them, start to feel special as a result of them. Becoming kinder, wiser, and more aware is the goal of life with full attention. That's what matters – not whether we have visions, unlock traumatic memories, or feel that our bodies are suddenly very large indeed. People seem to have these kinds of dramatic experiences earlier on in their practice of meditation. Gradually, as they become more integrated, everything starts to calm down.

The habitual body is the habitual mind

Body awareness is a journey from alienation towards integration and embodied consciousness. It is a path in itself, one that eventually leads to insight. Let's finally turn our attention to that, before we start to look at how to practise the first sphere of mindfulness in our day-to-day lives.

I tend to hold a lot of habitual tension in my guts. Relaxation and body awareness can help with this. I can notice the physical tension in my belly and keep letting it go – I can do this as I talk to a friend, attend a lecture, teach at the centre, or write these words. In meditation especially, I can release the tension very deeply. But – and there is a 'but' – the tendency to hold on in my belly has become instinctual. It goes into the very core of my being, far beyond conscious awareness. It has become how I hold on to 'me'.

The particular way we hold ourselves becomes hardwired. You can see this in how people walk. Some men walk like cowboys, others like nervous clerks; some women walk like timid librarians, others wiggle like film stars. Each walk expresses the person: they are quite unique and distinct. We hold our bodies, move our bodies, in a particular shape, a particular manner, and this becomes who we are. We identify with this shape. Even if it's uncomfortable, it feels like 'me'. We hold our bodies in a habitual shape that expresses our habitual self. Self is a habit – a habit of being a particular way, a tendency to react along particular lines. Who we are now is a consequence of what we have habitually done – whether we have habitually gotten angry, depressed, bored, intoxicated, argumentative, or ebullient. All this is inscribed in our bodies. My tendency to habitually react with anxiety and worry is my tendency to hold in the belly. We become who we are now by what we have repeatedly and habitually done in the past. Who we become in the future will be the consequence of what we do now. This 'me-making' is held in the body, somatized in the body.

Exploring how we hold the body – finding ways of letting that go – is loosening our attachment to self. At root, relaxation is a spiritual practice. If we really want to relax, if we want to stay relaxed, then we need to let go of self. Just notice how your body feels when you strongly want something – a pretty face, a sexy poster, a chocolate fudge sundae – notice what happens in your guts, in your shoulders. And feel what happens when you don't want something – when you wish that so-and-so would shut up! – notice how the body tenses up. Every time egoism arises, physical tension arises. The more self, the more tension. Egoism is painful. Don't take my word for it: cultivate body awareness and see for yourself.

From a Buddhist point of view, our most fundamental belief about ourselves is misconceived. We instinctively believe that we exist as a fixed and separate entity. We can't help thinking that behind our changing bodies – cells wearing out and being replaced, hair gradually thinning – behind our changing emotions, thoughts, and attitudes, there is an enduring 'self', a 'me' that all these changes happen to. But the Buddha said that no such self exists. It is an illusion, something we have brought into being by habitual mind-stories, predictable reactions, repetitive thought patterns. Self is the habit of being a particular way – which is also a habit of holding our bodies in a particular way. Let go of one and you let go of the other. As the great Zen patriarch Dogen said, when he recorded his experience of awakening, 'self and body quite dropped off'. We have nothing to lose.

Second practice week

Before I suggest practical, day-to-day ways of developing and deepening body awareness, I want to make sure we don't forget the basics: going for a run, getting an early night, eating a salad, avoiding junk food. This kind of thing may not seem very spiritual, but it is vital to wellbeing. At the risk of stating the obvious, let's briefly review some of the broader health issues of mindfulness of the body.

The health audit

Body mindfulness needs to include awareness of what we put into our bodies – what we eat and drink. It means, for instance, being mindful of not overeating. We need to make sure that most of what we eat has nutritional value. Dietary theories differ to the point of outright contradiction, but they all agree that fruit and vegetables should play a large part in our diet. When we consider that only 14% of men and 27% of women eat the recommended five portions of fruit and vegetables every day (not including potatoes), it's clear just how important this simple aspect of body awareness is. On top of that, many people only drink a fraction of the 2.5 litres of water that doctors recommend that we drink each day. Tea, coffee, and alcohol are diuretics, and this increases the likelihood of chronic dehydration.

Buddhism holds non-violence as a central belief. One relatively simple way of becoming more non-violent in everyday life is by becoming a vegetarian. The first ethical precept of Buddhism (as we shall see) is 'not to kill' – and as eating meat is killing, many Buddhists choose to become vegetarian. Whether or not we are moved by the moral considerations, it is fairly well documented that vegetarians live longer than meat eaters, and that vegans live longer than vegetarians. Vegetarianism and veganism are also more ecologically desirable and sustainable. By becoming a vegetarian or vegan, you are decreasing the harm you cause yourself, the planet, and all the beings on it.

We need to take regular exercise. This means doing at least 30 minutes of moderate aerobic exercise five times a week. 'Moderate exercise' means exercising to the point of getting warm, mildly out of breath, and mildly sweaty. Some studies show that the more vigorous the exercise the better, especially in preventing heart disease. In a way, it doesn't matter what exercise we do – though yoga or t'ai chi ch'uan have the added benefit of enhancing body awareness and aiding deep relaxation. At the very least, we should be regularly engaging in some enthusiastic gardening, or brisk walking. Once again, environmentalism and health coincide: what is unhealthy for the individual is unhealthy for the planet. The more we walk instead of drive, the better both Planet Earth and our bodies will be! The amount of sleep we need varies with age, life circumstance, and health, but many of us do not get enough. Our tendency to burn the candle at both ends has created 'so much sleep deprivation that what is really abnormal sleepiness is now the norm'.[8] Experts tell us that if we feel drowsy during the day – even when we are bored – then we haven't had sufficient sleep. If we routinely fall asleep within five minutes of lying down, we probably have severe sleep deficit.

I can only brush the surface of the health issues we need to face up to if we are to take mindfulness of the body seriously. It has now been shown, for example, that many food additives (such as E numbers) are linked with hyperactivity and disruptive behaviour in children.[9] A total of 67% of men and 58% of women are overweight and there is an epidemic of teenage obesity caused by the combination of junk food, lying on sofas, and playing computer games. It is estimated that one in five people drink alcohol to dangerous levels. If we include recreational drug use, monosodium addictions linked to fast food and over-reliance on stimulants such as caffeine, it's obvious that the physical health benefits of body awareness should not be overlooked.

This might be a good time to do a health audit on yourself, and, if they are willing, on your family. Use your journal. Create your own scoring system from 1 to 10 (1 being very poor and 10 being exemplary). Create categories such as: five portions of fruit and veg per day, regular aerobic exercise, 2.5 litres of water per day, 8 hours of sleep. See what your score is. You might also check the amount of alcohol you drink, and the number of cigarettes you smoke, if any. Do you use recreational drugs?

We often find that our good intentions are not borne out in actual experience. It's curiously easy to not notice this, as if we mistake intentions for actions. Because we mean to get to the gym or eat less junk food – even tell ourselves that that's what we're doing – we can fail to notice that we keep finding reasons for not doing it.

The mindful walk

The body is the anchor of our awareness. Every time we come back to the body, we are establishing ourselves in immediate sense experience instead of being 'somewhere else'. Tuning in to our physicality – the touch of our clothes, a cool breeze on our face, our feet striking the pavement as we walk – is a simple way of escaping toxic mind. Toxic mind is mind speeded up, stressed out, and compulsively active. In toxic mind, thoughts breed more thoughts; they proliferate into a noisy cacophony of recycled pop songs, negative self-talk, and repetitive views. Returning to the body is the first antidote to that.

But it would be unrealistic of me to ask you to be aware of your body all the time. Instead, it would be better to think of cultivating islands of mindfulness. These 'islands of mindfulness' will gradually affect your whole experience. So from now on I am going to ask you to take on specific mindfulness practices – practices that I will guide you through week-by-week. We are going to start by cultivating body awareness in a daily 'mindful walk'. I'm going to ask you to do this every day this week and then continue doing it until the end of the eight-week course. Of course you might forget, or you may choose not to do the mindful walk – we'll come to that later.

As the weeks progress, I'll be suggesting new approaches to the walk, approaches that explore the particular mindfulness theme we are exploring during that week. You will be more likely to remember to practise your mindful walk if you set up for it well – if you think ahead to the issues you are likely to face. As I've already said, if you plan carefully, you are more likely to succeed – and by 'succeed' I mean actually do it! Here's how to prepare:

Think of a walk you do every day. It's important, wherever possible, to choose a walk that you already do. If you add a special mindful walk to your daily routine, chances are you won't be able to keep it up. The walk should be no longer than 20 minutes and no less than five minutes. Over 20 would be too demanding, less than five would hardly be a walk at all! You might like to choose the first 10 minutes of your walk to the train station, or your walk to the bus stop, or nursery.

Describe your route. Using your journal, describe the walk you have chosen in as much detail as possible. Visualize it in your mind: 'I walk past the post office, the dry cleaners, and the supermarket, then I turn right down such-and-such a road with the park on my left...' Writing about it, visualizing it, you will remember to do it. It will serve as a prompt. I can't stress enough how remembering to be mindful is going to be the key to this whole course. So write it all down. If you can, draw a picture of your walk – it doesn't matter if you use stick men and lollipop trees – it will all help you to remember. The more detail, the better.

Jot down any issues you might face. Try to think of any possible obstacles you might face in trying to be mindful of your body during your mindful walk. For instance, you might meet people you know in the street, or you might have no set routine. Perhaps your routine is very different at the weekend? Perhaps you're a cyclist?

Try to think of creative ways of resolving those issues. What solutions can you come up with? You could plan a weekday walk to the train station and a weekend walk to the local park. You could dedicate the first 10 minutes of your bike ride to mindfulness – noticing your backside on the seat, and your feet on the pedals. You could park your car a little further away from work, or get off the bus a stop before your usual one. Write down what you decide. Be as specific as you can: one walk per day, for so long, with such-and-such creative solutions to such-and-such possible obstacles.

Review how it went. The mindful walk will be our daily practice in full attention. At some time in the day (perhaps last thing at night or as soon as you get into work), write down whether you remembered to do it and, if you did, what you noticed and how it went. I have provided a day-to-day review at the end of this chapter.

Walking mindfully is not about walking in a deliberate or artificial way. You don't even have to walk slowly. Yes, in some walking meditation practices, you walk very slowly indeed, and this has value (especially for continuing the effects of meditation), but you will look rather silly if you try to get to work like that! We have been walking perfectly naturally up to now; the only difference in our mindful walk is that we decide to pay attention to it. Here are some specific suggestions for how to do that:

Bring your attention into your body and its movements as you walk. Each time you get distracted, simply bring your mind back to your body in a relaxed and natural way.

Bring your attention into the soles of your feet. This is especially useful if you are speedy or anxious. Notice the weight of your body dropping through the soles of your feet and be aware of the support of the ground. Keep bringing your mind back to that.

Use a counting technique. You can use this along with awareness of the soles of your feet. It will help you stay with your direct physical sensations. Using counting is a really good way of doing walking meditation, especially if you are very distracted or stressed. It is also a useful method of building up concentration when you first set out on your mindful walk. What I suggest is that you count after each step, starting at one. Take a step and say, 'one' silently to yourself. Take another step and say, 'two', and so on up to eight. When you get to eight, count backwards after each step. Take a step and say, 'eight'. Take another step and say, 'seven', then, 'six', then, 'five', and so on. You could drop the counting after 5 minutes or so, or you could carry on counting for the entire walk.

Use words or phrases. Be aware of your whole body while you walk and add phrases that help you stay with your experience. You could repeat the words, 'walking mindfully', 'walking peacefully'. You might like to find your own words that connect you emotionally with the practice.

Walk and let go. Be aware of your whole body, paying special attention to any feelings of worry or anxiety, either physical or mental. See if you can just let go of those worries and relax your body and mind as you walk.

Bring an appreciative attention to your experience. This means tuning in to any pleasurable sensations coming in through the senses. Take pleasure in your body moving, the breeze on your skin, feelings of warmth or coolness. Notice pleasant sights and sounds – the colour of dahlias, the song of blackbirds.

Use your imagination. You might try using images, such as a lotus blossom opening under each foot as you walk, or the depths of the earth beneath your feet. This is a good way of getting interested in the walking practice.

The discrepancy monitor

All of us have what might be called a 'discrepancy monitor' – something that evaluates the discrepancy between how we are now (or how we think we are now) and some kind of model or ideal. The discrepancy monitor shows up the mismatch between the state of mind we actually are in, and the state of mind we wish, expect, or feel we should be in. This is inevitable and, often enough, helpful and healthy. It alerts us to the need for change, and stimulates the desire to reduce the gap between who we are now and who we want to be.

The problem is that many of the things that cause this sense of discrepancy relate to aspects of life where no immediate or obvious action can be taken – the desire to be happy or confident, for instance. All the mind can do is rehearse all the different possible ways of reducing the discrepancy. This can become a state of rumination – where we think we are trying to resolve the mismatch, but in fact we are making it worse. In this state of mind, we find ourselves constantly and painfully measuring what progress (or lack of progress) we have made towards closing the gap. This can cause an ongoing and undermining sense of always falling short of the mark, of not living up to our ideals, of not being who we should be. One of the challenges of spiritual life – of any life that involves the wish to move towards ideals, towards happier, calmer, wiser states of mind – is finding ways of activating change without becoming over-concerned with discrepancy. One of the antidotes to rumination (as we will see) is grounding our experience in the actual sensations of the present. The key to this is to bring the mind into the body.[10]

The daily body scan

You might find that taking up the mindful walk is enough for this week. Sometimes, it's best to decide to do one thing and to do it well. However, this would also be a good week to start a deliberate daily practice of body awareness. It will increase your felt-sense of the body and release pent-up tension. It will ground your energy in the body instead of allowing it to spin around in the whirligig of your mind. Practising the body scan will also help to set you up for next week, when I will be introducing meditation.

See if you can find 15 to 30 minutes each day to practise the body scan. Read how to do it carefully before you try it yourself. See if you can put time aside every day – you might find that you can do it as soon as you come back from work, or, if you work from home, you could do it in your lunch break. The body scan is about bring-ing your awareness into your body, filling the body with awareness. You are trying to notice what's there in the moment, bringing a non-judgemental awareness to whatever it is you can feel – com-fortable or uncomfortable, relaxed or tense. You are not trying to change your experience of the body, or even relax; you are just noticing what's there.

Lying down

Lie on the floor with your knees up and your feet flat on the floor and hip-width apart. Your head should be resting on a firm cushion, yoga block, or a couple of paperback books. Only the bony part at the back of the skull should be resting on the support – so you should be able to reach up and touch the back of your neck. You can get a sense of how far your feet should be from your backside by bringing the knees up to the chest, grasping them, and then letting them fall down with your feet flat. Basically, you are trying to find a place where you can balance your legs easily and naturally without having to grip. Have your elbows out to the side and your hands resting on your belly.

This is an excellent posture for your spine. Having your knees up like this means that the whole of the back rests on the floor (if you have your legs out flat, then the small of your back will rise up off the ground slightly). Having your head supported and your neck free means that the neck can fall back into alignment with the spine. Make sure you are warm enough. If you wear glasses, take them off, and put them on the floor above your head. If you put them on your chest, you might forget and roll onto them when you get up! When you're ready, close your eyes.

Scanning your body with non-judgemental awareness

Bring your attention into the body. Feel the warmth and weight of the body on the floor. Then cultivate conscious awareness, detailed awareness, of each part of your body in succession – starting with your feet and ending up at the top of your head: toes, soles of the feet, backs of the feet, ankles, shins, calf muscles, and so on... Try and be as detailed as you can (though this will depend on how much time you have put aside). Remember, you are trying to notice what you actually feel in the moment, not what you think you feel. You will probably notice that you can feel some areas of the body quite clearly, others hardly at all. That's fine. Just notice that – it's nothing to be concerned about. We are trying to educate our aware-ness to notice subtlety, nuance, and detail in the body, and this will take time and patience. So do what you can – work up from the feet to the top of the head, bringing your attention into each area.

Getting up

It is important not to jerk yourself forward to get up from this posture. You want to keep the alignment of your neck and spine. So, when you're ready, open your eyes. See if you can let 'the seen' just fall into your eyes without you having to look at anything. See if you can keep your awareness routed in your body. Often, when we think about moving, our mind jumps forward to the end of the movement – and this brings tension back into the body. So see if you can inhibit that tendency. You don't need to think about getting up at all. Your body will do that for you; just stay resting in your body, at home in your body. Let your eyes travel to one side and allow your head to follow; then let your whole body roll onto your side. Try to do this without lifting your head. When you are on your side, notice your belly – have you tightened your belly? Then, when you feel ready, roll onto all fours and then get up from there.

1. The mindful walk

Use the simple chart below to check if you remembered to do the walking practice. If you have time, jot down how it went. Were you able to work creatively (as you had planned) with the issues of doing your walking practice? How did the mindful walk leave you feeling – better or worse? Did you notice anything in particular about your body during the practice?

	Did you remember?	How did it go? What were the issues if you forgot?
Day 1	Yes/No	
Day 2	Yes/No	
Day 3	Yes/No	
Day 4	Yes/No	
Day 5	Yes/No	
Day 6	Yes/No	
Day 7	Yes/No	

2. The body scan

Were you able to do the body scan? If so, what did you notice?
Which parts of the body were you able to feel and which parts were
you less able to feel? How did doing the body scan leave you feeling?

Write your thoughts here

Awareness of the body and its movements is the first of the Buddha's four spheres of mindfulness. It is the bedrock of full attention. The body is our home. We can think of ourselves as living in such-and-such a place in such-and-such a town, but really, if we live anywhere at all, we live in our bodies. The first sphere of mindfulness is about becoming more and more at home in the body. All we need to do to feel a little bit happier is to go for a run, do some yoga, or take the dog for a walk. The body is our first port of call. If we want to de-stress or avoid becoming depressed, our first questions to ourselves should be: Am I getting enough exercise? Am I getting enough sleep? Am I eating healthily? The body is something we can always come back to – as you read this, attend a tricky business meeting, or drive to work. Whenever we are not sure how to cultivate mindfulness, we can just come back to the body and its movements – that's all we need to do. And of course when we notice the body, we start to notice how the body feels – whether it feels comfortable or un-comfortable, heavy or light, numb or tingly. So, in the next chapter, I want to explore this inner world of bodily sensations more deeply, and I also want to explore the feel, even the taste, of experience.

Feelings

What we can and cannot change

WE TEND TO ASSUME that happiness is a matter of avoiding unpleasant moments of experience and accumulating pleasant ones. But how wisely do we go about doing that? Let's look at the fundamental feel of life – pleasurable sensations, unpleasant sensations, and the sensations in between. Let's take a look, in other words, at the second of the Buddha's spheres of mindfulness: mindfulness of *vedana*.

Vedana is a Pali word. Pali is an ancient Indian language that only survives in Buddhist texts. It was once the everyday language of northern India – in contrast to Sanskrit, which was more scholarly. Traditional Buddhist texts come down to us in either Pali or Sanskrit. The word *vedana* is derived from the verb *vedeti,* which means both 'to feel' and 'to know'. *Vedana* is usually translated into English as 'feeling', but this can be misleading. When we talk about 'feelings', we usually mean 'emotions' – happy or sad – but this is not what *vedana* means.

Pleasant and painful vedana diary

The mindful walk

The breathing space

Working with physical pain

Setting up a meditation practice

Buddhism makes a distinction between our directly experienced feelings and the emotions we create out of those feelings. At first this difference might not seem very important. However, as we come to understand and practise mindfulness of *vedana*, we'll see that it has far-reaching implications.

Vedana is the texture of life; it is how life feels. Every sight, sound, smell, taste, and touch has *vedana*. To put it rather technically, all experience has a 'hedonic tinge'. We are aware of things – a tree, a friend, a summer's morning – and that awareness has flavour, has texture – it will feel pleasant, painful, or somewhere in between.

We experience an almost endless range of sensations. Take those different brands of chocolate you can buy at the lcoal shop. Some of them (usually the more expensive ones) will taste better than others. We will be able to taste the difference between a handmade Belgian truffle and a mass-produced Mars bar. We may not be able to verbalize that difference, but we will be able to taste it. And this is true for all experience, inner or outer; it has a particular flavour, even if we are hard-pushed to express that 'particular flavour' in words. Likewise with unpleasant and with neutral *vedana*; we experience life in a seeming infinity of degrees, shades, nuances, and textures. Life tastes. It might taste wonderful or mildly pleasing, horrible or slightly unpleasant. It might taste of nothing much at all.

This is as true for the physical senses as it is for the mind. Every memory we have, every thought we entertain, every idea we come up with, has *vedana*. Traditionally, Buddhism thinks not of five senses but six – the sixth being the mind. From a Buddhist point of view, thoughts and emotions are analogous to smells; they can be as pleasant as perfume or as nasty as the smell of cat pee.

All the things we experience – external and internal, mind and body, thought and emotion – have this feeling dimension. Mindfulness of *vedana* means bringing awareness to that, noticing how life feels, becoming more alive to the texture of experience.

The texture of life

Let's start by looking more carefully at unpleasant vedana. We do not like unpleasant *vedana*. We instinctively try to avoid it, push it away, get rid of it. We usually react to it as soon as we feel it. We react by getting into some kind of bad mood; we become angry, we blame other people or ourselves. A negative spiral easily develops. We experience unpleasant *vedana*. We react to that feeling with aversion. Aversion in itself is painful – it makes us feel even worse – and we react to feeling worse with still more aversion. Often there's a 'that's it' moment, a moment when we lose our temper, when we throw a screwdriver across the workshop, shout at the children, or decide that life is unbearable! All of this arises from an unpleasant sensation. If we want to become happier, we need to start there.

We cannot change unpleasant *vedana*. It is a fact of life. If someone cuts across us in traffic or spills hot tea down our trousers; if we're ignored by shop assistants or have to stand in crowded trains; if we get a headache or an income-tax bill, a parking ticket or a verbal warning, we will experience uncomfortable *vedana*. We cannot change the prickly feeling of fear we experience when we're about to give a presentation, make a speech, or teach a group of rowdy young students. *Vedana* is given. We cannot not have it. Of course, we can pretend not to have it, we can ignore the slight shake of the hand, but that's another matter.

What we can change is how we respond to painful *vedana*. We can notice that we are experiencing unpleasant sensations and then bring awareness to that. We can consciously investigate it, feel it through, taste it. When we do that, when we become aware of *vedana* as *vedana* – when we 'feel' and 'know' what we are experiencing – we begin to create a gap between what happens to us and the moods we get into as a result of what happens to us.

The Buddha used the analogy of two darts. The first dart, he said, is the dart of pain. It is unavoidable. Pain is inevitable – whether it is the agony of insomnia, the ache of lower-back pain, or the disappointment of failing a driving test. If we practise awareness of *vedana,* we can train ourselves to just feel it, bear it, be aware of it. But usually, the Buddha tells us, we shoot ourselves with another dart – this time it is the dart of our reaction to the first dart. As soon as we do that, we create more pain for ourselves.

Emotional pain threatens our wellbeing just as physical pain does. Our inbuilt response to feeling threatened is for the body to go into the 'fight or flight' reaction. Receiving a harshly worded email is a good example. We open it, and suddenly feel emotionally attacked. The body goes into fight or flight: dry mouth, butterfly stomach, tense muscles, increasing heart rate. This response is hardwired. It kicks off as soon as we feel threatened. We cannot make it not happen – although the degree of threat will vary depending on our temperament and mood at the time. Fight or flight has value; it concentrates the mind and prepares the body for action. The blood moves from the guts to the skeletal muscles, the eyes dilate so we can see better, adrenaline is pumped into our system. All this is vital if we are genuinely under threat. The difficulty is that this instinctive response, developed over millions of years of pre-history, cannot help us with so many of the things that modern life confronts us with – unpleasant emails, noisy neighbours, being kept waiting on premium telephone numbers. Full attention to unpleasant vedana therefore includes becoming aware of our fight or flight reflex and working so as not to exacerbate it. Unfortunately, like so many natural and automatic bodily responses, fight or flight can become a settled state – one in which we feel constantly on edge, physically wound up, restless, and short-tempered.

The problem of pain

Whether the cause is physical or emotional, we instinctively want pain to go away. We want it to stop now! This is fine for many of the experiences we have. It is an instinct for self-preservation that stops us causing ourselves harm, which we learn, rather traumatically, early on in life. However, after a certain point, aversion to painful vedana makes things worse. First, it tends to focus our mind on the object that we believe is causing the distress: the man having a loud conversation on his mobile, the, 'beat, beat, beat' of someone's mp3 player. Secondly, it makes us tense up our body. We generally tighten around painful physical sensations in an attempt to protect our- selves. Whilst this is fine for real injury, for everyday aches and pains this tensing merely contributes to our discomfort. Another aspect of this self-protective physical tension is that we do this when we feel emotionally as well as physically hurt. Sticks and stones may break my bones... but words can hurt as well.

It is difficult not to react to painful feelings, but it is possible. We can train ourselves to notice them and, counterintuitive as this may sound, relax into them. The alternative is to react with tension, frustration, irritation, and blame – which only makes the pain worse. Of course, one of the main reasons we push away unpleasant vedana is so we can make space for pleasant *vedana*. So let's move on to that.

The pleasure principle

When we invite friends around for a meal, we instinctively try to provide them with as much pleasant *vedana* as possible. We prepare tasty food, arrange the table with napkins and wine glasses. We intuitively understand the relationship between *vedana* and moods. We know our guests are more likely to be convivial company if they have lots of pleasurable *vedana*. Good moods and successful dinner parties don't automatically arise out of agreeable sensations – we know that – but they are more likely to.

And yet how much pleasure do we actually experience? However flavoursome the food, we have a tendency to only notice the first and last mouthful. The excellence of the dinner stays in the background of our awareness. And this is true for much of our life. We want pleasure – we spend money on it, rush through our to-do list to make time for it – but in the moment of having pleasure, we often forget to pay attention. We notice something is enjoyable only to move onto something else – we get embroiled in conversation, drink a little too much, start to think about how we'll get home. We complain of lack of enjoyment, whilst failing to notice it in the here and now.

So the first goal of mindfulness of pleasant *vedana* is relishing it, giving it our full attention. This direct awareness of pleasant *vedana* is the art of enjoyment. It affirms the spiritual value of innocent delight – the taste of rasmalai, the tingling of the skin as we slip into an ironed shirt. There is so much pleasure to be had in life, if only we can remember to turn our mind to it. I remember sitting on a park bench with my baby niece. I watched her watch two teenagers skateboarding. Every time they jumped, she'd giggle and kick out her legs with pleasure. It was a lesson in enjoyment. She'd not yet developed the predictive mind we adults have, the mind that says, 'Oh yes, I know what will happen next.' For her, each leap was an unexpected entertainment. We cannot get rid of our habit of prediction, but we can find our way back to innocent pleasure. I can do this most easily on retreat. On retreat I have the time to slow down and become receptive. I enjoy ordinary pleasures: a hare nipping into the undergrowth, the light shining through a jar of honey, reading a book. They are ordinary things. Nothing special. They are made significant by a mind that is calm, alert, inquisitive, and un-preoccupied – the kind of consciousness that meditation and mindfulness are helping us cultivate. Usually our minds are too distracted, coarse, pre-occupied, or over-stimulated to experience even a tiny part of the pleasures that surround us. Strange as it might seem, we need to cultivate the discipline of delight: the capacity to enjoy the simple things of life. This is more difficult than we think, because our habitual attitude to pleasure is so often counterproductive.

The discipline of delight

We are distracted from experiencing pleasure by wanting more of it. Just as when we experience unpleasant *vedana* we want it to stop, so, when we experience pleasant *vedana* we want to repeat it. We want more. This instinctual 'wanting more' takes our mind away from the pleasure we are actually experiencing. Our mind focuses on the idea of pleasure in the future, which means we don't fully attend to it now. It is the law of diminishing returns.

The law of diminishing returns is made especially clear if we think about our dinner-party scenario. Let's imagine we are one of the guests. The food is wonderful. As we near the end of the first course, we start wanting a second helping. As soon as we do that, we stop paying attention to the food on our plate. We experience a pang of anxiety. We worry that the other guests will get there first; that there won't be any left for us. So we begin to rush. The more we rush, the less pleasure we experience. The less pleasure we experience, the more we want seconds. The more we want seconds, the more anxious we feel that we might not get seconds. When our host finally replenishes our plate, it's never quite as good as the taste that prompted us to ask for a second helping in the first place!

It is this desire to repeat pleasures that causes the problem. Pleasure is addictive. The art of enjoyment, the discipline of delight, is to give our full attention to pleasurable sensations whilst not yearning to repeat them. This is quite a challenge. We evolved as a species in a wholly different set of conditions to those we find ourselves in today. For instance, we are predisposed to enjoy the taste of sugar. This predisposition was built up over millions of years of pre-history. For most of that time, food was scarce and sugar even more so. Enjoying sugar meant we would eat more of it, which in turn would mean we would be more likely to survive. It is only recently that sugar has become cheap, readily available, and plentiful. Our instinctive enjoyment of sugar is now a threat to our welfare. So when we are looking at our tendency to want more, we are looking at some of the most deeply encoded tendencies of the mind. The key to success is our capacity for awareness and reflection. The desire to repeat pleasure is in itself uncomfortable. We usually don't notice this. When we want something, our mind is preoccupied with what we hope to experience in the future, not what we are actually experiencing in the present. Because of this, we associate wanting with pleasure. But if we become aware of what it feels like to want, we'll notice it's actually unpleasant: it is a painful *vedana*, with all the tension that goes with that. And if we pursue pleasure too long or too ardently, it will inevitably become pain. Delicious food satiates and then bloats. And even refined pleasures – listening to classical music, for example – becomes painful after a while. Pleasure has in-built limits. No pleasure can be infinitely extended.

So we need to handle pleasure much more carefully than we think. Pleasure, to be genuinely pleasurable, has to have within it an element of restraint. The more we try to squeeze enjoyment out of experience, the more likely it is that what we end up with is pain. Piling pleasure on pleasure usually reduces the pleasure we actually experience. A frenetic weekend of retail therapy, cafés, and clubbing will leave us buzzing and excitable. Though we think we're enjoying ourselves, if we pay more attention to the quality of our experience, we often discover that we feel rather uncomfortable. Excitement is curiously similar to anxiety. It has the same physical tightness, restlessness, and agitation.

Excitement, like anxiety, makes it difficult to immerse ourselves in something. We cannot genuinely enjoy something unless we can abide in it, become wordlessly absorbed in it. In this sense, our richest pleasures tend to be the quieter ones – those moments of genuine and concentrated creativity, the appreciation of nature. Deeper pleasures have a distinctive inner radiance and softness. They feel different to superficial thrills. Deeper pleasures feel deeper – they have less 'self' in them. But this might start to ring alarm bells. Spiritual practice can easily be seen as pleasure-spoiling and over-earnest. Indeed, if spiritual life isn't understood properly, it can become those things. But training in full attention is training in pleasure, in what I call the 'discipline of delight'. An important aspect of life with full attention is learning the delicate art of maximizing pleasure without causing pain. The more we want, the less we get – it's one of those terrible laws of the universe. It is perfectly natural to want as much pleasure as possible. I certainly do. The question is how... and that 'how' takes us into the very heart of spiritual life.

Olives and cigarettes

If someone says something hurtful to us, we will experience unpleasant *vedana*. We cannot change that. What we can change is how we respond to unpleasant *vedana*. This is the key to spiritual life, the key to freedom.

There is, however, a dynamic relationship between how we respond to *vedana* and how we experience it. Take olives. I remember not liking them – their sour flavour and strange, fleshy texture. But then one day I tried to pay more attention to the actual *vedana* I was experiencing. I discovered that they weren't so bad. Before long, I was actually enjoying them. Similarly with smoking. When you first smoke cigarettes, they taste awful! They even make you feel nauseous. But soon you start to enjoy them. In both cases, the vedana seems to change. The context in which we experience *vedana* conditions the *vedana* we experience. My lower middle-class upbringing conditioned my response to olives – I came from a family that didn't go in for fancy, foreign food! It was as if the assumption created the unpleasant taste. Our expectations, even our prejudices, stop us examining direct experience. We mistake our reaction to things for the things themselves. With smoking, the addictive, biological factors change our feelings about cigarettes. We soon associate smoking with a break from work, with a little treat for ourselves; not with queasiness and coughing.

Vedana is experienced within a life context of association, expectation, and memory – and that will shape how we experience it. This means that as we change our reactions to experience – examining our assumptions and associations – we will change how life feels. We will gradually learn to stop confusing our reactions to experience with the experience itself.

The neutral in neutral

But perhaps much of our life is somewhere in between – neither especially painful nor particularly pleasurable. If asked how we are on this *vedana* level of experience, many of us would say, 'sort of, kind of, okay-ish'. Our day-to-day experience is often experientially neutral. This can be simply how things are – waiting for the checkout at a supermarket, emptying the dishwasher, 'just walking dully along,'[11] as Auden puts it, are not particularly painful or pleasurable experiences.

One habitual response to neutral *vedana* is to want pleasure instead – it's that moment when we slip away from our desk and go and buy a Kit Kat! If we have a lot of neutral *vedana*, we call this boredom. Boredom is more common, and more dangerous, than we usually

85

think. We will often go out of our way to avoid it. In many ways, our lives are an attempt to avoid suffering at one end of the scale and to evade boredom at the other. The classic formula for keeping the people appeased is 'bread and circuses' – bread to alleviate hunger and despair, circuses to stave off boredom. If the people become bored, they are almost as dangerous as if they become hungry!

Part of the reason for neutral *vedana* – why so much of our life can feel bland – is to do with lack of developed awareness. Our life slips by without our noticing it. We have not trained our mind to pay attention. Of course, there is much in modern life that militates against vividness. We are bombarded with information. Life is complex. People's attention spans are shorter than ever. All this contributes to a kind of frenetic and unstable energy that is incompatible with noticing nuance, shade, and subtlety. It is difficult to relish things.

The practice, here as elsewhere, is to turn our attention to *vedana* – stay with it, not react to it. However banal or routine life sometimes feels, we can still 'feel' and 'know' that that is what we are feeling. This is the practice of mindfulness of neutral *vedana*. We notice it, give our attention to it, explore its nuances and subtleties. When we do, we will discover that 'neutral' stops feeling neutral.

We could try this out by doing 'the raisin test'. Take a raisin. Look at it. Pick it up. Turn it over in your fingers. Smell it. Bring all your attention to it – the soft and crinkly surface, the shape, the faint perfume. Then put it into your mouth – give it your full awareness. You will find that the taste, which normally we would hardly register, becomes vivid. Our practice of mindfulness – body, *vedana*, and the other aspects of awareness we'll come on to – is a path of 'more life'. So often our wish for more life is expressed in a desire for more things. This is natural enough, but it doesn't really work. If we can deepen our mind, especially in meditation, we will find that 'less is more'.

The path of full attention means living directly – relishing the sparkle of street lighting on wet pavement, the jerky movement of squirrels, the taste of oyster mushrooms at a friend's dinner party. Whether *vedana* is pleasant, unpleasant, or somewhere in between, the more we notice it, the more we will create space around it. That space is vital to the art of happiness and to the discipline of delight. It is a space in which old habits die and new insights arise. If we can create a gap between our feelings and what we do with them, we are following in the footsteps of the Buddha.

Stages on the path

Each sphere of mindfulness is both a path in itself and a stage on the path. We can think about 'awareness of the body and its movements' as the first step, or as a complete way to Enlightenment. If we let go of the body entirely, we let go of self, and this 'letting go of the self' is the goal of Buddhism. But we can also think like this: first we develop awareness of our body, its weight and warmth, its movement – and then we deepen that awareness so that we notice how the body feels. In this sense, *vedana* represents a deepening of body awareness. It is the inner aspect of body, the inner aspect of life.

Vedana as a path to insight

The key to insight is the gap between vedana and everything else. Mindfulness of *vedana* means experiencing pleasant, unpleasant, or neutral sensations without reacting to them. This is the essential point of this chapter. It's easy to understand but difficult to put into practice. When we manage not to react habitually, we open up a gap, a creative space, between the incoming world, which we cannot change, and the outgoing self, which we can. In this gap, instead of merely reacting to whatever happens to happen to us, we respond. We choose the direction of our life. This gap between feeling pain and being angry, between wanting and grasping after what we want, is the point of freedom.

Freedom in Buddhism is essentially freedom from self. Much of the time we are a bundle of habits – repetitive behaviour patterns, ingrained habitual responses, unexamined attitudes. These habits dig grooves within the mind. Habit is our way of reinforcing self. Each time we notice *vedana,* we create a gap – and each time we create a gap, we transcend self. Self is nothing other than our tendency to react habitually to whatever happens to us. A life without reactive habit formation is a life free of self.

Freedom is what Buddhism is all about. We learn to bear the discomfort of a crowded train without getting ourselves into a bad mood, to enjoy the pleasure of a good meal without having to have seconds, to feel the tedium of decorating our bedroom without running out to buy lots of chocolate. This is going to be difficult. Like so many aspects of practice, we need to 'keep our respective hopes for the future within moderate, very moderate, limits'.[12] We need to be realistic. But if we train ourselves to notice *vedana*, we will gradually get better at catching the feelings out of which we build our emotions. As we do this, we will experience, at least from time to time, a new creative space opening between the pressures around and within us and our choices. The potential of freedom is always present. We can experience it at any moment.

Third practice week

Vedanas are the building blocks of our experience. They are what we build our moods and emotions out of. If we want to become happier, we need to learn the fine art of mindfulness of *vedana*. So I want to suggest that you take up quite a few things this week: a diary of pleasant and unpleasant events, reflecting on *vedana*, a daily breathing space, mindful walk, and meditation practice. That might seem rather a lot! See if you can do the daily practices and at least one of the journal exercises. It will be worthwhile. At the same time, make sure you're being realistic about what you can do – otherwise you'll simply create unpleasant *vedana* for yourself!

Pleasant and painful vedana diary

A useful way of exploring *vedana* is by keeping a pleasant and un-pleasant events diary in your journal. The diary will help you notice pleasant or unpleasant *vedanas* – catching them early before they have the chance to develop into moods or harden into attitudes. The diary will help you find ways of staying with your present experience rather than reacting habitually and unconsciously.

Noticing pleasant and unpleasant events

When we feel low, we have the tendency to stop noticing pleasant events. We overlook them and focus on unpleasant events and feelings instead. This can lead into a downward spiral. We start to feel that life is unfair, unpleasant, and un-enjoyable. The thoughts of being unhappy are in themselves painful and tend to lead to more pain. We stop noticing pleasurable *vedana*, and after a while almost feel immune to it. We can get so low that we can no longer take pleasure in things that we normally enjoy. The diary is a good way of counteracting this. We train ourselves to notice pleasant experiences at the time that they are happening. This helps us stay aware of pleasant experience rather than overlooking it or over-focusing on negative events. We have a strong tendency to react to unpleasant *vedana*. We often react with some kind of narrative; we say, 'Why does this always happen to me? Why are people always finding fault with my work?' Being aware of unpleasant *vedana*, and noting it in our diary, is about catching it early. It is about 'feeling' and 'knowing' that something feels unpleasant, and then leaving it at that. Negative states of mind are like lobster pots – they are easy to get into and difficult to get out of. The best way of not falling into them is to catch them early.

How to keep the diary

You could simply jot down pleasant and unpleasant experiences, using one page in your journal for pleasant events and another for unpleasant ones. Keep your journal with you. Try to feel the pleasant or unpleasant *vedanas* at the time they are happening. Become curious about them. Feel the texture of your experience in the moment. Make a mental note of them and then jot them down later on.

Alternatively, you might try something more thorough. Here's how.

1. Divide your diary into five columns. In the first column, write down, 'What was the experience?' For instance, say that one morning during your shower you noticed yourself worrying about work. Then, because you are practising mindfulness, you remembered to notice the pleasant sensations of being under the shower. So you write that down in the first column: 'stopped and noticed the pleasant feeling of taking a shower'.

2. Head the second column with, 'Was I aware of the pleasant feeling while it was happening?' So in this example, you would write 'yes'.

3. At the top of the third column, write, 'How did my body feel, in detail, during this experience?' The detail is important. Try to recall what the sensations felt like in your body, which of course implies that you noticed them physically, not just mentally. You might write about the awareness of your belly softening, the tingle of your shower gel.

4. In the fourth column, write down the heading, 'What moods, feelings and thoughts accompanied this event?' You might remember the feeling of relief and pleasure. You might have thought, 'How nice just to stop and notice' or, 'This is a good thing to do – before I was hardly aware of even being in the shower!'

5. Then finally, in the fifth column, write down, 'What thoughts are in my mind now as I write this down?' You might write something like, 'It was only a small thing, it took a few moments, but I'm glad I noticed it.' Or you might write, 'It feels good that I am taking myself seriously in this way. Even when I am busy I can find pleasure.'

Perhaps, after reading how to keep this kind of diary, it all seems a bit much; you're busy enough as it is without having to write a detailed account of your morning shower! Just do what you can. Notice pleasant or unpleasant sensations; feel them in the body, and help yourself become aware of them by writing them down. It doesn't need to take long; you can jot them down last thing at night or on the bus home. The diary is especially valuable if you are starting to feel low; it will help restore perspective. Try it out for a week. You might surprise yourself!

Learning more about vedana

If you have time, you might try using your journal to reflect on the week to come. As I have said, we tend to react to what happens to us along habitual lines. We tend to get into the same kind of scrapes – and if we are mindful, we can learn from this. So, on one page of your journal, write about a situation in the coming week around which you expect to feel unpleasant *vedana*. It might be commuting in the rush hour, or the daily battle of getting the kids ready for school. Try and think of a difficult experience that is likely to happen at least once during the forthcoming week. First of all, write down what usually happens, and how you feel when it happens. What are the particular flash points that you find unpleasant – being jostled on the tube, not being able to get a seat? Or is it the way your daughter always wants to go to the toilet just after you've left the house? Then leave the next page blank – we will write on that a little later on.

On the following page (after the one you have left blank), write down a pleasant experience you expect to have. Once again, try to think of something that will happen in the week, if possible more than once. Perhaps you are planning to go to a concert or you are in the habit of taking your mid-morning coffee break in a cafe. Jot down what it is you anticipate feeling. As with unpleasant *vedana*, try and be as specific as possible – the sort of feeling you expect to have in the body, the tastes, sights, the sort of mood associated with the pleasant experience, the kind of thoughts you tend to have.

During the week, when these things happen – the bus crush, the coffee break – try to use them as a cue to notice *vedana*. Having written about them and thought about them, you will be more awake to the experience when it actually happens. Then write what you actually experience on the page you have left blank. When you have a moment, compare the two. Is there a mismatch? If so, what can be learnt from that? How could you respond more creatively to the painful experience? How could you more fully enjoy the pleasant one?

The mindful walk

In this week's practice walk, I am going to ask you to pay particular attention to *vedana*. You could use the methods I suggested in the previous chapter, such as the counting technique. See if you can remember to do the walk each day, and, if you have time, jot down how it went in your journal. I've provided a review chart below for you to fill in as the week goes by.

But I want to stress that you're bound to forget to practise the mindful walk from time to time. You'll get to the bus stop or the office and realize you've forgotten all about it. No matter. Full attention often begins with remembering that we have forgotten. *Sati*, the Pali word for 'mindfulness', is related to the word *sarati*, which means 'to remember'. So the practice of mindfulness is to do with

93

remembering – both in terms of 'recollecting oneself' and in terms of remembering to be aware. Remembering that we have forgotten and not getting unduly frustrated about it will be an ongoing component in our practice.

Mindfulness can be like dieting: we're keen at first, but quickly lose enthusiasm. We need to be aware of this. We will probably have days when we simply refuse to do the walking practice. That's OK. We need to develop self-discipline and at the same time remember that, if our efforts are too willed, too tight, and too earnest, we'll simply react against the whole thing. Just have a go. Keep having a go. As the great Tibetan guru Padmasambhava said, 'Saying there are obstacles will get you nowhere; do what you can at the time.'[13] Try to get to know the texture of your experience, learn to tune in to it. Here are some suggestions:

Become aware of physical comfort or discomfort. As you walk, notice *vedana* in the body. What does comfort or discomfort actually feel like in the body? Try to make the distinction between what you think about it, and how it actually feels.

Become aware of the environment. As you walk, notice what surrounds you – an old lady with a shopping trolley, an advertisement for online poker, the sound of a truck revving at traffic lights. Become more attentive to your feeling response to these things. Notice the physical jarring caused by a police siren, the frisson of pleasure at the sight of a polka-dot dress. Feel how sights and sounds affect both mind and body.

Emphasize pleasant vedana. Pay particular attention to any pleasurable sensations of sight, sound, touch, and taste – the winter sunshine on your face, a dog running after a stick, the warmth of your coat. Actually look for pleasant sensations, however mild they might be.

The breathing space

A good way of cultivating mindfulness in everyday life is to practise the three-minute breathing space. You can do this anywhere – on the bus, at work, in the kitchen. The breathing space is particularly useful if you are starting to feel that things are getting on top of you. It's a good antidote to stress and negative states of mind. If you're stuck in traffic, if your computer crashes, if you're feeling overwhelmed – then this is something you might try. See if you can practise the breathing space twice a day.

1. *Stop whatever it is that you were doing.* If possible close your eyes. Sit with your feet flat on the floor and your hands supported in your lap.

2. *Gently scan through your body.* Notice the sensations in your feet and legs, the weight of your body on the chair. Are you sucking in your belly or tensing your shoulders? Soften your face, especially around your eyes.

3. *Become mindful of the sounds around you.* It might be the sound of a photocopier, or someone talking on the phone. See if you can broaden your awareness. You could listen to the traffic outside, the wind in the beech trees, a jumbo jet high above you.

4. *Then tune in to your breath.* Notice your breath coming in and going out. Follow a few breaths.

5. *Come back to your body and the sounds around you.* Then open your eyes and carry on with your day.

The breathing space doesn't need to take much time; two or three minutes is fine. And you don't need to make a big thing of it – you don't need to feel every single toe, or notice every sound. You just create a pause, an empty space. What often happens in day-to-day life is that everything speeds up – we multitask, we push on to get to the end of our to-do list. This can become addictive; every spare moment becomes an opportunity to send another text message or fire off a few more emails. When we get like this there is often an underlying sense of anxiety, which is fuelling our behaviour. This underlying anxiety tends to be experienced as feeling driven. This 'driven feeling' is to do with us – it is not to do with a particular task. It makes us feel on edge and uncomfortable. We usually don't want to stop and feel it. We'd rather press on and ignore it. Of course, pushing ahead to get things done can be exactly what we need to do – it creates a sense of mastery (as I mentioned earlier). It can even make us feel more relaxed: we no longer have that unwanted task hanging over us – the unopened bills, the difficult phone call. Sometimes our anxiety is to do with putting things off rather than getting things done. The difficulty is when 'pressing on' becomes a settled attitude, a basic fallback position; when our sense of accomplishment is only achieved by getting things done. We should be able to work, even work hard – but we should also be able to stop, relax, breathe, and forget all about it.

So the breathing space can become an island of calm and sanity in the midst of a hectic day. It creates a kind of buffer to our lets-get-on-with-the-next-thing attitude. It helps prevent it becoming addictive and counterproductive. We stop. We notice our body and the sounds that surround us. We breathe. Then we go back to our day a little more collected, a little less driven.

The path of meditation

We have probably already noticed how difficult it is to be aware. Even if we really value mindfulness, we often simply forget to do it. We get lost in thoughts, plans, and fantasies. Life slips by without our knowing – we are somewhere else. The systematic cultivation of full attention would be impossible were it not for meditation. Without meditation, it would be too much to ask ourselves to develop mindfulness in our daily lives. Meditation is a period of time set aside to cultivate awareness. It helps us know our mind and change our mind. Meditation is therefore indispensable to life with full attention. So, from now onward, I will be encouraging you to meditate every day.

Before I do that, however, I want to get a few things clear. Meditation is not primarily a technique – much less a recipe! It is not simply a matter of following a set of instructions, however useful those instructions might be. This is the reason why it is best to learn from an experienced teacher. A good teacher will exemplify the spirit of meditation. And it is this 'spirit' that is important. When I lead classes at the London Buddhist Centre, I am aware that I cannot really teach someone to meditate at all – at least not in the sense that I can teach someone to drive a car, or cook an omelette. My own teacher says that the spiritual life is, 'caught, not taught'. The same can be said of meditation and of mindfulness – you need to catch the spirit of it from someone who is in touch with that spirit.

This is not to say that technique is not important, that there aren't useful things to learn. Learning meditation is analogous to learning to sing. A good singer will learn their craft from other, more accomplished singers. They'll develop their vocal skills. They'll practise regularly. They will usually have ongoing tuition to help them refine their technique. They will learn about how to get out of, or not get into, bad habits. At the same time, a really good singer will go further; they will let something new come into being. This 'something new' is partly to do with their unique voice – with all the life experience that has gone into that voice – and partly to do with the potentiality of the moment, the inspiration of now. A good singer will take an imaginative leap, one that only occurs to them in the moment. It is backed up by skill, but it is more than skill. Meditation is like that. There is technique to learn and learn deeply. But we also need to be open to our own uniqueness – all the life experience that has led us up to now – as well as to the inspiration of the moment.

It is particularly in meditation that we turn our mind to the texture of experience. We learn to feel the distinction between the first and the second dart – between *vedana* and how we react to *vedana*. Much of the time we're caught up in thought – in repetitive self-stories and internal monologues. We are not usually mindful enough to notice the flickers of pleasant, unpleasant, or neutral *vedana*. In meditation, we train ourselves to search beneath the stories in our heads to the texture of *vedana* in our hearts.

We start with mindfulness of the body. We notice the weight of our body. We notice the grip of our jeans, the warmth of our hands, we notice if we are tightening our belly. We try to feel the body rather than think about it. Often we simply talk about the body in our mind; we say to ourselves, 'oh yes, toes'. We substitute words about experience for experience itself. Mindfulness of the body starts with directly feeling the sensations of the body in the here and now.

Then we deepen our awareness of the body by noticing *vedana*. We bring our attention to the belly, for example. We rest our attention there. We give ourselves time to tune in to *vedana*. And then we just wait. We might gently ask ourselves, 'Does it feel comfortable or uncomfortable, pleasant or unpleasant? Do any words naturally occur to us? Does it feel sore or tight, heavy or spacious?' Don't go looking for words; just rest in the sensation and see if any words or images spontaneously suggest themselves. Try to be patient and receptive. Then move on to another area of the body.

We may not be able to name all the sensations. That's all right – naming isn't so important. The important thing is to feel. Each sensation can be felt. This is true even of sensations we can't feel. Paradoxical as it might sound, absence of feeling can itself be felt. Things aren't simply missing from experience – erased – there's a felt-sense of absence. So, if we notice that we don't feel anything very much around our chest or heart area, we notice what that 'not feeling anything very much' feels like.

To do this, we need kindly awareness. When we meditate, we are not analysing our experience from a distance; we are trying to explore experience, feel it, allow it to open up to us. This means cultivating a sense of benign curiosity, a willingness to stay aware of ourselves – body, mind, and heart – with kindly awareness. The word 'mindfulness' can feel rather cool and cognitive. It might be better to call it 'heartfulness'. Our experience will not open up to us unless we can bring kindness to it. It is just the same as talking to someone – unless they feel that we have their interests at heart, that we are broadly sympathetic, they will not be able to open up to us. The attitude we bring to others makes all the difference. And this is the same with the attitude we bring to ourselves. We will probably need to work to cultivate this – consciously invest our attention with warmth. There are places in our minds that we do not like, that we have no patience for. There are places where we get thoroughly fed up. We need to take a kindly awareness into those places.

Working with physical pain

We need a gentle and kindly attitude if we are to feel pain and discomfort without reacting against it and thereby making it worse. We also need to be courageous. We need to be willing to move towards discomfort, rather than shy away from it.

We tend to polarize with pain in our mind; we feel it and at the same time don't want to feel it. So we need to consciously relax into pain – feel the discomfort in our shoulders or our back and breathe into it. In meditation, we can take our mind into a knot of pain and soften it from the inside, breathe into it, be with it. I sometimes imagine space coming into the painful area, or light. Or I just try to notice the changing sensations of pain. Relaxing into discomfort also means letting go of our stories about it: 'It's horrible! I can't bear it, it'll get worse.'

On one retreat, I was plagued by tinnitus, by a constant ringing in my ears. I was frightened the tinnitus would get worse, that I'd be driven crazy by it. The fear would arise in the meditation.

My internal narratives seemed to fill the universe: 'Is it still there? Will it get worse?' If I tried to ignore it, the 'trying to ignore it' was in itself a kind of focusing on it. But if I focused on it, I would become more and more hypersensitive to it and this would make it worse. I needed to acknowledge it with kindly awareness and then focus on relaxing and letting go. Every time a fear narrative would begin, I would notice it and then come back to softening my eyes and face. Very gradually, the fear subsided. So we may need to find the balance between over-focusing on pain, becoming hypersensitive to it and thereby exacerbating it, and simply ignoring it and wishing it would go away. Neither is effective. We need to remember that what we resist persists. We may well find that what we need to do is move between focusing with kindly awareness on painful *vedana* – being willing to relax into it and feel it – and then shifting our attention to a more comfortable area of our body. In this way, we acknowledge the pain and feel it, but without over-focusing on it.

For more help in working with pain, I highly recommend Vidyamala Burch's excellent and practical guide, *Living Well with Pain and Illness* (Piatkus Books, 2008).

Setting up a meditation practice

It's time to set up our daily meditation practice. We've looked at what meditation means, and why it's indispensable to a life with full attention. Now it's time to set up a routine so that we can actually sit down and do it!

Find time to meditate

Unless you already have an established practice, I suggest that you start by meditating for between 15 and 20 minutes a day. Most people can manage that. You will be more likely to meditate regularly if you build it into your daily schedule. Many people meditate first thing in the morning. But this is not a hard and fast rule. Just take a bit of time to think when would be best for you. When would you be most likely to actually do it? What's realistic?

Don't set yourself unattainable goals

If you set an unrealistic goal you will be setting yourself up to fail, and that will undermine your efforts. So don't decide to meditate for an hour every day before you go to the gym – you probably won't manage it. At the same time, don't be too floppy. I have heard that meditation teachers who have taught on death row at San Quentin state prison say prisoners sometimes complain that they don't have time to meditate! So be on the lookout for excuses – 'I'm too busy', 'I'm not a morning person.' See if you can meditate every day, or failing that six times a week, or failing that five times a week. Whatever. You don't need to get all het up because you miss a day. It doesn't have to be another failure. At the same time, try to develop the discipline.

Start and finish well

Pay attention to how you start and finish each meditation. A good routine will help. It's usually more productive to set regular time aside for meditation – rather than waiting till you feel like it. You might also like to create a place – a little corner of your room – that feels conducive to cultivating awareness. When you sit down to meditate, promise yourself that you'll try to explore your experience with benign curiosity, that you won't get all frustrated with yourself. And make sure you finish well. How you conclude the meditation will have a strong impact on how you feel about it afterwards. So don't get straight up and go and make a phone call. Pause. Take stock. Notice how the practice has left you feeling and see if you can take something of the meditation into your next activity.

This week's meditation diary

If you can, spend some time writing about your meditation in your journal each day. Just a few words will do. How did it go? How did you feel at the end? If you miss a day, just put a cross next to that day's meditation teaching. This is not to give yourself a hard time. Sometimes we think we're meditating regularly, when actually we've hardly done it at all! Crossing out the missed practices like this means that you can see how much your intention to meditate has been put into practice. And of course it means that you can come back and revisit those particular sessions later on. At the end of the book, I have written a brief description of two meditation practices you could use throughout this course, as well as a brief guide to meditation posture (see pages 318-323). But just for now, simply sit on a good, hard-backed chair – not a floppy armchair – with your feet flat on the floor, your lower back supported by a thin cushion, and your hands in your lap. In the first week of meditation, we will concentrate on the body and feeling. We are not trying to change anything just yet. We're just going to learn to attend, in a subtle and gentle way, to our experience.

Day 1. *Body awareness.* Begin by becoming aware of your toes and feet and then gradually work your way up to the crown of your head, becoming aware of each part of your body as you go. See if you can feel it, not think about it – even if you find you don't feel very much at all. Then rest in a broad awareness of the body for a minute or so.

Day 2. *Kindly awareness.* Become aware of your body as above, but this time consciously bring an attitude of kindly awareness to your experience – notice your sensations with a gentle, benevolent attitude. In your journal, jot down any differences you noticed as compared with yesterday's practice.

Day 3. *Noticing habitual tensions.* Cultivate body awareness as before. Then try to notice the more habitual and subconscious tensions in the body – especially in your face, neck, shoulders, and belly – take awareness into them, see if you can feel them more consciously. Then, without just wishing them away, see if you can relax into them and let them go.

Day 4. *Body and feelings.* Scan through the body once again. Start with awareness of your toes and work up to the crown of your head. Notice which parts of your body feel pleasant, which parts feel unpleasant (or less pleasant) and which feel neutral or numb. Just notice them with kindly awareness.

Day 5. *Consciously look for pleasant feelings.* Scan your awareness through the body as before. When you notice a pleasant feeling, dwell on that for a while. Remember: the feeling of pleasure might be quite mild – you are not looking for anything very pronounced. Keep coming back to pleasurable sensation. See if you can dwell in it.

Day 6. *Become aware of unpleasant sensation.* After scanning your body, try to experience discomfort more directly, without reacting to it with aversion. Let go of the thoughts around it, such as, 'I wish it would go away.' It might be tense shoulders or a sore knee. Do this for a few minutes and then notice a pleasant sensation. Alternate between awareness of pleasant and unpleasant *vedana*.

Day 7. *Awareness of sound.* Start by developing mindfulness of the body. Then, continuing with that awareness, include mindfulness of sounds. Notice the sounds around you without naming or judging them. The distant sound of a car alarm, voices from the street, rain spattering against your window.

1. Reflecting on vedana

Were you able to keep a pleasant and unpleasant events diary? If so, what did you notice? Did you feel you learned anything from it? Did you manage to reflect on an upcoming difficult or pleasant experience – if so, what did you notice?

Write your reflections here

2. Mindful walk

Were you able to remember to do the mindful walk? (I suggest you tick or cross these as you go through the week.)

	Tick/yes Cross/no
Day 1	
Day 2	
Day 3	
Day 4	
Day 5	
Day 6	
Day 7	

3. Breathing space

Did you remember to do the three-minute breathing space? If so, how often do you think you managed it?

	Tick here
Twice daily	
Once daily	
Often	
Regularly	
Occasionally	
Rarely	
Not at all	

4. Meditation

Finally, write down how your meditation went this week. Did you find time to do it? Did you enjoy it, or find it difficult? Did anything in particular strike you? Were you able to start and finish well? Did you cultivate kindly awareness?

Write your thoughts here

5. Mindfulness alert!

When you review your practice week, remember you are just looking for information – not evaluation and certainly not condemnation. You are simply checking how you got on, what the issues you were faced with were, and what, if anything, you have learned. Remember, you won't feel like you've learned something every day – that's unrealistic. If possible, talk to your mindfulness buddy about how it's going, share your experience with them. The fact that you have read as far as this is a success in itself!

We have learned that life has texture, has feel. Mindfulness of *vedana* is learning to stay with that texture without reacting to it with craving or aversion. *Vedanas* – pleasant, unpleasant, and neutral – are the building blocks of experience. They are the raw sensations out of which we build our life. But of course we don't often notice them. Usually we just find ourselves in a mood: a good mood, a bad mood, an I-can't-be-bothered mood. And perhaps we don't know why. It's as if it has descended on us from nowhere. We suddenly feel happy or grumpy, excited or listless, anxious or depressed. That's what we're usually dealing with. So, in next week's life with full attention, we are going to take a closer look at our moods, at our minds, at the kinds of things we tell ourselves. We are going to explore the third of the Buddha's four spheres of mindfulness.

Mind

Unhappy people in a happy world

IT'S STRANGE when we come to think about it. Many of us have never enjoyed so much wealth, health, and leisure time. Compared with the developing world, we are almost unbelievably affluent. And yet we are not happy, at least not in proportion to what we have and own. There is mounting evidence to suggest that, after a particular point, rising affluence actually causes unhappiness.

According to one survey, the UK has some of the worst road rage in the world. Typical behaviour includes aggressive acceleration, tail-gating, verbal abuse, and threats of violence. A total of 64% of workers have experienced office rage; 71% of internet users get so frustrated searching the net that they suffer net rage. One in four families experience frequent and heated rows about who controls the TV – remote rage.[14]

'Shopaholicism' is now a recognized addiction. Shoppers get so high on the fantasy and

Awareness of the mind and heart

Rumination is a cue for full attention

The mindful walk

The mindful moment

111

adrenaline that precede a shopping spree that they have the illusory feeling of being free from the problems of life. The psychologist Oliver James has popularized the term 'affluenza' for infectious over-consumption. Symptoms include high debt, overwork, the inability to delay gratification, obsession with externals, wastefulness, and stress.[15]

There are signs that depression is becoming epidemic. According to one report, 'Crippling depression and chronic anxiety are the biggest causes of misery in Britain today.'[16] The World Health Organization has predicted that by 2020, depression will become the second leading cause of 'disease burden' worldwide. In the words of Wallace Stevens, we are 'an unhappy people in a happy world'.[17]

It has never been so obvious that the cause of our unhappiness is to do with our minds. If we want to be happy – if we want to avoid losing our temper in supermarkets, running up massive credit card bills, succumbing to depression, or getting into a rage with our neighbours – we need to work with our minds.

Everything we experience, we experience through the mind. Our relationships with other people, our perceptions of the world, our work life, love life, home life – everything we have ever known and could ever know is mediated by our minds. It is our states of mind that make life interesting or boring, enjoyable or depressing, meaningful or futile. Understanding our minds, cultivating our minds, is therefore the key to happiness.

The Pali word for mind is *citta*. In English, when we use the word 'mind', we tend to mean 'brain' and 'thought'. We think of the mind as a sophisticated thought-processor. But the word *citta* includes heart as well as head. States of mind – *cittas* – have a thinking component, an emotional component, an action component, and an intuitive component. 'Mind' includes the more and the less conscious aspects of ourselves. It is this mind that we are cultivating awareness of in the third of the Buddha's four spheres of mindfulness.

In Marianne Moore's poem, 'The Mind is an Enchanted Thing',[18] the first line, running straight on from the title, goes on to say: 'is an enchanting thing'. What she is saying is that the mind is both casting a spell and under a spell.

The mind enchants. We interpret, distort, even contaminate our experience of the world around us. We do not see things as they are; we unconsciously fit them into pre-existing patterns of belief, expectation, assumption, and prejudice. We cast a spell on life. We call that spell, 'our experience', and believe in it as real and objective.

At the same time, the mind is itself enchanted. We are under a spell. We cannot tell if our thoughts are our own, or if we've picked them up from friends, workmates, family, or the media. We are mostly in the grips of the current zeitgeist of opinion: we think the sort of thing that most of those around us think we should think.

And yet we can learn to understand the mind. We can become aware of the difference between enchanting our experience and experience itself. We can become conscious of the second-hand nature of so many of our assumptions. And, as Marianne Moore puts it at the end of her poem, we can realize that the mind is, 'not a Herod's oath that cannot change'. We can recover from depression or addiction, we can become less prone to temper tantrums and resentment, we can become calmer, more generous, more grown-up. We can grow towards Awakening – towards seeing things as they really are. This is the vision of mindfulness of *citta*.

How we change

We need to understand what is meant by 'changing' our minds. When I set out on the spiritual life some 20 years ago, I was inspired to change. But the idea of change was appealing for two quite different reasons: first, because I saw the possibility of spiritual development, and secondly because I did not like myself as I was. I imagined that change would mean that I would become someone else – someone altogether nicer, kinder, less emotional. I thought that 'change' would mean getting rid of the old me.

When we think of change, we think of one thing changing into another thing: a seed changing into a flower. We know, of course, that the flower is encoded in the seed, that if certain conditions are met, the seed will become the flower. But we forget that. We think that we need to become something else – a beautiful flower rather than a dirty root.

So it's probably more helpful to think of 'growth' rather than 'change'. 'Change' is looking at the flower and marvelling at how different it is from the stem; 'growth' is the process whereby, when we grow spiritually, we grow into the best of ourselves. It is like light shining through stained glass – be it the flowing patterns of Art Nouveau, or the geometry of Art Deco. We become our unique potential. We become more of what we are. We become the best of what we are. We do not become someone else.

Expectations

The philosopher Karl Popper makes the point that when we approach day-to-day experience, we do so with pre-existing theories. What we are doing when we observe things, feel things, try to understand things, is to fit them into the theories we already hold about the world and our place within it. These 'theories', as he calls them, are pre-conscious; we arrive at experience with them, we look at life from them.

Take expectations. We cannot understand the world without expectations. People will sometimes ask us not to have them, but this is almost impossible. You will have expectations about this book, for instance. You'll expect it to be a Buddhist book, to not suddenly change into a maths textbook or a poetry anthology. You're probably not very conscious of your expectations, but you will have them nonetheless. And this is true of all our experience; we approach life with layer upon layer of expectation.

When we wait for a bus, to take a simple example, we know from experience that it is likely to be 10 minutes late. We get irritated if it is, but we only get really cross when the time we have subconsciously allotted for late buses has elapsed – in other words, when the bus no longer conforms to our predictive theory. But if we had been brought up in India, and if, instead of waiting for a bus in London, we were waiting in Delhi, our response would be very different. We would have different expectations: in India, a bus can be a day late! Wherever it is we are waiting for our bus, we are mostly unaware that we have expectations. We subconsciously expect life to conform to our expectations, and we can get very irate indeed if it doesn't!

We live in a state of pre-conscious expectation most of the time. We carry a kind of template in our head about how life should be, what should happen, and how people should behave. To respond to what actually happens means seeing that our expectations are just that. Mostly we only notice we have expectations when they are not met – when the bus is outrageously late. At the same time, our expectations have a terrible habit of coming true. Even when the outcome is painful, we can get perverse pleasure out of being proved right: 'I knew that would happen', 'I told you so.'

Assumptions

We appear in life with a whole host of assumptions. These assumptions, carried over from childhood and early conditioning, have a decisive effect on how we experience the present. When I was young, for instance, I assumed people didn't like me. This assumption was only partially conscious, and it had all kinds of consequences. It meant that I tended to be a people-pleaser – I wanted to make people like me because I secretly feared they would not or did not. Also, because I was on the lookout for feeling unwelcome, I tended to enter social situations with mistrust. People would pick up on this, and feel wary of me. They tended to back off, thus confirming my fears.

I cast a spell on my life: I looked at it through the distorted lens of self-dislike, but I didn't notice that that was what I was doing. I both misinterpreted and at the same time created my experience. We all do this in different ways. We mistake the spell that we cast on life for life itself, for how things actually are. Our assumptions about our lives shape our lives. The mind, as Marianne Moore puts it, 'is a power of strong enchantment'.

Predictions

We rarely experience life just as it is. Mostly we predict what could, should, might, will, happen next. This is especially true of painful experiences, but it is also true of positive ones. We really can think our run of luck will last forever; that the bonus we received last year will be repeated this year.

A good example of the power of the predictive mind is health – physical and mental. A friend of mine once convinced himself that he was having a heart attack. The thought, 'I am having a heart attack' will set the heart racing and the blood pressure rising; it makes the breath fast and shallow, and this causes pins and needles in the arms and hands. These symptoms will seem to confirm the truth of our initial thought: we are having a heart attack! This confirmation stimulates still more physical symptoms, which in turn re-confirms the thought... and so on. I remember saying to my friend, 'If you were having a heart attack, you would be in much more pain.' So, in his mind, not only was he having a heart attack – and this 'fact' was confirmed by his experience – but also the person he was with did not believe him! And this led to yet more feelings of panic.

Just as we can think ourselves into believing we're having a heart attack, we can hypnotize ourselves into painful states of mind. Part of what happens here is to do with the fact that thoughts have *vedana*, have a feeling dimension. So when we say to ourselves, 'I'm feeling overwhelmed' or, 'It's all too much' or, 'I'm about to have a breakdown, get ill, or relapse into depression', we shoot ourselves with the second dart. We shoot ourselves with a massive dose of fear and dread. This is painful in itself and makes the uncomfortable feeling of stress, fear, or unhappiness even worse. As with my friend's 'heart attack', the pain we provoke has the effect of confirming our prediction. We get locked into a negative feedback loop between painful feeling and painful thoughts.

We frighten ourselves by telling ourselves frightening stories. For example, we wave at a friend in the street and they don't wave back. We think, 'They don't like me. What's wrong with me? I'm a bad person. Nobody likes me.' It's as if we have a little demon whispering horror stories in our ear. The stories feel familiar; we have heard them over and over again. And they seem to be confirmed in our experience: we wave and they do not wave back – in fact they actually seem to frown! We forget they are too vain to wear glasses and have probably not seen us! Fearful predictions evoke the very thing we fear. It's like worrying about your blood pressure. The more you worry about it, the more your blood pressure will rise. If you then have your blood pressure checked, you will discover, 'It's gone up! I was right!' A thought that sends out still more adrenaline into your system, making your blood pressure go up once again.

Pattern-matching

Another way of understanding what happens in these kinds of experiences is 'pattern-matching'. As I say, we do not come into experience with a clean slate. Our minds are patterned by our history and conditioning. So when we enter a room, a friendship, a workplace, or a love affair, when we talk to a friend, watch TV, or go to the pub – we understand it by fitting it into the pattern of what we have been and known. We make sense of experience by matching it with other similar experiences.

When we perceive something, it's as though we flick through a massive catalogue of images, or a dictionary of shapes, to find which image or shape the new stimulus corresponds to. We do this especially if the initial stimulus is ambiguous or abstract – and therefore more in need of understanding. A classic example is noticing something long and thin lying on a path: is it a snake, or a piece of rope? In the moment of perception, we instantaneously pattern-match. We do this so as to understand what it is, how we should feel about it, and what we should do. We do not stay with mere perception. The meaning of the experience will depend on how we pattern-match it: snake (scream and run), rope (calmly walk away).

We can get it wrong, of course. We can think, 'Snake!', give ourselves a terrible fright, and then realize, no, it's actually a bit of rope. The very act of perceiving is bound up with our mind. To know something, to understand what it means – what we should feel, how we should act – is to fit it into a vast store of pre-existing images. But our pattern-matching is by no means always objective or accurate. If an elderly man asks us to move aside on an escalator so that he can get past, we will immediately pattern-match. We might come up with, 'Dad telling me off again', or, 'My maths teacher having a go at me' – we come up with patterns for authoritarian older men who have told us what to do. So we take it to be this type of experience, this thing happening again: a snake, not a rope. And we react accordingly.

Pattern-matching helps us understand why it is that we tend to repeat particular kinds of behaviour again and again. A good example is sexual relationships. We often find ourselves getting into the same pickle. Let's say our partner gives us a smaller than usual birthday present. We can understand our reaction in terms of pattern-matching. We have had previous relationships go cool – or we are prone to imagining that our relationships will not last, or that our partner will go off with someone else – and we make sense of the smaller-than-usual gift by matching it with that. We then react as if that is the objective content of the experience. It's the here-we-go-again rule. We pattern-match along habitual lines. We read the new experience as following the same trajectory as our previous ones, and this has the tendency to replicate them.

We have been exploring some of the ways in which we cast a spell on experience and then mistake that spell for the facts of experience. It is important to realize how deep this goes. Let's say we watch a man walk across a room, pick up his coat, put it on his head, then walk out. We cannot understand this by merely observing it. We have to have matching experiences; we have to be able to predict, assume, and expect. In this case, we know that he is about to walk outside, and we know that it is snowing, and that he is probably going to walk across a small courtyard and into another room. We know what it feels like not to be bothered to put a coat on properly, how it feels to have melting snow dripping down our necks. But 'outside', 'snow', 'getting wet', the extra little bit of bother of putting your arms into the sleeves, are not observable.

Mind creates world: the kind of world we experience is created by the sort of mind we have. Because our world, internal and external, is filtered through our mind, interpreted through our mind, made sense of through our mind – the state of our mind is the state of our world. The meaning of what happens to us, the motive for how we respond to what happens to us, is dependent on the mind. The smaller birthday gift is a sign of lack of money or lack of love. The man asking us to move aside on the escalator is either an elderly gentleman needing to sit down or another authority figure telling us what to do. Mind precedes world. As Marianne Moore puts it, 'it is a power of strong enchantment'.

How we are enchanted

Our assumptions, predictions, and expectations are, for the most part, shaped by our environment – by the attitudes and beliefs of our parents, the education we received, the religion we were brought up with, the people we mixed with, the newspapers we read. Our mind is shaped by history and culture, gender and sexuality, nationality and faith. Even our most intimate thoughts tend to originate elsewhere. Ideas, belief, and values are picked up from other people. They are like viruses – we catch them off the internet, from talkback shows and advertising slogans. Many of our views are repetitions of what our parents told us before we were seven. Like clothes and handbags, our attitudes are subject to fashion – we talk about 'authenticity' and 'being ourselves', whereas 100 years ago we would have talked about serving God and doing our duty. We tend to assume that the beliefs and values we hold supersede those that went before, and in this way are parochial in time as well as space.

Mind and world condition each other

The kind of world we grew up in conditions the kind of mind we have. The kind of mind we have conditions the type of world we experience. We do not know that we are under a spell; we do not understand how deeply we are a product of our conditioning;

we do not realize that what we are is largely what our conditions make us.

It is not yet clear, for instance, how new technology is affecting us. The novelist Doris Lessing talks about the effects of the internet. She asks, 'How will our lives, our way of thinking, be changed by this internet, which has seduced a whole generation with its inanities so that even quite reasonable people will confess that once they are hooked, it is hard to cut free...'[19]. Then there's the question of virtual violence. The University of Missouri recently conducted research into the effects of violent video games. They devised a way of measuring the emotional impact of what players see. The researchers concluded that, 'real-life violence troubled the players of these games much less than [it troubled] other children'. Manufacturers, as well as many of those who play, deny this, but if it is true – or even partly true – it is very alarming: 'five hundred million games of Halo 2 were played online, and $170 million worth of Halo 3 was sold in the first 24 hours after its release.'[20] Whatever the truth about the internet, or the effect of computer games, we rarely stop and consider the consequences for the mind. As our awareness develops, we will begin to feel the effects of our environment more vividly. We will become more aware of how external conditions affect us – whether that's mindless TV watching, hours spent on Facebook, or playing computer games. We might even conclude that we need to change those conditions, if they are making it difficult to practise. Perhaps we decide to reduce input (see page 44) or go off on retreat.

Self is a story we keep telling ourselves

Before we come onto how we change the mind, let's look briefly at the deeper, even more fundamental patterns within us.

We have probably had the experience of forgetting that we are in a bad mood. Perhaps we get absorbed in reading the newspaper, or something in the conversation catches our attention, and, for a while, we stop being in a bad state. Then a voice in our head seems to say, 'Now what was it I was thinking about? Oh yes, I was angry at so-and-so, I was resenting such-and-such, I was rehearsing what I was going to say to what's-his-name'... and we're back where we started. It's quite a particular feeling: we have this vague sense that the mind had been involved in something, then we recall what it was, and then take it up again. In this way, we rekindle the moods that spoil our lives.

Our states of mind are extremely changeable. We can be like a child who howls when their plastic duck is taken away and grows quiet once it's given back. How we fix ourselves – how we say this is 'me' – is by the stories we tell ourselves. Even when our stories are painful and unproductive, they are reassuringly familiar.

Self-talk is literally self-creating. This can be particularly obvious when we hear someone tell us his or her side of a story. They will tend to say, 'x did y, which meant that I felt z'; 'the bus was late'; 'my teenage son always leaves the kitchen in a mess'; 'I knew he was having an affair'. The stories people tell usually make sense; they are self-consistent. But if we get to know that person better, we start to notice that much of the story is missing. That the story they tell us is just that: a story that re-enforces their idea of who they believe they are. There may well be truth in the story. Usually there is. But it is rarely the whole truth. It is a truth that suits a particular self-conception – be it passive victim, or no-nonsense straight-talker. This can be easy to notice in others, but difficult to notice in oneself.

The aim of spiritual practice is freedom, freedom from the prison of self. Each time we notice a self-creating narrative, each time we let go of it, see it as just another story, just another voice – to that extent we transcend self. Conversely, each time we react with anger or blame or self-pity, we are defending 'self' – we are trying to protect 'the story of me' from the reality of others and of the world. Self is a story we keep telling ourselves.

Self and world

We can go further: self and world are both something we create. Earlier on, I talked about the snake/rope question. In Buddhism, that moment of naming and pattern-matching is called *samjna*. In the very act of perception, we create a thing that lies behind whatever it is that is being perceived, and we create another thing – a 'me' – that does the perceiving. We create an outside world of objects – snakes, ropes, bikes, tube stations – and an inside world of perception. We think of them both as separate and autonomous: a really existing world experienced by a really existing self that is separate from that world. But no such separation exists. Look up from this book for a moment. What do you see? Where do you end and where does the world begin? Where is the demarcation line between the sounds and you? And all the names we give to things – sights, sounds, tastes, touchables – they are not in the experience, are they? They are something we add to experience. When I look out of the window and see a few boys kicking a ball, or hear the mewing of a herring gull, there is no 'out there' in the perception. Mind and world are not two separate things.

Life is not commensurable with words, thoughts, and concepts; it transcends them, cannot be caught within them. Life is always more than we think. The insight of the Buddha is wordless, concept-less. There is nothing we can finally say about it because we can only talk about things – about 'inside and outside', 'self and world', 'this and that'. Self is a limitation. The more self there is, the more limitation we feel. What the Buddha taught was freedom – freedom from the illusion of self, and freedom to abide in the wordless mystery, the ever-changing beauty of the way things are.

Fourth practice week

Before we explore some specific practices for this week of mindfulness, I want to suggest some general approaches to knowing, and changing, the mind.

Awareness of the mind and heart

The first thing to say is that we cannot hope to have much success in working with our mind unless we have already cultivated awareness in the previous two stages of the path, namely mindfulness of the body and its movements, and mindfulness of *vedana*. We will also need an ongoing practice of day-to-day mindfulness, so that life runs smoothly enough for us to practise life with full attention in the first place!

It is difficult to be aware of the mind because the mind is our point of view; and we have no other point of view with which to compare it. We never see the world through another person's eyes. Our states of mind are so familiar to us that we don't usually notice them. In fact, it's not so much that we have thoughts and emotions, but that thoughts and emotions have us – they carry us along without much awareness on our part. We wake up into the thoughts and stories that are running (and sometimes ruining) our life. The Buddha knew this and was careful to train his disciples in body awareness and *vedana* as preliminaries. Once we've begun to establish ourselves in the first two spheres of mindfulness, we'll stand a far greater chance of cultivating the third: awareness of our mind and heart.

The fact that the Buddha has *citta* as the third sphere of mindfulness is a clue to how to work with it; we drop beneath the thoughts and emotions to how those thoughts and emotions feel in the body. In other words, we go back to *vedana*. We try to stay with direct experience rather than spiralling off into thoughts about experience – catastrophe narratives, blame stories, sob stories. We stay with the unpleasant sensations with kindly awareness.

If we are having particularly negative thoughts and emotions, we may need to drop back a stage further and re-establish mindfulness of the body. We might come back to the weight of our body, or the breath in our belly; we might soften our shoulders and relax our neck. Body awareness roots us in direct physical sensations; as such, it is a vital antidote to being caught up in painful thoughts. It helps us step back, and gives us a renewed sense of perspective and calm. Sometimes, trying to work directly with the mind ties us in even tighter knots. If we're waiting for an interview, for example, it's not worth asking ourselves why we feel anxious – it'll be much more fruitful to follow our out-breath, feel our feet, and relax. So, if in doubt, go back to *vedana* or back to body awareness. Once you strengthen these first two stages of the path, you will have more perspective on what's happening in your mind. This sense of perspective is especially noticeable after meditation. Once you have cultivated a more vivid experience of your body and your inner sensations, you will notice that troubling thoughts and repetitive narratives lose some of their power over you. You will be able to step back from them a little; not feel so caught up in them.

Mindfulness of *citta* is about noticing the narratives we tell ourselves. As I said in the previous chapter, we turn *vedana* into a whole state of being, into *citta*. One of the ways we do this is by telling ourselves stories. We don't just feel our experience, we extrapolate from it, generalize about it – often in an unhelpful way. We talk life up, or down, or round and round. We say to ourselves that the reason we're feeling bad is because so-and-so never listens, because such-and-such never washes up, because what's-her-name doesn't love us!

What we are trying to do with mindfulness of *citta* is become more honest with ourselves. We are trying to notice the monologues in our minds and recognize that they are our stories, that we are responsible for them. Yes, they may be partly true, they may even feel entirely objective, but they are stories nonetheless. This is the first goal. We take full responsibility for what we tell ourselves in the privacy of our mind – especially for those stories that feel horribly familiar, when we feel we have been here many times before. We will only be able to do this effectively if we cultivate self-esteem. We cannot be honest with ourselves without also being kindly to ourselves. The two need to develop in parallel. So we can start by simply asking ourselves whether the stories we tell ourselves are true or not. We can ask ourselves questions such as:

- Did the thought just pop up in my head out of the blue?
- Can I imagine thinking about the same thing in another way?

- Is there something about the story I am telling myself that could be questioned?
- Am I thinking in all-or-nothing terms?
- Am I blaming others or myself?
- Am I getting into negative or anxious speculation?
- Is what I am thinking really as true as all that?[21]

In this way, we can usefully reflect on the stories we tell ourselves. One of the most effective ways of escaping from negative narratives is by asking ourselves whether they are true or not.

To reflect in this way, we need to have developed sufficient mindfulness in the first two stages of the path; otherwise our intentions are liable to backfire. We'll end up 'putting out the fire with gasoline'. Say, for instance, we have a short temper. If we don't have enough mindfulness, our desire to understand our anger will actually inflame it – we start thinking, 'I'm angry with this person for these reasons. And I'm right to be angry.'

Mental states are like planets. They have their own gravitational pull. If our awareness is not strong enough, we will be pulled into their orbit. For mindfulness of *citta* to be effective, our mindfulness needs to be stronger than the *citta* we are mindful of. Otherwise we'll get into trouble. The way we make our mindfulness stronger is to practise the first two stages of the path of full attention. If we find that our attempts to be aware of the workings of our mind make matters worse – confirm us in our self-righteousness, or deepen our depression – then, once again, we need to backtrack; we need to re-establish awareness of vedana and the body.

Rumination is a cue for full attention

Another way in which our capacity for reflection can go wrong is rumination, or, as it is sometimes called, 'aberrant problem-solving'. Karl Popper thought of human beings as problem-solving animals. The history of science and technology can be thought of as a history of problem-solving – from the discovery of fire to the invention of the CAT scan. But when it comes to our inner life, this instinct to problem-solve can go wrong. What seems to happen for most of us is that we ruminate. We turn a problem over and over in our minds. We think we are solving the problem, whereas actually we are making it worse. There is a point when thinking about a particular problem, trying to solve it, becomes counterproductive – when thinking about the problem *is* the problem.

Rumination is to do with the discrepancy monitor I mentioned earlier (see page 68). We become aware of a mismatch between how we feel and how we think we should feel. This discrepancy shows up as a problem. We set about solving that problem by going over all kinds of possible solutions in our mind, and then measuring the degree to which those 'solutions' have narrowed the gap between what we experience and what we think we should experience.

An example from my own life might clarify how this works. I spent a fair chunk of my youth ruminating. I would ask myself, 'Why aren't I happy? Is it to do with this, or to do with that? What's wrong with me?' I'd go over it again and again. 'Should I do this or should I do that, is this the cause or is that the cause?' Obviously, there are fruitful ways of asking these kinds of questions, but it was the repetitive, habitual, almost neurotic way in which I did so that was so unhealthy – the sense of constantly measuring myself against some kind of standard of happiness. The way I thought about being unhappy became the reason for being unhappy.

When we ruminate, we return obsessively to a painful problem in our minds – the feeling of being a failure, the fear of being disliked – and this causes us to suffer all the more. We do not realize how powerful our thoughts are. Rumination is a kind of self-hypnosis. It's like saying to ourselves, 'I've got a problem', a thousand times over. It can be difficult to get out of because it really does feel like you're solving something. You feel that this time, this time, you'll get to the bottom of it, really sort it out, nail it once and for all.

You need to ask yourself: where does such thinking usually lead me? Have I thought about it enough now? Can I actually just feel how I am now in the body and be OK with that? Once again, it may be more fruitful to go back a stage. We notice we are ruminating – taking offence, nursing some hurt in our mind – and then we tune in to the *vedana* of that. We come back to *vedana* with an attitude of kindly interest and exploration. Or we draw our attention lower down in the body, into the sensation of the soles of our feet, or the support of the chair. Bringing our attention down like this is a simple antidote to the upward-moving energy of anxiety, restlessness, and stress.

Sometimes, of course, the best thing to do is distract ourselves. Thinking about something else, doing something else can be an extremely effective tool for overcoming negative thoughts. I have noticed that people attracted to personal growth have a tendency to believe that all mental states – particularly negative emotions – should be faced up to, examined, and learnt from; and that not to do so would be 'denial'. Of course, there is truth in this. Our negative thoughts and emotions can reveal things, which, when fruitfully examined, can help us grow. But the tendency to assume that pain is valuable, even (heaven help us!) 'deep', can fatally exacerbate any tendency to ruminate. If you find that you are in no fit state to usefully learn from what's happening in your mind, or if you're simply feeling grumpy, argumentative, or low, you do not need to work out what it all means. You can simply watch a DVD, read a novel, or help a friend!

The things we don't want to change

Sometimes, when people talk about their aspirations – what they want to develop, or how they would like to feel – the atmosphere becomes quite dispirited. What is happening here is that we make judgements about what we want to develop by focusing on what we feel we lack. We might talk about kindness, courage, and happiness, but our minds are actually focusing on not having those things, lacking those things. So how do we help ourselves feel inspired about cultivating more positive states of mind? Here are two suggestions:

1. Noticing what you have already developed

Using your journal, jot down some of the things you would like to cultivate. Then reflect about the ways in which you have already developed those things. As usual, try to be specific and detailed. Then write down how you might add in the future to what you have already developed. You might try using columns, such as my example on the next page.

Aspiration	How I actually live up to it	How I could develop further
- I would like to be kinder	- I look after the dog - I helped my mother clear out the garden shed last weekend - I give money to various charities	- I could be more patient with my mother when I go and see her - I could do the little jobs she asks me to do with more grace

With this exercise, you are likely to find that your aspirations – which are a vital aspect of life with full attention – feel more achievable, and that thinking about them is more enjoyable and inspiring. It will help you feel that you have already made progress, and this sense of achievement will affirm your sense that you can make more progress.

2. Things you don't want to change

Or you could jot down the things you don't want to change. Write, say, 15 things about your life that you don't want to change – for instance, 'my sense of humour', 'where I live'...

I don't want to change:

_____

_____

_____

_____

_____

_____

_____

_____

_____

_____

_____

_____

_____

_____

So, let's move on to the specific daily practices for this week's life with full attention: the mindful walk, the mindful moment, and our daily meditation practice.

The mindful walk

Use your mindful walk this week as an opportunity to notice internal commentary. As you walk, notice if there is anything particularly on your mind – are you worrying about something, going over an argument in your head, or craving for some future experience? See if you can become aware of the things you think about. Are they helpful or unhelpful? Do they make you feel happy or unhappy, angry or calm? And remember to do this in a relaxed and interested way. It's important not to be too analytical – you are not looking at your mind under a microscope – you're just trying to be mindful of where your thoughts are tending and working to make them positive rather than negative, helpful and growthful rather than repetitive or destructive. One way of doing this is by recapitulating what you have learned so far:

- Tune in to the body and its movement, notice *vedana*, and then just relax.
- Try to keep your mind free from any particular focus.
- Soon enough you'll find your mind wandering off.
- When you notice this – when you 'wake into thought', as I call it – try to become aware of what it is that you have been preoccupied by, what story you have been telling.
- Then see how it feels in your body to have those thoughts. Drop down into *vedana*. Notice what happens in your torso, in your heart area, your chest, shoulders, and belly. Notice if the effect of what you are thinking about is pleasant or unpleasant. Does it make you feel happy or unhappy, speedy or contented?

Then start examining the thoughts you are having. Are they particularly tenacious and hard to let go? Are the narratives you are experiencing familiar? Try to reflect on your experience. Be a bit careful how you do this. Make sure you are still in touch with yourself in a broad, relaxed, and kindly way. Then try asking yourself one or more of the questions below:

Is what I am saying to myself true? In a kindly, explorative way, become more objective about the story you are telling yourself. Is it true? Is it the whole truth? If it is true, decide what you are going to do about it, and then let it go (you might notice that even when you do this, your mind wants to go over it one more time!).

Can I think of narratives that contradict it? We often tell ourselves stories that suit us in a particular way, that serve a view we have of ourselves. Try to find other narratives that contradict what you are telling yourself, that don't fit into your story. Perhaps you often are the one who gets the milk and paper in the morning, but you hardly ever take out the rubbish or do the recycling.

Where does this kind of self-talk usually get me? The things we tell ourselves may be true, or partly true, but they may not be constructive. Many of the things we think about lead us nowhere. For example, it might be true that we have too much work on our plate, but thinking about it in this habitual and repetitive way only makes matters worse. It's like doing the task over and over in our minds.

Am I confusing a thought with a fact? For example: we can think that a smaller birthday present proves that our partner no longer cares for us. But this is a thought. It is not a fact. It might be true. But we don't know. We need to notice the difference between thoughts and facts. If it's just a thought – like so many other thoughts coming and going in our mind – then we can hold it lightly. We can let it go.

Do I have something invested in the narrative? Our inner narratives, especially negative ones, often have strongly held views behind them. In my workplace scenario, for instance, we sometimes want to believe that we're the only people who do any work! It suits us to think like that. If we're invested in a particular narrative, it's because it gives us something: in this case it might be the feeling of being important and therefore very, very busy. If this kind of reflective awareness becomes too cerebral or feels like a strain, just go back to body awareness. Body awareness is always an anchor for the mind; it keeps us in the here and now. It prevents mindfulness of *citta* becoming a mere cognitive exercise. Once again, I have included a review chart (on page 142) for you to note down if you have remembered to do the mindful walk.

The mindful moment

From now on, I'm going to encourage you to take up a specific 'mindful moment'. I suggest you choose a simple daily activity – your morning shower, brushing your teeth, the first time you turn on your computer – as a cue for full attention. Don't choose an activity that takes very long. And, if possible, try to think of an occasion when you tend to be alone, or don't need to interact with others very much, as that will make it easier.

Like the mindful walk, the mindful moment should be something you already do – not a mindful task you set yourself. Write in your journal the specific daily activity you plan to use, including when it begins and ends. Say, for example, you choose putting your pyjamas on at night – your starting point might be the point when you begin to remove your clothes, your cue to end could be the moment your head touches the pillow.

The simplest way to practise the mindful moment is to come back to your body. Here's an example:

- Notice the movements in your body as you remove your clothes.
- Try and feel the change of temperature on your skin.

136

- Notice what you do with your clothes – do you fold them neatly or leave them in a heap?
- Notice the sensations of putting on your pyjamas.
- Notice how your weight shifts from one foot to another as you pull on your pyjama trousers.
- Notice the temperature and touch of your nightclothes.
- How does it feel in your body as you get into bed?
- Feel the sense of physical relief as you lie down and rest your head.

As the weeks go by, you may want to change the activity of your mindful moment. We all need to alter our routine from time to time. And, if you have time, use your journal to jot down anything you found particularly striking. In the same way as with the mindful walk, I have provided a progress chart in the end-of-week review (on page 142). This will help you keep track of whether you have remembered to practise the mindful moment. Tick or cross the box provided at the end of each day. And remember: you are very likely to forget to practise the mindful moment. That's fine, just do what you can. You'll be trying to remember to intensify your awareness in the mindful moment every day from now on – so you need to approach it sensibly and patiently, without expecting too much from yourself on one hand, or giving up too easily on the other.

A useful way of noticing *citta* in your mindful moment is to become aware of the 'sticky thought'. Many of the thoughts passing through our mind are fleeting and associative – one idea or image sparks off another. If we turn our attention to something else – a detective story, a pop song, the taste of orange juice – they will simply dissolve. To say we 'think' is usually an exaggeration. Genuine thought is a noble pursuit - it lies behind much of what is best in human culture, science and technology. What we experience, much of the time at least, is 'sticky' thought. We get wrapped up in our thoughts; we stick to them; we find them difficult to shake off. So we could use our mindful moment to become aware of sticky thought, and to try to gain a deeper insight into it. Sticky thought is a cue for full attention, for the kind of reflection I have outlined above. We need to notice what it feels like to be stuck on these particular thoughts. We need to ask ourselves:

- What is it that makes thoughts sticky?
- Am I taking something too seriously?
- Have I lost perspective?
- Do I have some kind of subconscious investment in these thoughts?
- Are my thoughts sticky because they express needs that I am not aware of?

Another way of approaching the mindful moment is to use it as a cue to practise the breathing space (see page 95). Say, for instance, you have chosen the first time you turn on the computer when you get home in the evening. That would be a good time to do the breathing space. It only need take three minutes. Everyone has enough time to do that!

You could:
- Close your eyes (if that's possible).
- Tune in to the body as a whole. How does it feel – pleasant, un-pleasant, or neutral?
- Notice the sounds around you.
- Follow a few breaths in and out.
- Then see if you notice any particular inner narratives that you are involved in.

- Finally, come back to the sense of the weight of your body on the chair, and the sounds around you.
- Then carry on with what you were doing, whilst trying to stay in touch with the pause created by the breathing space.

This week's meditations

Meditation ripens our capacity to be aware. It strengthens our capacity to be mindful in everyday life. In particular, it gives us perspective. It is an invaluable way of stepping back from internal narratives, making space around them so we can look at them more objectively. We get so wrapped up in the stories we tell ourselves that we become the story. But we also know that when we are in a better mood, or even when we have gone for a run and consequently feel more grounded in the body, we can wonder what we had been so het up about. Meditation is about grounding our awareness in the present experience of the body and *vedana*. It is like altering the balance on the speakers of a stereo. Usually we have the head/thought speaker turned right up and the body/*vedana* speaker turned right down. We are trying to achieve a better, more harmonious, balance between the two.

In this week's meditations, see if you can sit completely still. Find a comfortable posture – you may have found that sitting on the floor is too uncomfortable and that you need to move onto a chair. Cultivate the discipline of sitting still – not moving, scratching, yawning, or shuffling. This will have a quietening effect on your mind.

Day 1. *Building up mindfulness.* Start with the body scan – scanning your attention into each area of your body from your toes to the top of your head. Then notice your experience of *vedana* (pleasant, painful, neutral). See how your body feels overall. Then try to feel your state of mind – are you in a particular mood? You can get clues about your state of mind from the sensations in your body – you might ask yourself, 'Is there anything in my experience that needs attention?' and then see how you feel in your body.

Day 2. *Working directly with inner narrative.* Build up awareness of body and feelings (as above), then gently ask yourself questions, such as, 'What is it that makes me happy?', 'Am I happy now? If not, am I telling myself a negative self-story?', 'When am I happy, and what does it feel like?' Try not to let it get too heady – ask and feel, pause, then ask again. It needs to be like throwing stones gently down a well. Drop in a thought and then wait and watch for any flicker of *vedana* in your body. At the end of the meditation, rest in body awareness.

Day 3. *Awareness of distraction.* Again, start with your physical experience – scan through your body as before – but emphasize awareness of what distracts you in the practice. When your mind wanders, notice where it goes. Are you preoccupied by something in particular? Does it feel familiar? If you are having sticky thoughts, what is creating the glue? Try to notice how your thoughts affect your body, and try to feel that. Then see if you can rest in the body again.

Day 4. *Letting go of unhelpful narratives.* Become aware of an unpleasant experience such as physical discomfort or mental unease. Notice the narrative you tell yourself about it, such as, 'This pain won't go away, it'll get worse.' See if you can let the narrative go and just experience the feelings with kindly awareness. Relax into it. Then rest in your body before getting up and continuing your day.

Day 5. *Letting go.* In this practice, just keep letting go. Build up awareness of the body as before. Then notice *vedanas* and relax into them, whether they are comfortable or uncomfortable. Notice your inner narratives and keep letting them go, relaxing in the body. A helpful method of letting go in meditation is tuning in to the out-breath. Try and follow the whole of the out-breath, imagining completely letting go as you do so.

Day 6. *Breathing and thinking.* After a few moments of tuning in to the weight of your body, notice the physical feelings of the in-breath and out-breath. When the mind wanders, notice what you are thinking about, let yourself carry on thinking about it and, instead of going back to the breath (and pushing the thought away), bring the breath to the thought. Consciously give yourself permission to think about what your mind wants to think about, but include the sensations of breathing as well. Then rest in the body.

Day 7. *Meeting needs.* In today's practice, sit very still – cultivate mindfulness of your body, *vedanas*, and mental states. Notice any inner narratives that arise. Try to feel them in your body and look for the need or value that they are trying to express. See if you can respond to that need in yourself. For example, if you are thinking about a good film, probably you want pleasure – could you experience pleasure in your meditation now?

1. Mindful walk

Were you able to remember to do the mindful walk? Put a tick or cross below the day as you go through the week.

	Day 1	Day 2	Day 3	Day 4	Day 5	Day 6	Day 7
Tick/yes Cross/no							

2. Mindful moment

Were you able to remember to practise the mindful moment? Once again, put a tick or cross below the day as you go through the week.

	Day 1	Day 2	Day 3	Day 4	Day 5	Day 6	Day 7
Tick/yes Cross/no							

If you were able to practise the mindful moment, how did it go? Did you notice anything in particular? Were you aware of sticky thoughts, or any particular habitual narratives?

Write your reflections here

3. Meditation

How did the meditations go? Did you manage to meditate regularly? If not, what prevented you? Could you meditate a little bit more next week? Is there any way you could strengthen your resolution to meditate – such as talking to your mindfulness buddy, or finding a way of practising with others? Generally speaking, were you able to notice any habitual stories? Perhaps you might like to jot them down here. Were you able to notice rumination and use it as a cue for full attention?

Write about your thoughts and inner narrative here

4. How are you getting on with the course?

You are now at the midway point of the course. It's worth remembering that this is the time when you are likely to lose motivation, stop reading the book, give up on the meditations, or react against being too self-improving! Probably your initial enthusiasm has run out. Well done if it hasn't! Don't worry if your motivation is down. One of the challenges of the spiritual life is finding deeper sources of motivation, and this often takes time. The inspiration that gets you going is often not the resolve that keeps you going.

So spend some time reviewing how you are getting on with the course. Do you need to back off a bit, become more flexible and less earnest? Have you turned the course into something of a chore? Perhaps you need to be less fastidious about filling in every single review box, or doing all the exercises I suggest. Do you need to find more supports – talking to your mindfulness buddy, for example? Perhaps you could get yourself on a retreat to refresh your inspiration. See if you stick with the course – developing the discipline of practice without at the same time making it all too onerous and humourless. Check, for instance, if you're giving yourself a hard time about not meditating regularly, or if you tend to be too laissez-faire about it.

The mind is an enchanted thing; it will take time, skill, patience, and application to work with it effectively. The mind is the undiscovered country. As we set out to explore it, we will face all kinds of obstacles. We might become alarmed at how much ill-will we harbour, how selfish we can be, how much our life is driven by craving or lust. But we will also discover wonders in the process.

We have a far better chance of working with our states of mind if we cultivate the calm and perspective that mindfulness of the body and *vedana* bring. These are the preliminaries. Then we can usefully become mindful of *citta*. As we do so, as we start to notice what is happening in our mind, we will need to bring to mind what is in our best interests. Instead of losing our temper, losing our nerve, or setting ourselves up for a big fall, we become aware of where our mind is tending – where 'thinking like this' usually leads us – and then gently bring ourselves back to what is healthy, fruitful, and productive. When we remember to breathe and relax when we notice we are getting stressed, when we ask ourselves if what we are thinking is a thought or a fact – each time we do that, we are moving onto the next stage in life with full attention: bringing the teachings to mind.

Bringing the Teachings to Mind

Virtues and strengths

We experience a special kind of pleasure when we do something that brings us into contact with our virtues and strengths. It exceeds the *vedana* of ordinary pleasurable activity – the first mouthful of cheesecake, watching a comedy programme on TV, going out clothes shopping. It is a deeper, richer pleasure, which gives a sense of gratification, fulfilment, and self-forgetting. An act of kindness or courage, the experience of learning, the sense of transcendence – they each give us a feeling of satisfaction that is qualitatively superior to ordinary pleasure. The American psychologist Martin Seligman calls this 'authentic happiness'. He imagines offering people a hypothetical 'experience machine'. For the rest of your life, this imaginary machine would, 'stimulate the brain and give you any positive feeling you desire'. Most people, he says, would refuse it. And that is because we don't just want positive feelings, 'we want to be entitled to our positive feelings'.[22] We want to earn our delight, our sense of accomplishment, our glow of satisfaction.

In exploring the fourth of the Buddha's four spheres of mindfulness, we are exploring 'authentic happiness'. We are moving on to the cultivation of strengths and virtues. We are entering the ethical life.

Mindfulness of dhammas

When we practise the third sphere of mindfulness – mindfulness of *citta* – we become more aware of our mind. We notice whether the things we tell ourselves are helpful or unhelpful, productive or counterproductive. As we become more aware of our mind, we start to notice how our mind feels – whether it's the pain of resentment or the pleasure of contentment. We notice that if we act generously, it feels like opening a door into our heart, and if we speak spitefully, it feels like slamming it shut again. Each time we become aware of this, we move from the third sphere of mindfulness to the fourth: from mindfulness of *citta* to mindfulness of *dhammas*.

Dhamma is a very important word in Buddhism. Many people will have heard the word in its Sanskrit equivalent, *dharma*. *Dhamma* can mean both 'teaching' and 'truth'. It can mean the ultimate nature of reality (which we will come back to in Week 8) and everything that leads to that. For now, it's best to think of *dhammas* as being aware of our experience in the light of what we have already learnt, or bringing the teachings to mind.

Mindfulness of *dhammas* means training ourselves to notice that when we act out of positive states of mind and emotion, we feel happier, more creative, tolerant, and expansive; whereas when we act out of negative states and emotions, we are liable to feel destructive, reactive, constricted, and unhappy. Positive emotions tend to make us feel more connected with other people – people like us better and friendships are more likely to develop. Negative emotions tend to lead to isolation. In positive states of mind, we are liable to be open to new ideas and experiences, whilst in negative states of mind, we tend to stick to what we think we know. If we want to experience authentic happiness, we need to discover ways of moving from negative mental states and emotions to positive mental states and emotions – that journey is mindfulness of *dhammas*.

The path so far

Body. Full attention begins with mindfulness of the body and its movements. This is the simplest and most straightforward way of developing awareness. You can do it now, reading this book. You can tune in to the weight of your body, your clothes on your skin.

Vedana. Then you can go deeper: you notice whether your experience of the body is pleasant or unpleasant, or whether you can't decide. This inner feeling of *vedana* is the gateway to depth. It brings you back to a more direct relationship with your experience.

Citta. Having noticed the inner feel of your experience, you observe how we build *vedana* into *citta*, into a complete state of mind. You become aware of your inner narratives and, with kindly attention, you try to gain a deeper insight into them: what do they say about your beliefs, expectations, and values?

The gap. This awareness of *citta* creates a gap. You stop. You take stock. You become aware of what your mind is doing. And then you choose how to respond.

Mindfulness unfolds naturally. Each new sphere arises naturally from the one before. So if you deepen your awareness of the body, you will inevitably begin to notice a whole inner world of feelings and sensations. In the same way, if you become more aware of your states of mind, you will inevitably notice the degree to which they are pleasant or unpleasant. If they are painful, you will naturally want to change them; if they are pleasant and fulfilling, you will naturally want to enhance and prolong them. Negative states of mind are painful and are a cause of further pain. Positive states of mind lead to authentic happiness.

It is as if we now have a guardian angel trying to prevent us hurting other people or ourselves. We notice this when we start getting wound up, short-tempered, or exhausted – a quiet inner voice urges us to calm down, take a break, or regain perspective. Even in our worse moods, we can be dimly aware of a voice urging us against it. Sometimes our guardian angel is happily walking beside us. Sometimes they're pleading for us to not act on our impulses. Mindfulness of *dhammas* means listening to that voice. But of course there is another voice urging us to do as we please. All the myths dramatizing the struggle between the forces of light and those of darkness play themselves out in the depths of our mind. For an alcoholic, for example, deciding to walk past a pub means engaging in mortal combat.

Awareness is the guardian angel. It is kindly, reflective, positive, and considerate of others. Genuine mindfulness – rather than mere concentration – has the taste of what I can only call 'goodness'. When we snap at friends, moan about working hours, gossip, backstab, gripe, or grumble, this is our mood speaking, not our awareness of it. Of course, we can decide to ignore the voice of awareness, override it, bury it, refuse to listen... but it is always there, like a child tugging at our sleeve.

The angel of awareness reminds us what is in our best interests. It reminds us that we want to be well and happy, that we want a heartfelt connection with other people, that we don't want to spend our lives arguing, feeling hard done by, or nursing grudges. The angel of awareness reminds us that generosity and kindness are better. We need to listen to that angel. We need to bring to mind the teachings, attitudes, and practices that help us live well. This is mindfulness of *dhammas*.

The mind is always involved. If it isn't involved in one thing, it will be involved in another. It is never free-floating. We can notice this when we're feeling bored. In this state, we're likely to start going over an argument in our head, getting drawn into sexual fantasy, planning our weekend, or worrying about our weight. Our mind searches past, present, and future for something to get wrapped up in. And it moves along habitual lines. It will explore the kind of thing we have been involved with in the past, familiar scenarios such as feeling misunderstood, indignant, defensive, or acquisitive.

The more our mind gets involved in something, the more it will tend to get involved in that thing. It is like monsoon rain. After the dry season in India, when the earth is baked hard and the dust kicks up in clouds at our feet, suddenly the rain comes. It pours in a great deluge, often for days at a time. And the water doesn't just soak into the ground. It digs channels. The deeper these channels become, the more water flows into them; the more water flows into them, the deeper they become. The mind is just like that. It flows along habitual and repetitive lines, digging ever-deeper ruts. 'Self' is nothing other than a pattern of grooves in our mind. Whatever we do (or don't do) digs a channel for self to flow down. We become who we are now through who we have been in the past. And who we are now creates who we will become in the future. We create ourselves by tending to feel, think, say, and do the same kind of things over and over again.

This means that we are not stuck with the person we are at this moment. If we can change our behaviour and mental habits in the present – if we can respond to experience with mindfulness instead of reacting automatically – then we will change our future. In this way, we will become happier and more fulfilled. Mindfulness of *dhammas* is about learning to establish ourselves in more openhearted attitudes, creative thoughts, and healthy, outward-looking volitions. Our lives are in our hands: what we do today subtly modifies who we will become tomorrow.

Recollection in the moment

A more traditional definition of *dhammas* is, 'recollecting the teaching of the Buddha'. Of course, to do so we will need to find out what *dhammas* are, work to understand them, and decide if they are true and helpful – and this may require studying and discussing them with others. But even when we have done those things, we will still find it hard to put the Buddha's teachings into practice. We'll discover that we are regularly overwhelmed by our habitual reactions. Mindfulness of *dhammas* therefore means bringing to mind what we have learnt in the moment when we need it. This is another reason why the Buddha enumerates mindfulness of *dhammas* after *citta*. First we notice the state of mind we are in, and then, whilst we are still in the grips of that state of mind, we cultivate a creative way of working with it. This really is a challenge. All of us have deeply engrained patterns that go right back to our earliest days and, who knows, even beyond that. By constant repetition, we have conditioned ourselves to react along habitual lines – we are quick to feel aggrieved; we blame others or ourselves; we find it difficult to stop working. And our habits are often confirmed, even entrenched, by other people. We have built up a massive pressure of habit. We will not be able to shrug that off or disown it – in fact, trying to do so is yet another bad habit!

When we practise mindfulness of *dhammas*, we are trying to get to grips with who we are in the moment of being who we are. If, for instance, we notice that we are just about to go into yet another 'poor me' monologue, we need to stop and remember that, when we do this, we only make ourselves miserable. By noticing what is happening in the mind, we find a new way of responding; it's the equivalent of changing the subject in a conversation.

And just as mindfulness of *citta* is a more advanced practice than mindfulness of *vedana*, so mindfulness of *dhammas* is more advanced again. If we try and change ourselves without enough self-knowledge, without enough mindfulness of who we are and what motivates us, we can go astray. We need to get to know our mind by practising mindfulness of *citta*. If we do not know ourselves sufficiently, we run the risk of dampening down our energies in the attempt to be a nicer, more 'spiritual' person. Our desire to change ourselves will be ill-informed. In practice, we will often need to go back a stage: concentrate on becoming benignly curious about the mind before working out how to change it.

And we would be wise to be clear-headed about the forces that we are taking on. Many of our habitual responses are backed up by powerful instinctive drives, such as self-preservation, power, status, sex, and greed. We need to be willing to feel these drives, not wish them away for religious reasons. At the same time, we need to train ourselves not to act out of them immediately – to feel them, but then to recollect how best to act. This can be difficult. In any given moment we are under enormous pressure – pressure from our environment, other people, and our habits. There is the pressure of our body, for instance. We are much more vulnerable to our negative tendencies if we are feeling tired, overworked, or ill. Then there is the pressure of the moment. Things are constantly being sprung on us: someone asks for a favour when we're particularly busy, a friend chooses a bad moment to criticize us, the car breaks down when we most need it. In the moment of pressure, or in the midst of multi-tasking, we often react without awareness. Mindfulness of *dhammas* is trying to get into that moment – become aware of it and change it. Unless we have the discipline of meditation and the previous stages of mindfulness at our fingertips, the pressures of the moment will probably overwhelm us.

Full attention of *dhammas* is a special kind of vigilance. We notice that the mind is flowing in a particular direction – towards an argument, away from a street beggar, towards chatting up a friend's spouse, against a telephone salesman – and we recollect what is really in our best interests. This word 'recollect' says it all really. It has two meanings. First, it means to bring ourselves together –

re-collect ourselves; secondly, it means 'to remember'. In mindfulness of *dhammas*, we are remembering ourselves and remembering what's really going to be helpful and fruitful for all concerned.

Meeting our needs

The mind is intelligent. It is trying to do something. Our inner chatter about promotion, romance, or film stars is the mind trying – often in a clumsy and incoherent way – to meet genuine needs. The same goes for our hate-fantasies, destructive urges, and critical impulses. Much of the pain we cause ourselves, and cause others, is created by the unwise and unhelpful nature of many of our strategies, not by the impulses that underlie them. The same is true of our values. Usually our values are not directly felt or clearly articulated. They are implied by our actions, words, and concerns. But the way in which we uphold our values can be boorish, boring, or bullying. Our needs and values have to be fathomed, like interpreting a dream.

One model for exploring this is provided by Marshall Rosenberg, the creator of Non-Violent Communication (NVC). For Rosenberg, conflict between people, as well as within oneself, is caused by not making the distinction between our needs and the strategies we adopt for meeting those needs. He believes that our true needs are life-connecting, universal, and growth-enabling. But these 'needs' are often, indeed mostly, subconscious. They have to be uncovered by honest self-examination and, where other people are concerned, with active, empathetic listening. This basic distinction, between needs and the various

155

strategies we adopt for meeting them, is very useful indeed. Unless we recognize the basic needs that drive our behaviour, we are bound to keep repeating that behaviour – including behaviour that does not meet our needs, which causes suffering. Having recognized the need, we will find it easier to let go of a particular unhelpful strategy – the inner diatribe, the people pleasing, the eating of too many biscuits.

Using reflection, imagination, and intuition, try and gain a deeper insight into the values and needs you are trying to express. Then see if you can find more fruitful ways of meeting those needs. All this requires a delicacy of self-awareness that is in tune with feelings, emotions, and body sensations. Try to think into experience, not skid along on top of it. See if you can look beneath your behaviour to the needs that your behaviour is trying to express – and then try to find more productive ways of meeting those needs.

Say in one of your meditations you keep thinking about a film. Notice that and drop beneath the images in your mind to the underlying *vedana*. Ask yourself, 'Why do I want to think about a film? What's in it for me?' Let's say you realize that the reason you're thinking about a film is because you want pleasure. To use the language of NVC, replaying the film in your head is a 'strategy', pleasure is a 'need'. So try to directly experience and meet that need – instead of merely fantasizing about it. Try to find pleasure in your experience right now. Direct experience of pleasure is intrinsically more pleasurable than thinking about something *associated* with pleasure. Of course, there may be aspects of the film that express your values – courage, kindness, beauty, playfulness. Can you stop and become aware of them?

Or perhaps you are having angry thoughts about someone at work. Perhaps they haven't done something with sufficient care, or they haven't helped the others on your team. Ask yourself what values you are trying to protect. Perhaps you value dedication and care, you appreciate excellence and teamwork. In this way, try to come into contact with the values that lie beneath your anger. Try to experience those values directly in your body and heart. Then think of a more creative strategy for expressing them. Getting into a row with your colleague isn't going to help foster team spirit! Perhaps the two of you need to talk and try and come to a deeper understanding.

The law of desire and the force of hatred

Let's look at the two main tendencies that shape our instinctive reactions: desire and hatred. When we work with the mind at the level of *dhammas*, we are especially working with these two supremely powerful forces. Our aim is not to feel guilty about them, repress them, or get hung up about them – our aim is to unlock the energy that lies within them. Mindfulness of *dhammas* is working with our mind so that we can do the most good and the least harm, to others as well as ourselves.

When we strongly want something, we see it in a distorted way. We distort our perception of, say, designer clothes, expensive meals, or exotic holidays, by concentrating on the pleasant aspects whilst neglecting or ignoring the unpleasant ones. We do the same with ideas of success, promotion, fame, money, and influence – we remember the big pay packet and sharp suits, but we forget for how long we end up stuck at the desk. Likewise with people. When we are powerfully attracted to someone, we tend to ignore or explain away the aspects of that person that we don't like or aren't attracted to. This accounts for some of the fallout that regularly sours the end of romantic relationships. 'Wanting' is our way of editing life; we leave the downside on the cutting-room floor. We edit it out. But, of course, it is still there to haunt us. Because we are not seeing things as they really are, we cause ourselves, and others, pain. The more we distort things, the more painful the consequences are likely to be.

And when we edit life in this way, we forget the law of diminishing returns. We forget that the experience of pleasure will soon wane into the taken-for-granted. Once our pleasure starts to ebb, we'll want to repeat it, we'll want something else, something new, and each time it will take a little bit more to give us the same thrill of delight.

We are often dimly aware of all this, but we tend to push that aware-ness aside or rationalize it away. In fact, the more we want some-thing, the more likely we are to override our awareness. We can get to the point where we are prepared to act irrespective of the conse-quences – sometimes with catastrophic effect. In this state of mind, our desire is more and more powered by the belief that the yearned-for object, sexual partner, new job, new home, is the only way to happiness. It will feel like 'we'll die if we don't get it'. Of course, we don't consciously think about it like this, but on a deeper level this is what's going on.

So part of our practice needs to be remembering that life has this twin aspect – a pleasurable aspect, which we over-focus on when we want something, and an un-pleasurable aspect that we tend to ra-tionalize away or dismiss as unimportant. Fruitful choices are those that bear both sides of life in mind.

Hatred is really frustrated desire. Not getting what we want is painful. It is painful right from the beginning. Our instinctive reaction to pain is aversion – from frustration and irritation at one end of the spectrum to jealousy and rage at the other end. We don't like pain. We want to get rid of whatever it is we think is causing it. For the majority of us, most of our pain is social and emotional. And by and large, we believe that aversion works. We think that raging against something will somehow put the world to rights.

Our reaction to pain has value: if someone steps on our toe, we are likely to push them off; if a wasp lands on our arm, we are quick to brush it away. The energy of aversion helps us act. It focuses our attention and gets us moving. It is the same with emotional pain. It tells us important things about our needs and values. It often points to a problem we need to solve – and we may well need all the energy locked up in our aggression to solve it. Perhaps we need to find the courage to stand up for ourselves, disagree with someone, request something, or make a useful criticism. The very act of problem-solving has an aggressive edge to it. Aggression can help us break through into new levels of skill or understanding. Athletes need it; artists need it; those practising life with full attention certainly need it.

But, when we react in this way, we tend to stop seeing things as they really are. Just as a wanting state of mind edits the world sunny-side up – focusing on what we desire whilst sidelining what we don't – so with hatred we exaggerate, embellish, and over-focus on what we don't like. We often do this to the exclusion of anything positive about the object of our dislike.

A negative state of mind activates a battle-station mode of thinking.[23] Its function is to isolate a problem, then eliminate it. Whilst this can be useful and serve a purpose, the battle-station mode tends to miss out on more creative solutions – it tends to polarize people and be defensive. It often means that we fail to see the positive points that someone is making because we have over-focused on those points that we disagree with – and this will adversely affect our capacity to make informed decisions.

We also tend to pile it on. We see a difficult person as irredeemably bad, with no saving graces whatsoever, or we make the object of aversion the cause of all our unhappiness. When we hate someone, even strongly dislike them, we tend to find it difficult to see anything good about them. We distort our experience by focusing on negative traits whilst refusing to be aware of positive ones. We can get to the point when we can't imagine anyone liking them. Not only that, but we almost wish those irritating little behaviour patterns into being. The person we don't like steps into the office and we're just waiting for them to say such-and-such. It's as though we constantly compare our righteous self with this person who's inevitably doing everything wrong. A large part of how we create our sense of 'self' is through this comparison. Hatred, the Buddha tells us, is like reaching a hand into a fire to pick up a piece of burning coal in order to throw it at someone. Our intention is to hurt, but the state of mind hurts us. Hatred is not in our best interests. We want happiness. Most, if not all, our actions have this one end. But when we are giving someone a good telling off in our mind, when we are in a rage about something or other, in that very moment, we are hurting ourselves.

In the West, we tend to think about ethics in legal terms: that our actions are judged, punished, or rewarded by some outside agency – an attitude that stems from belief in a creator God. But in Buddhism, the punishment *is* the crime. When we act out of ill will, spite, resentment, petty rivalry, and so on, we are causing our own unhappiness.

We do not need something or someone to mete out punishment – it happens naturally. It is a natural law, like gravity. This truth, so challenging in its implications, is self-evident. When we hate someone, our urge, more or less crudely expressed, is to see them removed from the surface of the planet – or at least as far away from us as possible. And yet in that very moment, they are as close to us as they can possibly get: they are right at the centre of our mind. Sometimes our negative feelings are so compulsive that we spend more time thinking of the people we hate than the people we love.

Mindfulness of *dhammas* means recollecting that hatred does not work and bringing this to mind in the moment we're just about to have a temper tantrum, get the sulks, or become monosyllabic. The answer is not to pretend we don't have hatred – to always meekly comply with the wishes of others, to step down from honest disagreement, or to refrain from constructive criticism. Mindfulness of *dhammas* means knowing that hatred does not add to our point; if anything, it detracts from it. The Buddha is saying that the only solution to hatred is love. How to love is a lifetime's endeavour. Sometimes we'll need to face conflict in order to love, sometimes we'll need to step away from it; sometimes we'll need to speak up, sometimes remain silent. However we learn, the starting point is recollecting that hatred is never conquered by hatred. 'This', the Buddha reminds us, 'is an eternal law.'[24]

Practising to be a Buddha

Mindfulness of *dhammas* requires us to do three things:

- Notice the state of mind we are in.
- Create a gap of honest self-reflection.

- Decide how best to act by bringing to mind the teachings that lead to authentic happiness.

It's worth emphasizing that cultivating this ethical outlook – developing 'virtues and strengths' – will have its challenges, especially if we have not developed sufficient awareness in the previous stages of the path. We might tend to neurotic guilt, complaisant rationalization in order to justify hurtful behaviour, moral sentimentality, or self-righteousness. All of these tendencies limit awareness and slow down spiritual growth. Like squabbling children, they are as bad as each other.

Buddhist ethics are natural. They grow out of awareness of the mind, out of our developing understanding that negative mental states are painful in themselves and tend to cause pain; that positive mental states are satisfying in themselves and tend to cause happiness.

Buddhist ethics are volitional. They are to do with the mental states that motivate our actions, not with how any particular society or culture views our actions. We can be deeply ethical and, at the same time, highly unconventional – in fact, sometimes, we may need to be.

Buddhist ethics are about practising to become a Buddha. A Buddha has seen – really and truly realized – that actions have consequences, that negative mental states are painful and cause pain. A Buddha has let go of the whole push-and-pull pattern that we are so fundamentally caught up in. This wanting and not wanting is how we create 'self' – pulling things (or people) towards us that we think will enhance our sense of self, and pushing things (or people) away from us that seem to threaten it. The Buddha has seen through all these tendencies. He is completely free. For him, there is only wisdom, compassion, and endless appreciation.

Trying to become a Buddha might seem an unrealistic aspiration. Certainly, we need to remember the old proverb, 'A journey of a thousand miles begins with a single step.' Cultivating strengths and virtues is a path of single steps – remembering to be a little bit more generous, patient, and helpful. At the same time, it's worth knowing that, from a Buddhist point of view, the Buddha is naturally ethical: he doesn't need to make an effort. The Buddha isn't trying to be compassionate; he is just being himself. The Buddha is fully awake to the true nature of things. So each time we are kind, learn something, or transcend ourselves, we are moving towards how things really are.

Fifth practice week

By practising mindfulness of *dhammas*, we are moving from exploring our experience to consciously and deliberately cultivating our experience – trying to bring new, more positive states of mind and emotion into being. The seeds of authentic happiness are already there. You already want to be kind, loving, happily connected with others, and courageously alive to new experience. You already value learning and growing, otherwise you would not be reading this book. Let's look more broadly at how to practise mindfulness of *dhammas* before we turn to the specific practices I recommend for this week, our fifth week of life with full attention. Let's look at the five Buddhist precepts, and at how we might start putting ethics into action.

Training in the five precepts

When someone becomes a Buddhist, they take what is known as the five precepts. These are not a set of rules or religious laws; they are not a stick to beat people, or a rod for our own backs. They are ethical guidelines – principles of training. They have a negative aspect – what we are trying not to do – and a positive aspect – what we are trying to cultivate. The positive formulation of the precepts was written down by my own teacher, Sangharakshita. His intention was to make clear the true spirit of Buddhist ethics. Only too often, people think of ethics as a list of 'shouldn't do's'. Of course, there *are* things we need to stop doing but, when we practise the five precepts, what we're really trying to do is develop virtues and strengths such as kindness, courage, patience, honesty, and the willingness to learn.

The negative and positive formulations of the five precepts form a spectrum ranging from the extremely negative to the supremely positive. Wherever we find ourselves on that spectrum, all we need to do is move in a positive direction. We can move from positive to still more positive, or from the negative to the little less negative. Here are the five precepts in their positive and negative formulations:

Negative *(what we are trying not to do)*	Positive *(virtues and strengths we are trying to cultivate)*
Refrain from harm	Cultivate love
Refrain from taking the not given	Cultivate generosity
Refrain from sexual misconduct	Cultivate contentment
Refrain from lying	Cultivate honesty
Refrain from intoxicants	Cultivate awareness

I suggest you consciously try to put the five precepts into practice this week. Give them a go and see how they affect you. Below are some suggestions for how you might do that.

Take a fearless ethical inventory of your life[25]

Using your journal and looking at the precepts above, explore which precepts you feel strong in and which you need to work on. Be specific. Nothing bland and universal like, 'I need to be kinder.' To be worth doing, your fearless ethical inventory needs to read something like, 'I was harsh and unappreciative when I visited my parents last week. I need to stop blaming them for my bad moods and take more responsibility for my life.' Go through each of the precepts and write down your reflections. You could ask yourself:

Do I steal stationery from work, skip train fares, fiddle my tax returns, or go off sick when I'm not actually ill? (second precept). Do I fail to return library books? Do I borrow a friend's bike, DVD, or books without asking? Taking the not given also includes taking people's time and energy – it means not buttonholing someone against their will!

Do I regularly get drunk or take drugs? (fifth precept). People take on this precept in different ways: complete teetotalism or drinking in moderation. Whichever way you decide to take it, the basic point is that you cannot develop mindfulness if you are under the influence of drugs or alcohol! And remember other things can be intoxicating too – money, success, status, or shopping. We can even be intoxicated by the simple fact of being young and rather full of ourselves. 'Intoxication' means anything that cultivates mindlessness.

What do I get up to sexually? (third precept). Am I cheating on someone? Am I trying to have casual sex with someone's husband/wife? Refraining from sexual misconduct means not causing harm, lying, or taking the not given as applied to your sex life. The issue here is not who you sleep with, but how you treat him/her/them. For most people, the principal ethical issues surrounding sexual activity are neurotic craving and unhealthy dependency.

How can I be kinder and more generous? (first and second precepts). Be careful not to focus too exclusively on the negative formulation of the precepts. Ask yourself, 'How could I cultivate kindness, generosity, truthfulness, contentment, and awareness?' Be specific: 'I could check out if my elderly neighbour needs me to get the shopping for her', 'I could help my friend sort out his computer', or 'I could give that book back'.

Go through the precepts in this way and see which ones you need to work on. Be fearless and completely honest with yourself. Just by doing this, you will be practising the fourth precept: you will be cultivating self-honesty. And remember to include the times when you are ethical: 'I didn't lose my temper in that meeting', 'I remembered my friend's birthday', 'I made tea for my grumpy boss'. The basic premise of Buddhist ethics is reducing harm and cultivating the good – for ourselves as well as all beings.

And watch out for irrational guilt – that sense of being somehow inevitably at fault. Guilt blocks awareness and ethical sensitivity. Also, be mindful of over-focusing on 'sexual misconduct'. I've noticed that many people tend to assume that ethics boil down to sexual peccadilloes and infidelities. It's often more productive to ask, 'Do I energetically contribute to the situation I find myself in?' Even if you are rather naughty in other areas, if you act generously, the whole of the spiritual life is open to you.

You could also simply put more effort into being a kindly, helpful, encouraging, and generous presence in the universe and then notice how that feels. Keep a checklist and write what you do each day in your journal.

Take a personal precept for a week (or more)

You could decide not to watch rubbish television, take recreational drugs, swear, eat junk food, or work on the computer after 10pm. Quite apart from the intrinsic value of not doing these things, there is the benefit of getting out of the habit of just doing whatever comes most easily. A healthy person has the mental muscle to resist things, to not always give in to passing desires.

Or you might decide to do something for a week – go for your mindful walk, meditate daily, eat healthily, spend more time with the kids. It needs to be something you can do. Don't choose something vague. If it's, 'spend more time with the kids', then make it specific: '40 minutes in the park as soon as I get back from work'. Use your journal to write down whether you managed to do it or not.

Buddhist ethics are saying that dishonest, destructive, or hurtful actions limit and constrict awareness, whilst positive actions expand and enrich it. Each time we take a day off sick for no good reason, for example, we limit our awareness and make ourselves uncomfortable in our skin. We cannot be fully mindful if we have a troubled conscience. Conversely, if we act positively, we will be happier and more fulfilled. We become someone our friends can trust and turn to.

Mindfulness and imagination

Mindfulness is an act of imagination. Imagination is not the same thing as fantasy. Fantasy is basically wish-fulfilment – we fantasize about having an affair with a film star, or winning the lottery. Fantasy is the ego getting what it wants. Imagination is the capacity to see beyond our immediate likes and dislikes, beyond the moment and its pressures, to the good, the true, and the beautiful.

A mindful person is imaginatively alive and imagines the consequences of their actions. They imagine the reality of other people – what they need, how they feel. They imagine the effects of their actions and lifestyle on the people around them and on the planet. They see beyond the surface of everyday life into the meanings and values that underlie it. In this way, the mindful person contributes to his or her own welfare and to the welfare of others.

Unethical actions are failures of imagination. When we act unethically, we fail to imagine the consequences of our actions. For instance, we fail to imagine the future – how drinking this much today will have consequences tomorrow. We fail to imagine the suffering we cause by eating a chicken leg or by wearing a leather jacket. We forget to imagine the consequences of wastefulness. We forget to notice how being in a bad mood makes life more difficult for our friends and loved ones. Even leaving our breakfast bowl in the sink is a failure of imagination: we forget to imagine what it's like for someone to have to wash it up after us.

If practising the five precepts is the telescopic view of life – seeing it in the broadest possible perspective – then practising the four forces is the microscopic view. The four forces are how we cultivate mindfulness of *dhammas* from moment to moment. We'll be concentrating on these four forces for the rest of this week – in our mindful walk, the mindful moment, and in our meditation. First of all, let's get acquainted with them and their traditional formulation.

- *Eradicating* already arisen unskilful mental states.

- *Preventing* the arising of as yet un-arisen unskilful mental states.

- *Cultivating* the arising of as yet un-arisen skilful mental states.

- *Maintaining* already arisen skilful mental states.

The first thing to make clear is what is meant by 'skilful'. In Buddhism, positive mental states are skilful, whilst negative mental states are unskilful. The word 'skilful' makes it clear that when we practise mindfulness of *dhammas*, we are learning a craft – like carpentry or ceramics. As with any craft, it will take time, application, and patience. Calling a new apprentice's joinery bad is both discouraging and unfair; he has only just begun. But if we encourage him to develop his skills, seek help, and learn from his errors, his craftsmanship will improve. The same is true of mindfulness of *dhammas* – skilful action is something we learn with the help of those with more experience. If we are harshly critical with ourselves, if we expect unreasonably high standards, we will undermine our capacity to learn. At the same time, if we don't make an effort, we will not make progress.

In some ways, it's more helpful to approach the four forces back to front. Our aim is to dwell in states of creativity, positivity, warmth, and awareness. In other words, at best, all we need to do is maintain already arisen skilful mental states. If we don't manage that, we work backwards: we cultivate un-arisen positive states, then prevent ourselves from getting into still more negative states than the ones we're already in. Finally, we try to shake off and overcome – eradicate – unskilful states. Let's briefly look at how we might work with each. I'll enumerate them in their traditional order.

Eradicating arisen unskilful mental states

We are often unaware of being in a negative frame of mind. It's not so much that we get into a bad mood, but that a bad mood gets into us. So, first of all, we need to be present and receptive to our experience. We need to 'feel' and 'know' what we are experiencing, and this means cultivating the previous stages of the path. When we are unhappy, we tend to blame someone, fall into self-pity, or distract ourselves. This means that we don't fully own up to the bad mood we're in and therefore don't try to change it. Taking full responsibility is crucial. Often, we don't make progress simply because we haven't really and truly owned up to our negative states of mind. As soon as we do that, in that very moment, we are already eradicating them.

We have learnt so much. We've learnt how to notice *citta* (our states of mind), and to notice the narratives we tell ourselves. We've learnt to drop beneath *citta* into *vedana*, and we've learnt how not to react to uncomfortable *vedana*. We know that mindfulness of our body is an antidote to toxic mind. So we can bring all that to mind now, in the moment we need it.

Preventing the arising of as yet un-arisen unskilful mental states

The best way of preventing the arising of as yet un-arisen unskilful states of mind is to be enjoying positive states of mind! Genuinely good moods – rather than mere ebullience – have the effect of protecting us from negative mental habits and tendencies. Below are a few suggestions for putting this second force into action.

Our personal psychology is not always the cause of negative emotions. The cause can be simple and practical – to do with the kind of issues we explored in day-to-day mindfulness. If you haven't prepared for a meeting, if you don't have a good filing system, if you forget your train pass, you are likely to get yourself into a bad mood. So notice the things you need to do in order to stay well. Start with practical stuff of day-to-day mindfulness, and then work out from there. It might be that you need to make sure you spend enough time alone, or get enough exercise, or have something creative on the go. It might be that you need fairly regular experiences of worthwhile communication, rather than lots of socializing.

We need to get to know ourselves. It's as if we are complex and mysterious machines. We need to learn how this machine works – what helps it run smoothly, and what makes it blow a gasket! This is not as easy as it sounds. We need to fathom ourselves. This means learning the lessons that life teaches us – learning about our moods, our lights and darks. Self-knowledge is knowing about the shadow places and learning how best to stop ourselves going there. It's about knowing what we need to do in order to keep in positive states of mind and protect ourselves from negativity. It's about fathoming our needs and finding creative ways of meeting them.

Watch out for those early, tell-tale signs that you are getting into a bad mood: the slide into self-pity, the shift from working effectively to overworking and anxiety. Look out for signs that your mood is going down: not eating properly (taking snacks on the run) or comfort eating, not bothering to open your mail or do the washing up, isolating yourself, not enjoying things you normally enjoy, giving up on going to the gym, changes in your sleep pattern, feeling tired all the time. Notice if you're getting into a battle-station mode of thinking, or if you are starting to feel aggrieved, misunderstood, or unappreciated. We all tend to have our own early warning signs. So part of, 'preventing the arising of as yet un-arisen unskilful mental states' is learning what the triggers are for you, and then working out how to respond. If you notice early warning signs and take evasive action, you will be much more likely to prevent the downward spiral into negativity. The key is to catch bad moods early, before they dig in and take hold of your mind.

Cultivating the arising of as yet un-arisen skilful mental states

These are all the things that help you get into a positive state of mind: altruism, communication, meditation, listening to relaxing music, going for a walk, running the marathon, clearing up your bedroom, making a to-do list and then doing the first three things on that list. Cultivating 'as yet un-arisen skilful mental states' means practising life with full attention – mindfulness of the body and *vedana*, not taking our inner narratives too seriously, bringing to mind the teachings in the moment that we need them. We easily forget to prioritise the things that help us get into a positive state. Putting time aside to play badminton, meet a good friend, read a novel, or spend some quiet time at home easily drop off our to-do list. Those things can be the first to go when we feel stressed or over-worked. Sometimes, of course, we have to focus on urgent tasks. But we need to be careful that this fire-fighting attitude doesn't become our basic mindset. Making time to do things that put us in a good state of mind is important. A well-lived life is one that focuses on what is important, not just on what feels urgent.

Maintaining already arisen skilful mental states

This is what we are aiming for: to dwell in positive, creative, ener-getic, aware states of mind. We are trying to make positive states of mind our fundamental habitat – the natural bent and inclination of our being. But, when we feel happy, we often lose our mindfulness; we become intoxicated. Much of our happiness might be better ex-pressed as 'egoistic triumph' or simply 'getting what we want'. There is nothing wrong with this. It's pleasant, even extremely pleasant, to succeed. For most of us to feel happy, we need to feel some sense of success in our life – whether at work, at home, or on the sports field. When we get intoxicated, however, we forget the darker side of life. We distort our perception in the ways I have outlined above: we over-focus on the upside of life, and this stores up trouble for ourselves in the future. When we are in a good mood, we tend to think that we don't need to be mindful anymore, because every-thing is just great! And, as we all must know by now, intoxication comes before a fall.

The other thing to watch out for is thinking, 'At last, I've got some energy. I'm out of the slough of despondency, the painful am-bivalence. I've stopped putting things off. Now I can get on and

173

do everything!' This is where we go from one extreme to another, without learning that one extreme leads to the other! We are in a good mood, our energy is back, and we really go for it... then get exhausted, bad-tempered, or depressed again. Alternating between 'boom and bust' can become a habitual and undermining tendency. If we are prey to this, we need to be especially mindful when we are in a happy, 'can do' mood.

The mindful walk

Working with the five precepts and the four forces might seem like enough to be getting on with for this week! But remember: don't worry about trying to make time to explore all the different teachings introduced in this course. Just reading about them will help. Having said that, if you can make time to explore one of them – such as 'making a fearless moral inventory' – then all the better. Life is an ethical situation. We are constantly called upon to make ethical judgements. Making better, kinder, wiser judgements is the art of mindfulness of *dhammas*. We'll continue developing virtues and strengths in this week's specific practices, starting with the mindful walk.

The mindful walk and the four forces

Notice if you are in a good mood and see what you can do to maintain that. You might focus on the pleasant feelings and let them grow naturally by simply giving them your attention. Try doing this without grasping, without trying to make them grow, as this will be counter-productive.

Do you need to cultivate a positive state of mind? You might notice that you are preoccupied by a particular problem or situation. See if you can shift your attention to a more positive experience/sensation: sunlight in the cherry blossom, the sound of someone's radio. Look for an uplifting, unusual, or funny experience/sensation. Or you may need to question your inner narratives (see week 4). Alternatively, you could drop back into *vedana* and see how it feels in the body to be in a negative state of mind – notice what it does to your belly, your shoulders, and your face. Stay with those bare sensations.

Do you need to prevent unskilful states from arising? Sometimes we are on the edge of a bad mood. We can feel it, like some great pit opening in front of us – we almost want to jump in. See if you can 'look elsewhere', so to speak – coax your mind into getting involved in something more positive. Notice trigger points that are making you vulnerable to bad moods – a nasty cold, sleep deprivation, one meeting too many – and see if you can take evasive action. 'Evasive action' means noticing where your mind is tending and responding appropriately. You might notice that you are starting to see things negatively, even cynically – try to consciously bring to mind something positive and appreciative. Depressed people, for instance, have a ratio of one negative thought to one positive thought. Non-depressed people have a ratio of one negative thought to two positive thoughts.[26] So you can take evasive action by simply bringing in more positive thought.

Are you already in a bad mood? Try to fully acknowledge your state of mind without self-condemnation. Really try and own it – your point of view may be justified, but your anger, self-pity, or resentment is not. You need to decide what you are going to do about the point you are making in your mind, and then let go of the negativity surrounding it. Tune in to the uncomfortable *vedana*. Breathe into it. And let it go. Keep letting go in a gentle, non-judgemental way.

Working with anxiety

Let's look more closely at a mental state that we all experience: anxiety. The word 'anxiety' comes from the Latin 'angere', which means 'to press tightly'. It is associated with words meaning 'to narrow, constrict, or choke'. When we're anxious, it really does feel like we're choking. We feel alienated from our emotions and, because our thoughts are speeded up and fragmentary, it's hard to think clearly. We tend to go over the same fretful narrative again and again. Anxiety has a lot of energy tied up in it. But that energy tends to spin about in our head. One way of working with anxiety is to cultivate its opposite. So, if we notice anxiety on our mindful walk, we can:

Take the attention down to the soles of the feet. The energy of anxiety goes up, as it were, into our fevered brain. Bringing the attention down in the body is a simple antidote to that.

Consciously relax the body. Either systematically – starting from our feet and working upwards to our face – or simply by relaxing the shoulders and belly. Notice if you're leaning forward, as if your mind is already in front of you. Notice if you're frowning or screwing up your face. Keep coming back to softening the belly.

Use the breath. As you walk, count your out-breath. Let your in-breath be completely spontaneous and free, and as you breathe out, count, 'one, two, three, four, five'. Gradually lengthen the out-breath by adding another digit with each successive out-breath. See if you can get beyond 14. But remember: don't strain or snatch at the in-breath – that would mean you are forcing it. Lengthening the out-breath like this has a calming and relaxing effect on the body.

Use sentences that cultivate the opposite of anxiety. You might say to yourself, 'I am walking calmly. I am walking peacefully'. Come back to the body, and then drop in the sentence again.

Slow down! Anxiety speeds things up. So a simple way of working with anxiety is slowing things down. If you're cycling, go slower, let the cycle couriers overtake you!

As usual, use the review chart at the end of this chapter to note down whether or not you remembered to do your mindful walk.

The mindful moment

Use your mindful moment to fully acknowledge your state of mind. Are you happy and relaxed, or unhappy and irritable? Bring to mind the four forces. What do you need to do: maintain, cultivate, prevent, or eradicate? In your journal, note down what state you are in. It will help you get to know yourself better. You might notice that you keep getting angry, or anxious, or just plain fed up.

Because anxiety is such a common and painful state of mind, let's carry on exploring it. The Sanskrit word translated into English as 'anxiety' is *kaukrtya*. It is a state of mind that we frequently experience but have no English word for. Literally translated, *kaukrtya* means something like 'something-not-done-ness' or 'something done that should not have been done'. It's a feeling that can be ethical, which tells you something is up: you feel troubled because you have lied about being a student to get the concessionary rate. Or it can be practical: you leave the house with an uncomfortable feeling then realize you've forgotten your house keys. *Kaukrtya* is our psychic alarm. Often our life is so fast and complicated that we don't have time to hear it. We just have this uncomfortable sense of something not done, or of something done badly. If we don't become aware of the cause of *kaukrtya*, it can become a settled state of mind: the alarm stays on.

So in this week's mindful moment, try to focus on any background sense of *kaukrtya*. See if you can feel it, reflect on it, and find out what it is trying to tell you. See if you can allow whatever is up to come into full consciousness. Notice if something has not been done – you've not sent off for your visa or you've not done that odd job you'd promised your partner you would do. Or notice if you have done something that – with hindsight – feels uncomfortable. Try to clarify what it is. Of course you may not be able to find the cause. It may just be a settled state of discomfort. Use *kaukrtya* as a cue to deepen your awareness. Below are a few pointers to help you.

When we have done something we're ashamed of or feel embarrassed by, we have a strong desire to keep it secret. This is natural enough. We want to avoid pain. But secrets tend to stifle spiritual growth. They stifle energy and isolate us from others. Being able to unburden ourselves to a trusted friend can liberate our awareness and unblock our energy. It can make us feel alive again. Sometimes it's not a case of unease alerting us to something done or not done. There's just this ongoing, niggling feeling of something up, wrong, or missing. This is a good time to take a breathing space:[27]

Become aware of what's going on. Name it: 'I'm in a fury with my friend'; 'I'm dreading starting my new job'; 'I feel irrationally guilty.' Try and fully acknowledge what is happening in the moment. Feel it in your body.

Gently redirect your awareness to your breath. You might use words like, 'coming back to breathing – inhaling, exhaling' to help you focus. Or you might count at the end of the out-breath – in, out, 'one', in, out, 'two'... and so on up to ten.

Expand your awareness. Try and expand your awareness to your whole body. Notice any feelings of discomfort or resistance. Try and breathe into them and let them go. You might say, 'It's OK. Whatever it is, let me feel it.'

As usual, use the review chart at the end of this chapter to note down whether or not you remembered to practise your mindful moment.

This week's meditations

In this week's meditations, notice what state of mind you're in and apply the four forces. Remember to be on the lookout for positive states of mind. Some people assume that going deeper in meditation inevitably involves facing up to emotional trauma – and, of course, sometimes it does. But this attitude can make the difficult aspects of our experience stand out all the more. We are, in effect, looking for trouble, and this will have a distorting effect on our awareness. So, to counteract this tendency, try assuming that positive states of mind lurk in the shadows waiting to be acknowledged. We can experience very powerful positive states of mind in meditation –

ecstasy, rapture, and bliss. These exalted states of mind can even be a bit scary at first. They are a clue to how much positivity and energy is locked up and repressed within us. The way to move towards positive states of mind is to keep an eye out for pleasure – deepening into that pleasure, and nurturing the seeds of calm. A simple way to become more absorbed in meditation is by using a counting technique. You can use the mindfulness of breathing practice in appendix 1 (page 318). Or, in this week's practice, after you have spent some time developing mindfulness of body and *vedana*, you can spend a few minutes counting the out-breath. Let the breath come and go quite naturally. At the end of the out-breath, say, 'one'. Then let the breath come in and out again, and then say, 'two' – and so on up to 10. If you get to 10, simply start at one again. And if you lose count or go beyond the count, just notice that with kindly awareness, and start again at one.

Day 1. *Acknowledgement and acceptance.* Once again, settle into your body and feel your breath coming in and going out. You may like to use one of the counting techniques above. Notice what happens in your mind when you lose contact with your breath. Try to acknowledge and accept whatever thoughts arise. A self-condemning or impatient attitude in meditation is counter-productive. Notice what's going on, name it, and gently come back to the breath.

Day 2. *Cultivate the opposite.* Today, emphasize becoming aware of where your mind goes off to as you sit in meditation. If you notice an unhelpful state of mind, see if you can cultivate the opposite. If you are sleepy, try opening your eyes and bringing your attention high in your body; work at improving your posture – lift your chin slightly and straighten your back. If you are feeling anxious, sit very still, relax, and bring your awareness down in the body – feel the uncomfortable *vedana* and breathe into it. If you are feeling hatred, see if you can cultivate patience – soften the face and belly, root your awareness in the weight of the body.

Day 3. *Enjoy the breath.* Focus on your breathing, perhaps by using the counting technique above. Look for pleasure. Bring to mind how the body is being massaged from within by the breath; or that the breath is like the breeze blowing through the branches of a tree. All you need to do is relax and let the breath breathe you. When you get distracted, see if there is pleasure in what you are distracted by. If there is, see if you can drop beneath the narrative and try to feel the pleasure directly, without the surrounding imagery or story. Feel the pleasure in the body. Remember, pleasure can be very subtle indeed; it can just be the mild sense of ease caused by the warmth of your meditation blanket.

Day 4. *Use reflection.* Settle into the body. After you have relaxed, start noticing the inner sensations around your heart, chest, and belly. Then, whilst noticing this *vedana*, see if you can reflect on positive emotion. You might ask yourself, 'Can I remember a time when I felt really alive, connected with others, or happily absorbed in a meaningful activity?' Notice any response or non-response in your heart, chest, and belly. Think of a time when you were kind, or generous, or simply felt connected with someone. Remember: you're not looking for big emotion here – just a heart-flicker of response. Alternatively, you might just say to yourself, 'May I be well, may I be happy', while focusing on the sensations (or lack of them) around your heart.

Day 5. *Just sitting.* Today, just sit entirely still. Think of meditation as something entirely receptive, and not as anything you need to do.

Start by cultivating mindfulness of the body. See if you can intensify that. If you are feeling a bit low, you might spend a few minutes saying to yourself, 'May I be well and happy.' Then relax. See if you can rest in the body, and when the mind wanders away – as it will do – just notice it, be receptive, and then come back to the body. I think of this approach as 'just waiting in the body'. You are not trying to do anything. There is nothing to change.

Day 6. *Gratitude.* After you have set up the first three stages of mindfulness – how you are in your body, at the level of *vedana*, and what your state of mind feels like – bring to mind people you feel grateful to. Anchor your mind with your breath and then just bring to mind those people – parents, teachers, partner, or friends – that you feel grateful to. Notice your inner response with complete openness to whatever arises.

Day 7. *Appreciation.* In this meditation, use your breath to anchor your awareness in the present. Start the meditation with five minutes of counting after the out-breath. Then, while you carry on being somewhat aware of the breath, see how you can bring to mind the things you already have – health, sense of humour, friends and family. Bring to mind the things you like doing – the book you're enjoying, playing with your child, a funny story you heard at work. Then bring to mind your friends and bring to mind what you appreciate about them. See if you can gently foster this sense of appreciation while keeping some of your awareness on your breath.

Week 5 Practice Review

1. Mindful walk

Were you able to remember to do the mindful walk?

	Day 1	Day 2	Day 3	Day 4	Day 5	Day 6	Day 7
Tick/yes Cross/no							

Write your reflections here

2. Mindful moment

Were you able to remember to practise the mindful moment?

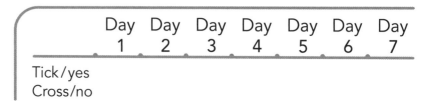

	Day 1	Day 2	Day 3	Day 4	Day 5	Day 6	Day 7
Tick/yes Cross/no							

Try not to get disheartened if you forgot your mindful moment – absolutely everybody does. See if you can find a way of reminding yourself: put a post-it note on your bathroom mirror (if you have chosen brushing your teeth), or put a little Buddha figure in your car (if you use the first five minutes of your drive to work). You may need to change the occasion of your mindful moment, or perhaps you could set your watch alarm for a certain time as a reminder.

3. The five precepts and the four forces

How did you get on with putting the five precepts and four forces into practice? What did you do, how did you cultivate them? Did you notice any issues that arose – such as guilt or resistance? Were you convinced that cultivating positive emotion is the key to authentic happiness?

Write your reflections here

4. Meditation

How did your meditation go this week? Did you manage to do it? How did you feel after the meditation? Did you try counting at the end of the out-breath?

Write your reflections here

Mindfulness of *dhammas* concludes the path of full attention. We don't need any more stages; we don't need a fifth sphere of mindfulness. All we need to do is keep bringing the teachings to mind until we have gained insight into those teachings – until we have seen that hatred is never overcome by hatred. Insight is direct knowing. It is not primarily an intellectual understanding. It is intuition, imagination, thought, and direct perception all in one. We can only 'know directly' if we apply the Buddha's teachings to our emotional lives, if we allow our understanding to transform our hearts.

At the same time, there is a possible danger. We can think of mindfulness as something private – something we do for our own benefit. If we approach mindfulness in this spirit, it becomes overly inward-looking and self-preoccupied. True awareness shines out to the world around us and to other people. So it is time we turned our attention to the beauties around us, to nature, objects, and works of art.

Sandpiper

The roaring alongside he takes for granted,
and every so often the world is bound to shake.
He runs, he runs to the south, finical, awkward,
in a state of controlled panic, a student of Blake.

The beach hisses like fat. On his left, a sheet
of interrupting water comes and goes
and glazes over his dark and brittle feet.
He runs, he runs straight through it, watching his toes.

–Watching, rather, the spaces of sand between them,
where (no detail too small) the Atlantic drains
rapidly backwards and downwards. As he runs,
he stares at the dragging grains.

The world is a mist. And then the world is
minute and vast and clear. The tide
is higher or lower. He couldn't tell you which.
His beak is focused; he is preoccupied,

looking for something, something, something.
Poor bird, he is obsessed!
the millions of grains are black, white, tan, and gray,
mixed with quartz grains, rose and amethyst.

Elizabeth Bishop[28]

Nature and Art

Appreciation as a way of life

When he taught the four spheres of mindfulness, the Buddha was saying that a well-lived and meaningful life is a life of full attention. He taught the path of awareness so that we could explore the mysteries of consciousness and realize our potential for Enlightenment. But any system leaves things out. Life is too big. Our lives are too messy, unpredictable, and multifaceted to be encapsulated in any teaching or philosophy.

So when we look at the four spheres, two things are missing: the environment and other people. By 'environment' I mean countryside and city centre, spaniels and herring gulls, pot plants and artichokes as well as objects – the laptop I'm working on, the mug next to me, the pencil on my desk. Just as mindfulness of the body means caring for the body – going for a swim, eating vegetables – mindfulness of the environment includes caring for the environment: leaving the car in the garage, not leaving the tap running whilst

Cultivating wise attention

The mindful daytrip

The mindful walk

The mindful moment

Creating a shrine

we brush our teeth. The environment also includes works of art and architecture: the riff of a guitar, the fortissimo of a tenor, the pink triangle on a blue square in a painting by Kandinsky.

So, in this chapter, I want to explore the value of seeing things, hearing things, touching, smelling, and reading things. I want to explore the value of art and poetry. I want to emphasize the need to preserve the natural world. Awareness of the environment is a vital part of life with full attention.

Elizabeth Bishop's poem, 'Sandpiper' (quoted at the beginning of this chapter), is a wonderful example of mindfulness of the natural environment. She describes a sandpiper looking for food along the coast. It's a familiar enough sight – one that we might have seen on a family holiday, or glimpsed from the window of a train. But how vividly do we engage with such sights? Do we really see them? We are usually so engrossed in the story of ourselves – our internal narratives and chatter – that the natural world only registers dimly on the periphery of our awareness.

Elizabeth Bishop sees with extraordinary clarity and feeling. Her poem reminds me of the fact that true mindfulness is vivid and sympathetic, concrete and imaginative, intelligent and emotional. In other words, mindfulness is integrated perception. It is the whole person wholly attending. The mind-clearing detail:

a sheet
of interrupting water comes and goes
and glazes over his dark and brittle feet

combines with a gentle sense of comedy:

He runs, he runs straight through it, watching his toes. [...]
Poor bird, he is obsessed!

How many of us can enjoy nature with such keen-eyed warmth?
'Sandpiper' also speaks of connectedness and intimacy. The bird is
not seen as existing 'out there', a mere ornithological specimen; it is
relished and identified with. Bishop's poem begins with:

The roaring alongside he takes for granted,
and every so often the world is bound to shake.

And of course, this roaring is also the roaring of the world – the
sounds of the 20th century, of war and hardship. The poet knows
only too well that the world is bound to shake. But she also knows
that this propensity for shaking is true of her own life – from her
mother's insanity to the suicide of her lover.[29] All through the poem,
we sense a deep connection between the bird and the poet. But this
identification is outward-looking and appreciative. She is not using
the bird as an excuse to talk about herself. The sense of fellow feeling
arises from a vivid engagement with the seen. In this true seeing,
the division between 'self' and 'world' begins to dissolve – things
become animated with mind. Both are experienced as more meaningful and more alive.

Bishop describes her sandpiper as a 'student of Blake'. She is thinking
of William Blake and his famous line, 'To see the world in a grain
of sand'. This is our aim in mindfulness of the natural world – to see
everything reflected in anything: 'the world in a grain of sand'. And
this is precisely how the sandpiper sees:

The world is a mist. And then the world is minute and vast and clear.

'Sandpiper' reminds me of a quality I know from Sanskrit: the quality of *vidya*. *Vidya* can be translated as, 'analytic appreciative understanding'. It is a kind of 'relishing of things', a purified sense of appreciation without any trace of acquisitiveness. *Vidya* is also a word for 'wisdom implicit in true appreciation'. When we see with *vidya*, we see that the world is not a sequence of discrete, material things existing out there. We see that everything fuses with everything else, partakes in everything else – that outside the limits and limitations of self, everything is interconnected.

I want to emphasize appreciation as a way of life. By appreciation, I don't mean being so hothouse delicate that we can't do a hard day's work, dig a trench, or run for a bus. But I also don't mean a life of activity with the odd evening set aside to watch a DVD or visit the ballet. I mean appreciation as an absolutely central attitude to life. Our aim should be to simply appreciate life, to stand back and enjoy it all. Yes, we need to work and plan. Sometimes we need to push ourselves beyond the comfort zone in order to grow, do whatever we can to help others, or take on projects and responsibilities. But we shouldn't take all this too seriously. There needs to be a certain playfulness, a certain lightness of touch. If we do everything for a reason – because it's good for us, because it will help us win friends and influence people, because the planet needs our help – then we will take all the joy and spontaneity out of life. We need to remember to enjoy things. Our basic attitude to life should be aesthetic.

This 'appreciative mode' has radical consequences: we become less preoccupied with worldly concerns. We do what we need to do in order to live and make a contribution to the lives of others. But we choose to live a simple, uncluttered life. Appreciation needs quietude to blossom. It needs a kind of spaciousness, a freedom from complexity and over-timetabling. This is why it is so much easier to experience appreciation on a retreat. On retreat, you live without many possessions. You turn off your phone and put away your laptop. Each day follows a simple programme of meditation, discussion, and free time, so you don't waste time and energy making choices. You live a simple life – communal, uncomplicated, in touch with the natural world – in order to relish simple things: your breath in meditation, the sight of a blackbird, or the poetry of Elizabeth Bishop.

The spiritual value of the appreciative mode is in its non-utilitarian, non-acquisitive nature. Appreciation is an end in itself. It is its own reward. And as we develop this appreciative mode, we start to become sensitized to how so much of modern life is ugly. We notice how banal the media can be, how unpalatable harsh speech, cynical ideas, and snide remarks are. We start to notice that egoism, in all of its myriad guises, is not very productive – we see how uncreative it is, how coarse and predictable. True appreciation is a letting-go of self, a letting-go of egoism. When we are absorbed in the appreciative awareness of a tree, or a poem, or a sandpiper, we forget ourselves and, by doing so, we transcend ourselves. Or to put it another way: in our moments of deep appreciation, self becomes relational. Instead of tending to be entrenched, repetitive, and habitual, self becomes open-ended, spontaneous, and creative. In Elizabeth Bishop's 'Sandpiper', self and world modify and animate one another.

Appreciating nature

We need to develop the capacity to take pleasure in things, to let things be as they are and enjoy them as they are. It is so tempting to focus on what we haven't got: the holiday we can't afford, the boyfriend that got away, the free time we wish we had more of. We can build our sense of self around the feeling of being overlooked or hard done by. To counteract this, we need to cultivate interest in – and appreciation of – what is right in front of us, right now. And we can start with the natural world.

Interaction with other species is good for us. Pet owners show fewer signs of stress than those without them. They experience fewer minor ailments, and have lower blood pressure. According to the American Heart Foundation, after just a 12-minute visit from a dog, heart-failure patients will experience significantly decreased levels of anxiety, reduced blood pressure, and diminished release of harmful hormones.[30] 'Pet therapy' has been used to help people with mental health problems, violent prisoners, and problem teenagers. It seems that any contact with other species can have a positive effect, whether it's keeping terrapins and koi carp or going out bird watching.

Studies have shown that hospital patients with a window overlooking a garden recover more quickly than those who have to look out at a wall. Similarly, you are liable to get better sooner and have fewer side effects if you can see a tree from your room. Gardening is being increasingly recognized as having all kinds of psychological and physical benefits. Even houseplants are good for us; they help us become calmer and more optimistic and, according to research in Norway, they reduce fatigue, coughs, sore throats, and cold-related illnesses.[31]

As we cultivate life with full attention, we start to experience nature as something valuable in and of itself. This kind of genuine feeling for nature takes time to develop. It is not primarily ideological. It is not 'environmentalism' as a political cause – however needful that may be. It is more akin to love.

I remember going out into the countryside on my first retreat. I tried to take pleasure in the sight of a wren, or the crimsons and golds in a sunset. But if I was honest with myself, I found it all rather dull. I preferred sex and cinema. It was only after practising mindfulness for a number of years that I started to feel that unforced and genuine enjoyment of nature that is the hallmark of true appreciation. As I developed and deepened my awareness, I started to feel a certain resonance with things – with sunlight glittering on willow leaves, or the flight of a wood pigeon. This resonance wasn't something I thought into being (though reflection played its part) – it was more a willingness to let the natural world enrich and modify my consciousness. I can't remember when my feeling for landscape changed but, gradually, I began to notice a new sense of connectedness. I increasingly felt part of nature, rather than a bored or dutiful observer of it.

This kind of feeling for the natural world is important in its own right. Once it is developed and established, it is a hallmark of spiritual maturity. The German philosopher Immanuel Kant said that, 'The love of nature for its own sake is always a sign of goodness.'[32] The key point here is: for its own sake.

At the same time, we need to connect our developing resonance with nature with a willingness to forego those things that contribute to its destruction. We need to honestly examine our greediness, wastefulness, and selfishness in relation to the planet, and see what we can do to reduce our impact on it. More than ever, it is obvious that our acquisitive mode of being – our 'getting and spending' as

Wordsworth put it – is destroying our world.[33] We urgently need to learn the value of selfless appreciation. A life with full attention is a life where we need less in order to make us happy.

Appreciating the arts

One of the ways in which we can cultivate appreciation of the natural world is by developing our appreciation of art. Cyprus trees have never looked the same since Van Gogh painted them; Monet helped us to see the colour of shadows; and Rembrandt to relish the glow of human skin. Painters can help us notice patterns and connections, affinities and ambiguities, subtleties and nuances. People talk about 'a painter's eye' – the drama that Constable relished in storm clouds over Salisbury cathedral or the strange beauty that Morandi saw in his collection of dusty old bottles. We need to develop this 'painter's eye' if we are to cultivate mindfulness of our environment.

And poetry can help too. A good poem will help us see, in our minds eye, with new clarity. The 'finical' and 'awkward' movements of a sandpiper described by Elizabeth Bishop make us think, 'Yes, I've seen that, I didn't know I'd seen that, but now I can see it in my mind.' By simply connecting one thing with another – which is basically how a metaphor works – we can suddenly see things afresh.

To be healthy human beings, we need to keep travelling between two worlds. The first world is our world of work and rest, earning and spending. The second world is like the first world except that it is transfigured by the imagination of the novelist, poet, or playwright. This second world is a counterbalance to the first world. It bears its countervailing weight against the chaos, banality, tedium, and pain of so much of our lives.[34] The second world of the imagination presses back against the day-to-day reality of the first world, thereby consoling and refreshing us.

The spiritual value of art is to be found in the pleasure it can give us. That pleasure is (or can be) of a particular quality. It can be innocent – by which I mean not based in egotistic desire or hatred. We can read a poem or look at a painting and feel uplifted. We can come away from watching *Macbeth* or *The Cherry Orchard* and feel we have gained a deeper understanding of what it means to be human. This is what Seamus Heaney calls the 'redress of poetry': that the arts can give us back our life, purified and absolved by the imaginative vision of the artist. It's a rare kind of pleasure, but it exists. At best, the arts can give us access to a kind of satisfaction that unites pleasure and meaning. When we say something is 'beautiful' we mean that it is both pleasurable, and at the same time, meaningful.

In the seen, only the seen

The appreciative mode is an antidote to the prevailing mode in the West – the acquisitive mode. We can start practising it now, by stroking the dog or pruning the forsythia. We can cultivate a love of the natural world and a willingness to do whatever we can to preserve it. We can enjoy what we have, instead of longing for what we don't have. We can go on retreat. We can go for a walk. We can read those writers who take us into the other world of imaginative appreciation.

And we can move towards *vidya*. There is a famous Buddhist text in which the Buddha communicates the essence of spiritual life, the culminating insight of life with full attention. It is a very simple teaching, at least intellectually. He says: 'In the seen, only the seen, in the heard, only the heard.'[35] This is experience with nothing left over, with nothing of 'me' added on. It is pure, selfless appreciation. When we see things in this way – without describing, grasping, or referring everything back to me, me, me – we see with *vidya*. And when we see with *vidya*, the world starts to shine. We look at a building or a mop bucket or a bramble hedge, and there seems to be something *more*, it seems alive in a way we can't pin down. The life in the world 'out there' seems connected to the life 'in here' – both seem more vivid, and at the same time more mysterious. The chasm between the world and the self has begun to disappear. We know, at least theoretically, that matter is not dead, inert stuff. When we see with heightened awareness, we begin to percieve the mystery of life. There is experience, full experience, but it is ungraspable, un-sayable, un-nameable. At moments like this, we intuit a whole new way of experiencing the world. We move towards wisdom.

Sixth practice week

I would like to start our week of mindfulness by suggesting some general approaches to becoming more aware of our environment. After that, we'll turn our attention to the daily mindful walk, the mindful moment, and to sitting meditation. But before I do any of that, let's look at an important Buddhist teaching called *dhamma*, which I have briefly mentioned before and is particularly relevant to this week's practice.

Wise and unwise attention

I have suggested that sometimes the best thing we can do if we are slipping into a bad mood is distract ourselves. But calling something 'a distraction' is to put it negatively – as if the real thing is the bad mood, and distracting ourselves from it merely an evasion. Of course, distraction is often an evasion: we eat too many biscuits because we're depressed or lonely or we shop for computer software to get away from that dreadful empty feeling inside.But this is not the whole story. Sometimes 'distraction' – or the shifting of attention – is exactly what we should be doing, especially as a short-term solution. We naturally distract toddlers when they cry because their parents are out. We use distraction as a deliberate, short-term strategy, knowing that the child is in no real danger, and that her tears, though real enough, do not need to be taken too seriously. We are not so very different. Consciously shifting our attention onto something more constructive can be a valuable strategy for working with the mind. The question is: how do we know when we should face up to things and when we should turn our attention to something else? This question is answered by the Buddha's teaching of wise and unwise attention.

Going back to the four forces for a moment, unwise attention causes un-arisen negative states of mind to arise and makes any negative mood we are already in worse. When we ruminate, we are giving our thoughts unwise attention – digging over childhood traumas, replaying painful narratives. When our focus of attention makes us angrier, more depressed, or resentful, our states of mind have become the object of unwise attention.

Unwise attention also relates to our environment. We can give unwise attention to seductive advertising, cynical chat shows, gossiping work colleagues, or sensationalizing newspapers. A lot of the things we give our attention to in modern life will provoke, and even encourage, negative states of mind. The question we need to ask ourselves is this: is the effect of giving my attention an increase or a decrease in suffering?

When we give something wise attention, negative states of mind don't arise, and any bad mood that we're experiencing disappears. Incidentally, this may be one of the values of the various kinds of psychological therapies – a good therapist will support your wise attention by encouraging you to experience difficult emotions without exacerbating them at the same time. Certainly, this is an aspect of friendship, as we shall see.

The art of happiness is learning how to arouse wise attention and avoid unwise attention. This is precisely what this course has been encouraging you to do for the past few weeks. When we are absorbed watching our breath in meditation, we are abiding in wise attention. A meaningful conversation, a walk along the seafront, singing in a choir – they can all be aspects of wise attention. One of the reasons we get into bad moods is because we often don't have enough positive outlets for our energy. This is why cultivating sustaining interests is so important to our psychological health. Whether we join an amateur drama society, learn the foxtrot, or read books about quantum physics, we need to find positive outlets for our energy and interest. If we don't find positive outlets, we will find negative ones. The main thing we are trying to do in our life is become interested in whatever takes us forward, in what contributes to our own welfare as well as that of others.

The appreciative attention we give the world around us – listening to music, going mountain biking, enjoying a wall covered with graffiti – protects us from our habits of unwise attention. We can learn from Darleen Cohen who teaches people who live with chronic pain. She says, 'If you have chronic pain, your job is to (1) acknowledge that pain and its burden and (2) enrich your life exponentially.' If managing your pain is one of five things in your life, five major themes, then you're going to get into trouble. It needs to be one of at least ten. Managing pain is only one part of managing pain. The other nine parts are the things we need to do that stimulate our thinking, enrich our emotions, and spark off our imagination. We need to make life 'so rich that no pain can commandeer it.'[36]

SOME IDEAS FOR CULTIVATING WISE ATTENTION

An environmental week

You could use this week to help protect the environment. You could decide not to use the car. You could mend an object rather than throw it away and get a new one. You could take bottles to the bottle bank, turn the central heating down, or change to eco-friendly light bulbs. You could recycle cardboard and start composting. You could cycle to work. And why not turn off all electronic devices when you're not using them? If we all did that, we would save thousands of pounds of carbon dioxide every year.[37] You could plant a tree (a single tree will absorb one ton of carbon dioxide in its lifetime) or plan a holiday that doesn't include flying. These are small things. They will not in themselves save the planet. But they might help. Of course, you could go further and start sharing. You could move into a house-share and share the washing machine, the dryer, the fridge, the vacuum, and the heating.

See if you can use this week to set up positive habits that will continue into the future. The usual guidance for this is the three Rs – Reduce, Re-use, Recycle. Do what you can to reduce your consumption: re-use rather than take away and throw away; recycle as much as possible.

Improve your cultural diet

Just as many of us need to improve our nutritional diet – renouncing burgers for vegetables and mineral water – in the same way, many of us need to improve our cultural diet. The quality of what we put into the mind is just as important as the quality of what we put into the belly.

So, this week, have a look at the kind of things you do for relaxation and entertainment. Ask yourself honestly: do they have any 'nutritional value'? Do they help or hinder the path of full attention? How much time do you spend surfing the web? Do you spend your commute reading free papers or playing games on your mobile? When you get home, do you watch any old rubbish on TV? Ask yourself when you last read a decent novel or visited an art gallery. You can tell the 'nutritional value' of something by how it leaves you feeling at the end – bloated or satisfied, narrowed or enlarged, coarsened or uplifted. Here are a few suggestions:

Say, 'no' to the men standing outside tube stations handing out free newspapers. Instead, keep a slim volume of poetry with you. Read one or two poems on your journey each day. Read each poem two or three times, not just once. Good poems need time and space to be appreciated; they can't be speed-read. Poems are like those signs that light up on country roads just as you're coming into a village – the ones that say 'slow down!' They slow you down and help you stop and appreciate things. And it doesn't matter which poems you choose. There are lots of good anthologies. You might explore a particular poet: Philip Larkin, Seamus Heaney, or Elizabeth Bishop. If you want to try something more 'difficult', try Wallace Stevens or Paul Celan. You could read Ruth Padel's book, *The Poem and the Journey*.[38] She introduces 60 contemporary poets and explores a poem from each of them. It's a good way of introducing yourself to new writing. If you don't commute to work, see if you can read a poem every night before you go to sleep or first thing in the morning before you meditate.

I often go and look at one of my favourite paintings in the National Gallery in London: 'An Autumn Landscape with a View of Het Steen in the Early Morning' by Rubens. Rubens is never very popular, so I can always get a place on the bench in front of it. I look, and I look, and I wait. Sometimes I wait for so long that the guards get edgy. I'm waiting for the picture to come alive. It's not difficult. I just give it my attention. It's like meditation; all I need to do is keep coming back to the object of attention. And as I do that, I notice how Rubens has caught the glitter of silver birch leaves or the distant view of wet fields. I don't need to know anything about baroque art. I don't need to know when Rubens painted it or why (though that's interesting enough). I just wait until I feel an affinity with the painting in front of me.

Some people may find art galleries intimidating and feel that art is all too highbrow and difficult. Actually, there's plenty to enjoy. We just need to remember that artists paint for us – to give you and me pleasure. So this week, see if you can visit an art gallery. If you don't have a gallery nearby, then make a date in your diary for a daytrip. Have a look at the gallery website. See if you can find one or two paintings that you like and respond to. You don't need to know anything about them – you can find out more later if you feel like it. If you can't decide which paintings to look at, just choose one or two of the gallery's best-known works. Choose one painting – two or three at most. An important fact about any of the arts is that they need 'quality time'. They cannot be thoughtlessly consumed. You can't make yourself appreciate art, but you can at least give it the time of day.

How to look at a painting

Go to the café first. You need to do this in order to change gear from the day-to-day world of ordinary life to the world of imagination. Treat the café as a chance to relax – soften the belly, drop the shoulders and let your mind settle. You can take a three-minute breathing space – it will help to get you in the right state of mind for appreciation.

Choose one or two pictures. Look at each of them for at least 10 minutes or just look at one painting for 20 minutes. You might like to choose a painting that has a bench in front of it!

Stand further away and then close up. Spend some time stepped back from the painting so that you can take in the whole thing. Also spend some time standing closer up so you can enjoy the fine details. Then go from one to the other a few times.

Look at the abstract elements. All paintings, from Giotto to Picasso, are built up of formal abstract elements – the shape made by a figure, a horse, or group of trees. Try and see how these abstract elements relate harmoniously across the surface of the picture. Notice how these abstract relationships – between foreground and background, smaller and larger shapes – create patterns, rhyming and mirroring.

Discover the meaning of the painting. Painters use these formal abstract elements to add to the meaning, message, and focus of the picture. Linking the hillside with the Madonna in a Raphael painting creates a pleasing feeling of harmony and calm, which is part of the meaning of painting. It also gives the Madonna a monumental quality – it invests her with stability, security, and grandeur.

Notice handling and colour. Notice how the paint is applied – is it laid on in thick impasto (as in Van Gogh), or in thin mists of colour (as in Turner)? Is the use of colour bright and discordant, or soft and glowing? Does it have a particular 'colour world' – bluish-grey or brown? How is colour distributed across the painting? Again, try and notice how these things contribute to the meaning and atmosphere of the painting. Each element of a painting will be adding to the impact of the whole.

Play with the meanings. All of the above need to be explored in the spirit of play. When you look at pictures in a gallery, you want to feel that you are standing in your slippers – completely at home, unbuttoned, and relaxed. Play with the meanings: what do the shapes, colours, and textures remind you of? What association do you have with them? So in Raphael's 'Madonna', for instance, she is wearing a warm red gown that covers her chest and heart, which suggests her emotional love and kindness.

Find the meaning in your own experience. This is vital. Find a personal connection with the work. What does it mean to you? Does it embody values that are important for you? And remember: this sense of value doesn't need to imply belief – I can enjoy the Madonna's gentleness, grace, and warmth without believing she is the Mother of God. Play with the metaphors of the painting and see how they connect with your life. This takes time and sensitivity to how the painting makes you feel – what it sparks off in your mind. Any connection will help: the flowering meadow reminding you of a picnic, the view in a Rubens painting reminding you of your hill walking. Find intimate connections, meaning, and resonances.

Try another painting or another day. Of course, you can do all the above and still not feel much sense of connection. Meaningful aesthetic experiences are created by a mysterious interaction between the quality of the object (in this case, the painting), the quality of your attention, and the particular patterning of your life history and values. No one finds every painting moving. Even great masterpieces can be boring. So you might try another painting, or come back on another day when you are in a different state of mind. And, as you become more accustomed to looking at paintings, see if you can extend the range of your interests. Don't just stick with the Impressionists.

Try to have at least one evening this week when you just read a book. Resist the television. The trick is not to turn it on; once it's on, it's much more difficult to turn off! Don't have any music on in the background and turn off your mobile phone. See if you can read for an hour or more without getting up to do anything else, such as making tea, or checking your emails. Spending more time with a book means spending less time on other leisure activities. So set aside your glossy magazines, Sunday newspapers, computer games, or web blog. The idea is to create a concentrated period of uninterrupted time to enjoy reading. Once again, you may need to enlist the support of your partner or roommates. Someone who came along to classes at the London Buddhist Centre decided to suggest to her partner that they had one silent evening that week so they could read and relax. So you could try that too.

A reader's starter kit

When I was young, I wanted to enjoy poetry and literature but I had no idea where to start. My education had been fairly rudimentary so I tended to think that the 'high arts' were beyond me. Looking back on it, I would have appreciated a reader's starter kit introducing a few books and poems to spark my interest and get me going. So, at the risk of sounding patronizing or of inflicting my own particular taste upon you the reader, I thought it might be helpful if I suggested a few things that I have enjoyed. I make no attempt to be exhaustive or objective. This reader's starter kit consists of works of imaginative vitality and intellectual weight. It is based on the kind of books I have happened upon and appreciated. Who knows, you might like them too!

Poetry

John Keats: *Autumn*
W. H. Auden: *The Mask of Achilles*
Elizabeth Bishop: *The Moose*
Seamus Heaney: *District and Circle*

Fiction

Tolstoy: *War and Peace*
Emily Brontë: *Wuthering Heights*
Vikram Seth: *A Suitable Boy*
Kazuo Ishiguro: *Never Let Me Go*

Non-fiction

Bryan McGee: *Confessions of a Philosopher*
Simon Schama: *Rembrandt's Eyes*
Martin E.P. Seligman: *Authentic Happiness*
Sangharakshita: *Who is the Buddha?*

Many people find that it's best to follow a thread of interest when they explore the arts. So, for instance, reading Auden led me to reading Marianne Moore (they were friends), which led me to reading Elizabeth Bishop (Moore acted as Bishop's mentor for a while). Looking at Van Gogh led me to Cézanne, which in turn led me to the Renaissance painter Piero della Francesca, whose style of painting seems almost to prefigure Cézanne's. The thread doesn't need to be highbrow. I first got into opera by listening to Malcolm McLaren's post-punk fusion of Madame Butterfly and 1980s' rhythm and blues. So find your own thread of interest. Follow where it leads you. It might take you to reading biographies. After all, works of art are best understood within the context of the artist's life and times. But remember: the main thing, spiritually speaking, is to discover genuine enjoyment, intrinsic interest, palpable delight. It may take some effort, but it will be worthwhile in the end.

Go on a mindful daytrip

Make a date in your diary for a daytrip – or pilgrimage, as I prefer to call them, even though that might sound too religious and
austere for some people. When you go on pilgrimage, you visit a
sacred place such as Bodhgaya, Lourdes, Santiago de Compostela, or
Mecca. This place manifests your values – the shrine of a saint, the
birthplace of a Buddha – and the journey takes place on two different levels: outward and inner. Christian pilgrims will often walk
a special pilgrim way, stopping at a church or oratory to offer up
prayers. In pilgrimage, inner purification and outward journey are
united.

So choose your sacred site. You could choose to visit a bird sanctuary.
You might take your binoculars and see if you can see an avocet. This
particular kind of bird was once extinct in the UK but now, miracu-
lously, they're back! Seeing an avocet, watching a flock of lapwing or
arctic tern circling and landing: that's a sacred sight, so long as you
give them your undivided attention. Bird sanctuaries express values:
the wonder of nature, its endless variety and beauty.[39] Or you might
visit one of the great cathedrals, an ancient stone circle, or a famous
museum. Think of a place that communicates value to you.

This is how I do it: I try to be mindful of my walk to the station. I
see if I can catch the fine details that I so often miss – the shadow-
show of leaf patterns on a white van, the blue swirl of a tattoo on
a stranger's forearm. In the train, I notice the weight of my body, I
allow my belly to soften. I become aware of the other passengers, the
free newspapers left on vacant seats, the empty milkshake carton
rolling about on the floor. When I get into town, I go for a croissant
and cappuccino. I taste the coffee. I enjoy gathering up the last of

the froth with a plastic spoon. And, in my journal, I write the things that strike me – two terriers getting caught up in each other's leads, a homeless man carrying a sleeping bag and some cardboard, a crocodile of Chinese school children making their way to the National Gallery. Then, when I've established myself in mindfulness, I go into the gallery and look at a painting.

You will all have your own sacred site. Wherever it is, my advice is: go alone, or with a fellow pilgrim that you can share your experience with. Take your journal. Go in the spirit of pilgrimage, which means that the journey and the arrival, the inner voyage and the outer coach trip are all equally valid. And you could decide – as you sit in the tearoom of a favourite museum, or hide behind a bush in a bird sanctuary – you could decide to write a poem about it, or a short story, or a day diary. Think of it as a day of full attention. After all, it's the quality of attention that makes something sacred.

The mindful walk

All the above are things you could do this week, or at least plan to do. Of course, you could simply spend more time gardening, looking at your tropical fish, walking the dog, or re-potting your yucca tree. However you go about it, bring your awareness into the world around you. Relish things. Cultivate wise attention.

We easily forget to pay attention to what is around us; we may feel stressed, over-stimulated, or uplifted by it – but we often don't really look, listen, touch, or hear. We may find ourselves reacting negatively to our environment – the packed concourse, the filthy streets, the driving rain – without noticing that we are tensing up against it, or moaning about it in our mind.

So, this week, carry on with the daily walking practice as before (you might want to look back at the list of ways of approaching it to refresh your memory), and whilst staying aware of the body and its movements, try to bring more attention to the environment.

Try to see things as they are. Notice bus stations, shop fronts, or litter without reacting to them. Just notice. Include sound in your awareness – birdsong, a truck revving at traffic lights, a baby crying in a buggy. Bring more awareness to sight and sound as you walk. Try to remain in touch with the weight and movement of your body at the same time.

Mutual conditioning. See if you can notice the extent to which the environment conditions your mental state – how it's easier to feel cheerful when the sun is shining; how miserable you can become if it keeps raining. Notice how advertisements can stimulate discontent, how they can make you want to buy something. Become mindful of the effect of a police siren, or a poster for underwear. Notice how the environment affects your body – do you tighten your guts, hunch your shoulders, screw up your eyes? Likewise, notice how the mood you are in affects your perception. We have a marked tendency to project our mental states onto the world around us. If we feel grumpy, things tend to look ugly. If we feel rushed, traffic lights seem to always be on red and shop assistants seem to be especially slow!

Visiting from another country. Carry on your normal walking meditation route, but see if you can take in the things you don't usually notice, the things you have become blind to – it might be the architecture above the shop windows, or the iridescent neck of feral pigeons. You could imagine that you are visiting from another country, or another planet. Bring a poet's or a painter's eye to your experience. After all, mindfulness is about enhancing the senses – experiencing the world with more vividness.

Remember you are trying to be aware of the environment in an integrated way – at home in your body, aware of how you feel, sensitive to what you see, hear, taste, or touch. You are trying to extend the circumference of your awareness to include inner and outer world. As usual, use the review chart at the end of this chapter to note down whether or not you remembered to do the mindful walk.

The mindful moment

Use your mindful moment as a cue to become aware of your surroundings. Try to intensify your awareness of the things you live amongst. If you use your bedtime ablutions as your mindful moment, really taste your toothpaste, feel the soap in your hands. If it's the first time you turn on your computer, then notice the things on your desk: the Scotch-tape snail, the highlighter pen, the paperclips caught up in each other. Nothing is insignificant in the gaze of mindfulness.

And use your imagination. You will probably need to find ways of keeping your mindfulness practice interesting. You might want to change your mindful moment, or find new triggers to remind you about it. You could write a little story about your toothpaste or the icons on your computer – so that each time you see them, you are a bit more aware of them. Sketching the objects on your desk, or describing them in your journal could help to trigger your awareness.

Try spending 10 or 15 minutes looking at the environment. You might just look out of your window. I sometimes do this first thing in the morning. Or you could sit in the park and watch the squirrels. If you're a keen gardener, you could just sit in the garden for a while.

Resist the urge to do that last bit of weeding. Get yourself a cup of tea, stop, look, and listen. Don't do anything. Just become gently aware of what is around you.

You are trying to enter a state of reverie, where you let go of things to do, people to see, and business to deal with. So remember to turn off your mobile phone. If you have the phone on, you're always subliminally aware that someone might call, that you might have a particular task to do or think about, which prevents your mind from opening out and relaxing. Part of maturing as a person is learning how to start – how to get over the hump of resistance and apply yourself to a task – but it is also about learning how to stop.

Or you might decide to listen to some music. Choose a CD you find beautiful and just listen to it, without washing up, ironing, or sorting out your papers. Try to listen deeply and un-distractedly.

Meditation – creating a shrine

It is important to set aside a place to meditate. We need somewhere quiet – without the television on, or a jazz riff seeping through the walls. We need somewhere comfortable – not very cold, but not hot and stuffy either. We need somewhere we won't be disturbed. And, if possible, we need somewhere aesthetically pleasing. The main shrine room at the London Buddhist Centre has a glowing maple floor. Lights can be dimmed, and we burn candles and incense. It is uncluttered and spacious with a shrine to sit in front of.

The word 'shrine' means 'place of peace'. It is a place that embodies your values. So, this week, you might decide to make a little 'place of

213

peace' in your home. You might, for instance, spend some time tidying your room, freeing space where you can sit and develop peacefulness. You might open a window to let in some fresh air. You might buy yourself some meditation cushions to sit on.

And you could build a shrine. When I was a student, I made one with a tatty bit of old curtain slung over a box. I enjoyed lighting candles and burning incense – it became my little ritual to set myself up for meditation. So why not build a shrine of your own? You could decorate it with things that are important to you – a postcard of somewhere you find beautiful, a few roses from the garden, an image that inspires you. Or you could create a shrine using traditional objects such as:

Candles   symbolizing the light of the Buddha's wisdom

Flowers   symbolizing impermanence, the essence of Buddhist teaching

Incense   symbolizing the positive, perfuming effect that men and women who practise life with full attention can have on the world

Preparing a shrine before meditation is a good way to change gear, to move from the external world of activity to the inner world of receptivity and exploration. Lighting candles and incense helps us to slow down. It signals a transition. And it helps us value meditation. Creating a shrine is a way of saying, 'This is important to me.' Many people put a Buddha statue on their shrine. The Buddha is usually depicted in meditation. Placing flowers and candles around this figure is a way of saying to ourselves, 'This is the kind of tranquillity and aliveness I aspire to.'

This week's meditations

How are you getting on with meditation? Have you been doing it, or have you rather given up? Are you finding an appropriate and regular time to meditate? Or do you find yourself always putting it off and thinking you'll do it later, but never quite getting round to it? This week, see if you can do a little more meditation. If you only managed once last week, see if you can meditate twice or three times this week. If you have been meditating for 20 minutes every day, see if you can sit for a little longer (without forcing it). Remember: if you get time, briefly note down in your journal how the meditation went.

Day 1. *Mindfulness of sounds*. Start by developing awareness of the body. Work through the body systematically from your toes to the crown of your head. Then, remaining in touch with your body, listen to the sounds around you. Sounds do not have labels attached to them such as 'music from a car radio', 'birdsong'. They are just sounds. So try to notice sounds without attaching labels to them, without describing and naming them in your mind. Just relax. Be aware of the body and let noises around you just be as they are: 'in the heard only the heard.'

Day 2. *Sight and sound*. Start your practice with your eyes open. Let your eyes focus softly a few feet in front of you. Become aware of what is coming in through your eye-sense, but without looking around or trying to stare at anything. Again, see if you can let go of the naming and describing. Let the seen be only the seen. Let things just fall into the back of your eye, so to speak. Then close your eyes, and become aware of sounds as before. Include your body and finally notice your breath. Feel your breath in your body. At the end of the practice, come back to sounds and then sit with your eyes open without moving for a minute or so.

Day 3. *Just being aware.* Start with awareness of sight in the way you explored yesterday, then close your eyes and become aware of sound. Sit in awareness of sound for a few minutes. See if you can become aware of how you assume that 'sound' comes from outside. But is that in your awareness? Or is that something you are adding to your awareness? Ideas like 'inside' and 'outside' are thoughts: they are not in direct perception. Then bring your attention to your other senses. Can you smell anything: the flowers on your shrine, someone downstairs making toast? Is there any taste, however nondescript, in your mouth? And what about sensations of touch: the warmth of your legs, the slight coolness of your forehead? Then see if you can notice feeling tone (*vedana*), and inner narrative (*citta*). And then just sit and relax in full awareness.

Day 4. *Exploring the breath.* In today's meditation, see if you can explore the subtlety and nuance of the breath. Start by developing body awareness as usual. Drop away from the front of your head. Relax your eyes. Soften your brow. Tune in to the weight of your body on the chair or on the cushions. Then explore your breath. Where do you feel the breath most strongly: in the chest, the belly, the nostrils? Does the breath feel rough or smooth, deep or shallow, quick or slow? Can you feel the breath right down in the pelvic region, in your lower back, in your sides? As you relax more deeply, explore the subtleties of the breath. See if you can feel the breath in the back of your throat, or even in your hands and legs.

Day 5. *Appreciating your world.* Once again, start with your eyes open. Then close your eyes and tune in to the sounds around you

– a car changing gear in the street, a plane banking in the sky above, school children squealing outside. See if you can take an appreciative awareness to it all – as if you were listening to music. Try and feel the effect of sound in your body. Then, maintaining this broad awareness, include the body and the massaging sensations of the breath. Again, see if you can consciously cultivate appreciative awareness. Try not to react negatively to unpleasant sensations or grasp after pleasant ones. See if you can establish yourself in a relaxed, appreciative awareness.

Day 6. *Cultivating wise attention.* As before, cultivate awareness of sight, then sound, taste, touch, feeling, and breath. Try to cultivate the broadest possible awareness and then gradually focus on one part of the breathing cycle. You might focus on the breath at the tip of your nose, or right down in the pit of the belly. Remember: when you focus, you don't need to forcibly ignore breadth. Just allow the focus to emerge out of the breadth quite naturally. Then see if you can dwell with appreciative attention on the specific aspect of the breath that you have chosen. If you get distracted, consciously turn your attention to what is distracting you. See if you can cultivate wise attention: why are those thoughts interesting to you? What are you wanting? Can you feel the inner *vedana* of the narratives in your mind? Notice if you slip from wise to unwise attention. Notice where the mind goes and cultivate wise attention. Then come back to the breath.

Day 7. *The magic moment.* Once again, set up mindfulness of the senses: what can you see, hear, taste, touch, and smell? Then close your eyes and relax into your body. Ground yourself in this first sphere of mindfulness. Then bring your attention to your breath. Use the counting technique to count from one to ten at the end of each out-breath. Do this for about five minutes, starting again at one every time you lose count or go beyond the count. Then drop the counting and feel the whole breath in the body. When you get distracted, notice the moment when you notice you are distracted: this is the 'magic moment'. It is a moment of pure awareness. If you can notice it directly and without getting frustrated that you have got 'distracted', it will take you deeply into meditation. All you need to do is have more and more of these magic moments. You can even say to yourself, 'It's good to get distracted: it means I can experience more magic moments!'

Week 6 Practice Review

1. Mindful walk

Were you able to remember to do the mindful walk?

	Day 1	Day 2	Day 3	Day 4	Day 5	Day 6	Day 7
Tick/yes Cross/no							

2. Mindful moment

Were you able to remember to practise the mindful moment?

	Day 1	Day 2	Day 3	Day 4	Day 5	Day 6	Day 7
Tick/yes Cross/no							

Did you manage to extend your mindful moment and spend some time looking out of the window, sitting in the park, or listening to music? If so, how did it go?

Write your reflections here

3. Writing exercise

Without thinking about it too carefully, jot down below five aspects of the environment – objects, nature, and art – that you especially noticed this week.

I especially noticed...

4. Meditation

Are you noticing any patterns arising in your practice? Do you quickly get bored or frustrated with yourself? Do you need to do more to build up your concentration – such as perhaps counting at the end of the out-breath – or do you tend to force your mind to stay with the meditation? Reflect on the trends you are noticing in meditation.

Write your reflections here

We have explored the value of appreciative awareness and how the whole of the spiritual life could be thought about in terms of enjoying things as they are, without wanting to own, use, or exploit things. This is a path to wisdom. I mentioned at the beginning of this chapter that the Buddha's four spheres of mindfulness don't include awareness of the environment, at least not as an explicit aspect of the path. Perhaps the Buddha and his disciples felt that this kind of awareness was so self-evident that it needn't be stressed. But I also mentioned another area of awareness that seems to be missing: other people. It's time to turn our full attention to them.

Other People

Love is the awareness of another person

Our lives are inextricably bound up with other people. Our parents and grandparents, brothers and sisters, teachers, work colleagues, lovers, and friends have all made and continue to make an indelible impression on us. They shape our emotional attitudes, our patterns of beliefs, our positive or negative outlook. And everything we do affects other people. When we talk about 'experience', 'life', or 'the world', what we mean most of all is 'people'. If we want to understand our life, if we want to change our life, we need to understand and change our relationships with other people.

And yet the Buddha did not include this in the four spheres of mindfulness. He probably saw no need to. After all, in ancient India, there was no welfare state, health care, police; there were no pensions, hospitals, or schools, at least not in the way we understand those things today. Your very capacity to survive depended on an extended network of fam-

Mindfulness of others

Working with a difficult situation

The mindful walk

The mindful moment

223

ily, friends, and social obligations. Whilst the Buddha taught that friendship could develop beyond mutual helpfulness into a love of virtue, he would have taken ongoing social interaction, friendliness, and positivity for granted. He could not have imagined how isolated we would become – how billions of people would end up living separate lives, in separate rooms, in big anonymous cities where we sit hunched over computer screens, for hours on end.

The Buddha assumed that any kind of spiritual life involved intimate friendship. He even went so far as to say that, 'Friendship is the whole of the spiritual life.'[40] But friendship is not what we normally associate with Buddhism. Buddhism is linked to meditation, and meditation is something we do on our own with our eyes closed. So it's easy to assume that Buddhism is an exploration into subjectivity – a journey of inner discovery, a private concern. But this is one-sided. Buddhism starts with our mind. It gives us the tools to understand and change our mind. Yet it doesn't end with our mind – at least not in the personal, subjective sense. Its ultimate goal is Enlightenment for the sake of all beings; its aim is selfless love.

Whether or not we have cultivated life with full attention, we have each of us undergone a journey of awareness. When we were babies, there was no distinction between our mother and ourselves. As growing children, we necessarily saw the world from our own perspective, unable to imagine that other-world of grown-ups. Since then, we have been travelling the long journey from seeing our parents as authority figures and pocket-money dispensers to relating to them as fellow human beings. Growing up therefore means growing out of self-centredness and into harmonious, adult relationships. If self-centredness is primarily the symptom of immaturity, selflessness is the sign of full human maturity. Love is the ripening of awareness.

Awareness of others means relating to each person's unique individuality – not to their social status, race, gender, wage-earning capacity, or amusement value. When we practise this awareness, we use the inner experience we have developed in the four spheres of mindfulness to imagine the inner experience of other people – how they feel, what they need and value. When we are fully and deeply aware of another person, we cannot help but love them. Love is the awareness of another person.

Have we become less selfish?

The way we know if we have made progress on the path of full attention is to ask ourselves whether we have become less selfish. Have we become kinder and more considerate? Over the last seven weeks, we might have missed meditations, forgotten to do our mindful walk, got fed up practising the mindful moment, discovered our ethical life is not up to scratch – but if we can say that we have become a little less selfish, then we have made progress. The rest is secondary.

Having said that, there can be a legitimate period of increased self-absorption, even selfishness, in the early days of practising life with full attention. There certainly was for me. Like many people, I came to Buddhism rather out of touch with myself. I was 24 and mixed up. I had all kinds of ideas about the kind of person I was – a good-time party person – that didn't really stand up to examination. Mindfulness and meditation soon revealed that. So I turned in on myself. I felt people wanted me around for entertainment value, so I stopped telling jokes. I stopped trying to please people. I became terribly serious, which was fine for a while as it was a necessary stage, a corrective.

But there is a danger that is especially evident in anything that encourages introspection: it is the danger of spiritualized selfishness, which tends to manifest through particular symptoms. It stresses introspection at the expense of activity. It tends to see getting things done as worldly and point-missing. People who have slipped into spiritualized selfishness tend to talk a lot about 'depth', they often use jargon, either spiritual or psychotherapeutic, they are apt to lose their sense of humour, and they tend to be sickly. It is a danger that all of us on the path of full attention need to be on the lookout for. The problem with spiritual selfishness, as opposed to ordinary selfishness, is that we will tend to use the very words and teachings of spiritual life to rationalize it. We will tend to talk about, 'being in touch with ourselves', 'caring for ourselves', 'not beating ourselves up' – but we will be using those words to confirm self-absorption rather than liberate ourselves from it. It can be difficult to tell if we have drifted into this. We need to ask our friends, get a second opinion, and watch out for the symptoms I have listed above. Of course, the best way to avoid self-preoccupation is by turning our attention to other people.

From self-orientation to reality-orientation

As we move through the four spheres of mindfulness, we move from a psychologically orientated approach to spiritual life to a transcendental orientation. In the early stages of spiritual life, we are likely to be motivated by the need for personal happiness and freedom from pain, especially emotional and social pain. We will see mindfulness as a way of becoming happier in our skin and more at home in our world. Practising mindfulness will help us achieve this, so long as we learn carefully and practise regularly.

But our motivations can change. We might discover that our quest for personal happiness has become limiting and, after a certain point, self-defeating. We might start to feel motivated more by the suffering of other people than by our own. We might even start to realize that the only way to true happiness is to transcend self altogether. This is the transcendental orientation of Buddhism. A Buddhist approach to mindfulness takes into account a psychological orientation but will always guide us towards a transcendental one. Buddhism is emphatic in saying that it is only by liberating ourselves from our belief in a separate self – separate from others and from the world – that we will finally be happy.

So you might want to pause to consider this. Do you want to move towards a more transcendental approach to spiritual practice? I ask this not to make the more psychological approach negative in any way, but because Buddhism assumes a self-transcendent attitude to spiritual practice, and this is increasingly my assumption as our course in mindfulness progresses. Not that you literally move from one orientation to another – like getting off one bus and jumping onto another. It's more like a gradual shifting of emphasis, a willingness to look at your life from a different perspective, a greater desire to concentrate on the well-being of others. After all, the royal road to selflessness is altruism – and the way to altruism is other people.

Focus on gratitude

We can feel positive emotion about the past, present, and future. Positive emotion about the past includes satisfaction, contentment, fulfilment, and serenity. Lack of appreciation of good events in the past coupled with an over-emphasis on bad ones

227

(such as childhood traumas) undermines our capacity to feel content. The way to develop positive emotion about the past is to focus on gratitude and forgiveness. Gratitude amplifies the positive experiences we have had, building their richness in our mind and increasing the frequency of good memories. Forgiveness prevents us from becoming embittered about the bad events. Here are three suggestions for cultivating gratitude:

Five a day. Set aside a few minutes before you go to bed to think about anything that has happened that day that you feel grateful for. See if you can write down five things. They might include things about your family or friends, aesthetic appreciation, or your good health.

The gratitude book. Use your journal to begin a book of gratitude. Write down 15 things you feel grateful for. Do it straight away if you can. Include everything that comes to mind, whatever you can think of. And try to be specific by writing down the reasons why you're grateful to a particular person. Then for the rest of the week, see if you can keep adding to the list. You might especially think of your parents, your teachers, your mentors – all the people who have helped you in one way or another. Then, at the end of the week, read them over one by one. Read them slowly, bringing each one to mind.

Express gratitude. Find an opportunity to express gratitude. You might write a letter to your parents, or invite a friend over for a meal and say thank you to him or her. You might write to one of your teachers. You could send out, say, five postcards to people you've not been in touch with for a while but to whom you feel grateful. If your parents' wedding anniversary is coming up, you could create a gratitude book with appreciative letters from all their children and friends. Or you could write a speech enumerating their qualities and telling them how much you value them.[41]

Loving all beings - Starting with ourselves

Let's explore how to practise mindfulness of other people; then, as usual, we can move on to this seventh week of full attention. But before we think about other people, perhaps we should start with ourselves. I say 'perhaps' because the belief that we should learn to love ourselves before we can love others can often be counter-productive. It is true that we can only truly love others if we love ourselves but, usually, we need to do both.

Many people have difficulties with self-esteem. One symptom of this is complexity. When you don't feel happy within yourself, life becomes complicated – especially your relationship with other people becomes complicated. You will tend to misread situations. There will be a marked tendency to compare yourself with others, to perceive threats, criticisms, lack of respect, or lack of love. You will feel these kinds of things quite readily. You will be sensitized to them and on the lookout for them. And all this has complicating effects. So, if your relationship with other people constantly feels difficult, it is likely that you have issues with self-esteem. Lack of self-esteem doesn't go away very easily. In fact, trying to make it go away usually makes it worse. I suspect that lack of self-love is a habit that people remain vulnerable to. We may need to learn to manage it, in much the same way as people learn to manage addiction.

Of course, the question is: how? One answer is to practise the four spheres of mindfulness. Lack of self-esteem is a self-story, a narrative, a symptom, very often, that we are mistaking a thought for a fact. So we need to step back from it, regain a sense of perspective, and mindfully examine the stories we are in thrall to: in other words, we need to cultivate mindfulness of the body, *vedana*, *citta*, and *dhamma*. Lack of self-esteem is one of those 'down the plughole' mental states: just about anything can get dragged into it. Even trying to cultivate self-love can become part of the problem, as if there really is an empty self-love tank in our psyche somewhere needing to be filled up. We can end up taking our stories of self-dislike too seriously, too literally, which of course exacerbates them.

This week, I'll be introducing a meditation that directly works on self-esteem. But for the meantime, it's best to forget all about it. Get absorbed in something else. Give your attention to whatever it is you enjoy, to what enriches and enhances your life. If you focus on the lack of self-esteem without making a concerted effort to be conscious of your inner narratives (as I've suggested in Week 4), you are likely to make matters worse. This is the 'down the plughole' scenario. So make time for the things you love. Caring for something – a cat, a pot plant, a friend – will affect your sense of self-worth. As the poet John Burnside puts it, 'What we love in ourselves, is ourselves loving'.[42] Our moments of enjoying something, cherishing something or someone, gradually change how we feel about ourselves.

Of course, the other vital ingredient in loving ourselves is the fact of knowing that we are loved by others.[43] We need to surround ourselves with friends who care for us and who are emotionally positive.

Cultivating friendship

Friendship is giving someone your full attention. The first rule of friendship is: if you want a friend, be a friend. According to Buddhist tradition, the Buddha was always the first to smile when he met someone. Usually, in social situations, we check someone out first: we decide whether we like them and whether they like us. We rarely just give ourselves. We rarely smile first. So we need to go out and make friends.

If I had to think of two ingredients for cultivating friendship, I'd choose time and attention. Friendship grows slowly. It takes time to mature. So find any reason to be with your friend: live with them, work with them, go on holiday or retreat with them, go to the cinema with them, go for a walk with them. Give them your time and your attention. If you do that, your friendship will flourish.

And see if you can make friends especially with people who, like you, want to develop strengths and virtues. Aristotle, the ancient Greek philosopher, said that friendships tend to be based on one of three things: usefulness, pleasure, or the good.[44] Those based in usefulness tend to be work-based – where the connection arises out of common usefulness and purpose. When the usefulness ends, the friendship dwindles. Friendships based in pleasure are those social, pub-banter friendships concerned primarily with enjoying each other's company. They tend to stay at a particular level. At worst, they are fair-weather friendships, which survive so long as pleasure does.

But then there are friendships based on the good. They may well be pleasurable and even useful, but they will not be based on, or defined by, usefulness or pleasure. What defines friendship based on the good is a common striving for virtues and strengths. This kind of friendship will support you in your attempts to grow and change; a good friend will encourage you in your efforts, even challenge you if needs be. Friendship based on the good is the best support if you want to practise life with full attention.

People we feel neutral about

Of course, most of the people we come into contact with are not friends or family, enemies or workmates, drinking buddies or lovers. Most people are just people – crowded concourses, bustling shopping centres, thriving cafés. If we live in the city, the majority of the people we meet as we go around the shops, catch a train, or stop for a coffee are people we have never seen before, people we feel neutral towards. That is unless they bump into us, refuse to serve us, or get in our way. Or unless we find them sexually attractive.

Auden talks about, 'our kindness to ten persons'. That about gets it right – two parents, a few siblings, our partner, a couple of friends, and our children. But when we practise mindfulness of others, we are consciously trying to expand the circumference of our awareness – to reach beyond our kindness to ten persons. Mindfulness of others means seeing the person, not 'the people'. People don't exist. There are only unique individuals with hopes and fears, wishes and desires, feelings and values. Mindfulness of others means trying to see that, not just as a nice idea or a cliché, but as a felt reality.

This felt reality needs to be acted upon. This means being pleasant to bank clerks, not losing your temper with traffic wardens or those people who try to clean your windscreen when you're stopped at traffic lights. Of course, it doesn't imply being gullible or naïve. It means relating to a person as a person, whatever their age, gender, skin colour, or sexuality. It means being friendly however we feel in ourselves, whether we are having a good or a bad day.

Overcoming hatred

But then there are those people we don't like. Sometimes, when we practise life with full attention, we start to notice how regularly we react with irritation, anger, and hatred. This can actually be a sign of progress, as we often repress our darker feelings. We want to believe that we are a kind, reasonable sort of person, so we tend to ignore feelings that don't fit in with that self-view. But, as our mindfulness develops, our capacity to edit experience – to repress and disown the unpalatable side of our nature – is weakened. The light of awareness shows us to ourselves. And this can come as quite a shock. We need to value it. If we internalize our feelings of aggression, we are likely to become depressed. Our desire to cultivate positive emotion will result in dampening down our energies, prematurely softening and sweetening ourselves because we feel guilty about our darker drives. Being mindful of people we dislike means being open-eyed to our aversions and hatreds; it means feeling and owning them.

Mindfulness means becoming aware of our negative emotions without being consumed by them. Often we have experience without awareness. We are angry or feel sorry for ourselves without being meaningfully aware that that is what we are feeling – we are simply driven along by our moods and reactions. Either that or we stoke the fires of our bad moods by telling ourselves negative stories. As we

233

develop mindfulness, we feel things directly – including the darker side of our nature – with awareness. This means not falling into unhelpful rumination, or harmful self-preoccupation. But it also means not pretending we are a nicer person than we really are. Feeling our anger and hatred is not the same as acting on those feelings or repressing them. As soon as we act on feelings of hatred, we have temporarily resigned from the life of mindfulness. We have put ourselves beyond the pale. So our first responsibility, if we are about to lose our temper, bully someone at work, or say something cruel – is to remove ourselves from danger by going for a walk, calming down, and breathing. If we act out of hatred, we will make life worse for ourselves and for others. Of course, there is a whole gamut of ways in which we express hatred: from silent resentment and passive aggression to physical violence. But they all undermine our virtues and strengths, as well as our hopes for authentic happiness.

There's a wonderful Zen story that illustrates the effect of positive and negative emotions. According to the story, a samurai warrior went to visit a Zen abbot. He wanted to know what heaven and hell were. The abbot said, 'How would you know, you great oaf! It's far too sophisticated for a blockhead like you to understand.' He carried on insulting the samurai in this way until the samurai got so enraged that he raised his sword to cut off the abbot's head. 'That's hell,' said the abbot. The warrior, seeing the meaning of his words, put the sword slowly back in its scabbard. 'That's heaven,' said the monk.

How we prevent hatred from arising, how we stay in heaven rather than go to hell, is one of the fine arts of mindfulness. Once again, we need to catch our states of mind early, and this may mean finding the courage to speak instead of stewing in resentment. Sometimes, putting off saying something out of fear of conflict actually creates conflict later on. We need to find ways of communicating that are truthful and kind – that do justice to our own feelings as well as to the other person's. We need to approach communication in the spirit of exploration rather than accusation. Once we find ourselves in an argument – as distinct from a discussion – we no longer learn anything: both parties simply become entrenched. Anger can be skilful – it can be a way of breaking into communication – but we need to be very mindful and emotionally positive to use it in this way. As my own teacher put it, 'The only way to avoid hating one's fellow men is to love them.'[45] Loving doesn't mean liking, much less agreeing; it means seeing beyond our reactivity to a deeper sense of shared humanity.

Focus on forgiveness

When we talk about 'the past', we are talking about *memories* of the past. How we feel about our past depends entirely on our memories. Just as dwelling on good events in the past creates a sense of satisfaction and happiness, ruminating on real or imagined wrongs creates vengefulness and bitterness. Frequent and intense negative thoughts about the past block happiness in the present. Whatever the objective truth in our feeling of being done down, betrayed, or overlooked; if we want to be happy, we need to forgive. Forgiveness is the only way to heal ourselves of the toxic effects of resentment and bitterness. I am aware that some people have experienced terrible cruelty and violence and, in such situations, forgiveness can seem impossible. The eminent American psychologist Everett Worthington created a five-step process of forgiveness for those who want to forgive but find they cannot. His own mother was violently murdered, so he is well aware of the struggles involved in trying to forgive. He is aware that forgiveness is not easy or quick. He calls his five-step process REACH:[46]

R is for Recall. Try to recall the event in a way that is as detailed and as objective as possible. (You might want to precede this with a breathing space to create calm and perspective.) Be careful not to fall into self-pity or righteous indignation. Try to be clear about what happened.

E is for Empathize. Try to understand what happened from the other person's point of view: why did they hurt you, what was going on for them? You may need to remember that when other people feel threatened, they lash out, and that bad conditions often create negative behaviour.

A is for Altruism. Bring to mind occasions when you have acted badly and when others have forgiven you. Remember what a gift that forgiveness was, how much you needed it. Try to give forgiveness, not so that you can feel better but for the other person's welfare. Give forgiveness fully, not begrudgingly.

C is for Commitment. Forgive publicly, as it were. You might write your forgiveness in your journal, tell a friend about it, or write a forgiveness letter (which you may or may not want to post). In Buddhism, we sometimes perform rituals in which we ask for and are given forgiveness. So you might want to create your own forgiveness ritual.

H is for Hold. This is important. Painful memories are bound to recur. You will need to hold to your desire to forgive so you can keep forgiving. When the bad memories recur, watch out for vengefulness or wallowing in painful memories. Remind yourself you have forgiven. As Isadora Duncan said: 'The best revenge is a happy life.' You can only have a happy life if you release yourself from bitterness and the desire for revenge.

In one study on forgiveness[47], those who focused on taking offence less and on revising their story of grievance in the ways suggested above experienced less anger, less stress, more optimism and better health. At root, forgiveness is a spiritual act: it is a voluntary letting go of self, a renunciation of revenge and retaliation.

All beings

All our relationships – with family, friends, lovers, or shop assistants – will fall into one of these three categories: we like them, dislike them, or feel neutral about them. This brings us back to everything we have learnt about *vedana*. Our capacity not to react to *vedana* really comes into its own in our relationship with other people. After all, it is people that we react to with craving, aversion, or indifference. Earlier on in Week 4, we learnt that, when we see things with desire or hatred, we distort our experience either by over-focusing on the positive when we want something or by fixating on the negative when we don't. All of this is especially relevant to our relationship with others. So much of what we have learned on this course has its most far-reaching consequences in our relationships with others.

Full awareness is inseparable from love. When we give our complete attention to an azalea, a blackbird, a mountain ridge, or a person, our heart goes out to them. Full attention includes head and heart, sympathy as well as discernment. Love is the awareness of another

237

person. Our aim, as we cultivate mindfulness of others, is to extend the circumference of our concern beyond our love of ten persons. We develop feelings of loving-kindness for all beings: young and old, happy and unhappy, those being born and those dying away. We cultivate an all-embracing heart that reaches out impartially to all men and women, to the animal kingdom, to birds, fish, insects, and to the natural environment. Mindfulness of others is about trying to develop an all-embracing heart. This is the goal of life with full attention.

Seventh practice week

Mindfulness of others

Mindfulness of others means making a conscious effort to see things from other people's point of view. It is an act of imaginative sympathy. We often relate to people superficially. We don't really take them in, look at them, listen to them, or trouble ourselves to understand them. If we become aware of another person as a person, we will find that feelings of concern and appreciation naturally arise. This week, I suggest you become more mindful of two people: someone you like (a friend) and someone you dislike. But before I introduce you to that, let's look at relationships with your parents and partner.

Becoming more mindful of your parents

It might seem strange to say, but we often don't really know our parents. What we do know is our reaction to them. We visit them for the weekend and, as soon as we step over the threshold, it's as though we become a child again and we get into the same arguments. So developing mindfulness of your parents needs to involve noticing your habitual reactions and working to overcome them:

Notice your intentions. When you go to see your parents, are you trying to improve them in some way, setting yourself up for a fight, or nursing grudges? Are you intending to watch TV and let your mother wash your clothes and cook all your meals?

Do your intentions create problems? If you intend not to do much, does that mean that you get irritable if your mother asks you to do chores? Do you use home as a base, dumping your bags and spending all your time seeing friends? Notice how your intentions, expectations, and assumptions contribute to any tension between you and your parents.

Concentrate on understanding your parents. Be mindful of not thinking about your parents in terms of yourself: how they don't understand you, appreciate you, or aren't sufficiently interested in you. Change the emphasis to your relationship with them, seeing your mother or father as a person in their own right, getting to know them, taking an interest in them.

Spend time with your parents individually. Family gatherings are not usually conducive to deepening your awareness of your parents. So see if you can spend time alone with just your mother or your father.

Express gratitude. Parents are not perfect, but they have given you so much. They deserve your gratitude. See if you can express that. Be careful to be mindful of them when you do this. Some parents find protestations of love and thankfulness confusing, embarrassing, or painful. We shouldn't brush this aside simply because we value saying what we feel. At the same time, if we can express our gratitude in words, all the better. The most important thing is to show gratitude.

So, this week, become more mindful of your relationship with your parents. When you phone them -- and make sure you do phone them -- notice any habitual reactions you have to them and see if you can be more patient and understanding. When you next visit them, see if you can make it a practice of full attention. Give them your time and attention, and make a contribution.

I am aware that some of you might have a difficult relationship with your parents. Some parents might have been unpleasant, even cruel to their children. But a positive, healthy relationship with your parents is an essential aspect of wellbeing. Who you are now is a direct consequence – biological and psychological – of who they are. Having a negative relationship with your parents is tantamount to having a negative relationship with yourself. However they have acted towards you in the past, if you want to live well and be happy, you need to forgive them (if needs be) and learn how to love them and express gratitude. This doesn't mean idolizing them. It means going out of your way to establish the best possible relationship.

This holds true even if your parents are dead. Memory tends to be highly selective, so try to become aware of things you normally edit out, such as how you behaved in relation to them. See if you can gain a deeper insight into why they acted in the way they did. Having accepted the reality of your past, you will need to work with your memories of it. Dwelling on real or imagined harm only creates passivity and bitterness, and this will undermine your desire to be happy.

Becoming more mindful of your partner

Many of the above points apply to your husband, wife, or partner (if you have one). Like our parents, we often get stuck in habitual reactions to our partner's behaviour, especially if it is a long-term relationship. And we often need to stress seeing things from their point of view, rather than insisting that they make allowances for us. Buddhism's attitude to sexual relationships is pragmatic. It sees them as primarily social contracts that entail duties and responsibilities. Buddhists have been celibate, married, monogamous, or polygamous. So there are different options open to you. You need to decide if you want a sexual relationship, and then be clear about the ground rules. At the risk of sounding like an agony aunt, here are some ways in which we can usefully become mindful of our sexual relationships:

Cultivate fidelity. Try to make the nature of your relationship conscious and discuss what you expect from each other. Make sure you enter the relationship freely. If you want to be monogamous, make sure both parties genuinely agree. Then stick to the relationship you have agreed upon. This often means consciously limiting your choice: deciding not to be on the lookout for someone else, not flirting at office parties, or keeping someone in the background as a possible replacement. Stick with the relationship and work through difficulties.

Emphasize liking each other. There can be a wonderful period of falling in love at the start of a relationship. Enjoy it. But as that begins to settle down, emphasize getting on well together, liking each other in an ordinary day-to-day way. Falling in love is exciting but unstable. Freud called it, 'the psychosis of normal people'.[48] It often doesn't help relationships stay together.

241

Time together, alone, and with others. You will want to spend time together so that you can enjoy each other's company. At the same time, you need to spend time alone, and with friends outside the context of the relationship. It can be tempting to spend all your time as a couple, but this puts undue pressure on the relationship. Watch out for always meeting in couples, as this tends to militate against deeper communication.

Listen and validate. Couples often misunderstand each other because they don't listen carefully enough. Defensiveness, a quickness to blame and find fault are fatal to good relationships. The key to communication is validation. Make sure you let the other person know that you have understood. This is not merely to do with listening to the content, but looking beyond the content to the needs and values that are being expressed. Make sure you say things like, 'I can see what you mean', 'Yes, that's true', 'That must have been difficult for you.' If needs be, paraphrase what the person has just said to show them you understand and have taken on board their point of view – especially if you are getting into an area that you often disagree about.

Practise the 'government of the tongue'.[49] This means talking through difficulties, resisting the temptations of blame and acrimony, and trying to reach a deeper understanding. At the same time, be aware that, generally speaking, the genders have different needs in this respect – women tend to gather information by talking; men tend to keep silent and hope for the best. Watch out for assuming that your approach to working through difficulties is necessarily the right one. The government of the tongue also means not slipping into nagging and fault-finding, not humiliating your partner at dinner parties, and not passing on secrets once the relationship is over.

Cultivate supports. Relationships work best if both parties are independent and have their own friends and enthusiasms. So make sure you give time and attention to developing external and internal supports. External supports include friendship with other people, especially of the same gender, so that you have other committed relationships in which you can communicate and gain understanding. Internal supports include cultivating interests and passions other than the relationship.

Be more conscious of your sexual relationship this week. Look at the suggestions above, and see what you need to work on. Do you pressurize your partner into telling you he loves you? Do you become monosyllabic and refuse to say what's up? Can you talk openly about the sexual element of the relationship: is it working for both of you? Are you over-investing in the relationship? When was the last time you saw a friend? When did you last go out together without the kids in tow?

Focus on generosity

The Buddha said that if you are generous, the whole of the spiritual life is open to you. You can have many faults and shortcomings but, if you are generous, everything is possible. Generosity is a practical and immediate way of improving your self-esteem. When we feel bad about ourselves, we become self-absorbed. Self-absorption is one of the major symptoms of depression. A simple antidote to this painful self-preoccupation is generosity.

Generosity is something you can practise in any state of mind; you don't need to be in a good mood. You can help a work colleague move office, help your nephew with his homework, or cook a meal for your mother. When we give, we get immediate feedback that we have something to give. Negative states of mind are barren – they make us feel we are lacking and need things from others, which in turn fosters passivity. If we can give – even in small ways – we create a sense of inner fullness and plenitude. Generosity creates positive relationships with others, which is vital to our happiness. Here are some ways to practise generosity this week:

Take an interest in someone. Give someone a little bit more of your time than you normally would. Take an interest in them, listen to them, and ask them about themselves.

Give affection or encouragement. Be willing to express affection. It might simply be in the tone of your voice or in your eyes. The Buddha talked of looking at people 'with kindly eyes'. Touch people. Elderly people often suffer from a lack of touch. So give your father a hug when you next see him. Even a warm hand-shake can express affection and give encouragement. Try to be enthusiastic about your friends' aims and passions.

Give on a busy day. When we are busy, we tend to become overly task-orientated and our focus of attention narrows. We often become tight, tense, and irritable. So see if you can look around a little. Offer to make the tea, or go out and get the sandwiches. Do something for someone. Probably they are busy and stressed, and therefore isolated as well.

Welcome someone. If someone new starts at work, buy them a card and some chocolate. Leave it on their desk for when they arrive at work. If you invite someone around for a meal, be a good host and show them around, prepare nice food, be ready to welcome them. Cultivate a welcoming attitude when your partner comes back from work, when your children come back from university, or when your friend comes back from holiday.

Volunteer. Volunteer at the local school, help out at the local hospice, do the washing up, or deal with the recycling. Volunteer to do something that benefits other people. Think in terms of giving back.

Just give! If your friend is hard up, give them some money. If your spouse is exhausted after work, pamper them a little – run the bath, cook supper – and try not to say how you've been busy as well. Find any excuse to give money, objects, recommend books, or pay for the cinema.

Mindfulness of two people

Having looked at your relationship with your parents and partner, let's move on to this week's particular practices. My suggestion is that you concentrate on becoming mindful of a friend and a difficult person. Be careful not to be overt about this: it's not very pleasant to feel experimented on!

Choose a friend you will spend time with this week. If that's not possible, choose someone you are in regular contact with, preferably by phone rather than email. The friend should be about your age – not old enough to be your parent or young enough to be your child. They should be someone you are not sexually attracted to or in a relationship with. And, if possible, choose someone of the same gender. The idea is to choose someone as much like you as possible: a close friend of the same gender and about the same age.

Also choose a difficult person. This person needs to be someone you actually know, not a public figure you love to hate. Don't choose someone you really despise, as this will be too difficult. Choose a person you have face-to-face contact with on a regular basis or, if that's not possible, someone you are in contact with by phone or email. If you can't think of anyone you dislike, my advice is: think again. Think of someone you would want to get away from if they came and sat next to you in the staff canteen. If you really can't think of anyone, consider someone in your immediate family (you can usually find one there!) The difficult person could also be a friend you're having problems with at the moment. Find a way of imagining them and bringing them to life in your mind. You could write a day's diary entry for each person, imagining their day. You might include each sphere of mindfulness.

- How does their body feel to them?
- Are they tense or relaxed, habitually tired or over-strained?
- What *vedana* do they experience?
- What kind of states of mind do they inhabit?
- What values are they trying to express?

If the exercise feels too difficult, just jot down what they do, where they go, how they feel, and who they are in relationship with. Write it in the first person, as if you were your friend or the difficult person. Include how they feel about you. This will help you be mindful when you meet them. Use seeing the friend or difficult person as a cue for full attention. When you come into contact with them, become more aware of them and of yourself in relation to them. You will be more likely to be able to do this if you spend some time bringing them to mind in the way I have suggested above. Then try to put the following into practice:

Look at them. Many of us get into the habit of not looking at someone when we talk to them. Notice if this is true for you and, when you meet your friend this week, look at them and take them in. Let them see your liking for them in your eyes. Make sure you look at the difficult person. When we have an ongoing difficulty with someone, we tend not to meet their gaze, which they of course pick up on. So try not to avoid looking at them; try to see and understand them and let them look at you.

Listen to them. So often, 'conversation' is really mutual monologue – we are waiting for our turn to speak. So see if you can listen instead of rehearsing your reply. Listening means deepening your awareness of another person, noticing the thoughts, feelings, values, and needs embedded in the words that someone uses. Listening to someone means putting aside your personal agendas and hobby horses to give them your full attention. If you do this, anything you say will arise out of real awareness of them.

Become interested. With the difficult person, make a particular effort not to react in the usual irritated, dismissive, or fearful way. We often make situations worse by reacting habitually to what we don't like or approve of. Use this week as a chance to hold back on your own way of seeing things. Try to learn at least one thing from the difficult person. With your friend, try to resist the temptation of dragging the conversation back to you. Find a way of deepening the communication and of becoming more fully interested in them.

Do something. If possible, and without making a fuss about it, see if you can do something for them. Real awareness leads to action. You don't just become aware that someone is thirsty; you go and get them a glass of water! Try to do at least one thing for each person. If your friend or the difficult person is struggling with a suitcase or an online job application, try to help them with it. You could replace the ink cartridge in your boss' printer or take a small gift when you meet your friend. Don't make a big deal out of it; just find a quiet way to give.

Try to maintain awareness of these two people during the week. You might put a photograph of your friend on your shrine, or you might write their names on a card and keep it with you in your wallet. However you do it, find ways of reminding yourself about them and, at the end of the week, review how it went using the table at the end of this chapter.

Working with a difficult situation

You might feel that the above feels like too much effort. So another way of becoming more mindful of someone is by concentrating on a difficult encounter you are likely to have, such as a work meeting or spending time with a friend you are having problems communicating with. Difficult situations have three aspects:

Anticipation Thinking about the difficulty beforehand, often unhelpfully;

Encounter Reacting in the moment by becoming physically tense, or emotionally defensive;

Recall Going over and over what was said or done, or compulsively thinking about what you should have said or done.

In this way, a difficulty with someone can spread and affect gradually more aspects of your life. Try to work towards feeling the painful *vedana* in the present tense without reacting to it, and not dwelling on it fruitlessly before and afterwards. Here's a brief guide:

Anticipation

Be present and receptive. Notice how you feel in your body and notice *vedana*.

Be aware of the inner narrative. Ask yourself if what you are thinking is true. And if it is, how you can communicate it effectively? What is the subjective reaction and the objective truth?

Rehearse a more creative strategy. Think more creatively about how to work with the situation, or a more useful way of communicating your point of view. Shift your perspective and try to see the difficulty from another angle.

Encounter

Be present and receptive. Focus on any physical or mental discomfort. Try not to react negatively out of it. Consciously relax the body, especially the shoulders and belly. Sometimes, this is as much as you can do.

Stay connected. It is tempting in difficult situations to cut off from other people. This diminishes awareness and causes more pain. So make a conscious effort to listen and understand. Check with the other person if you have understood them correctly. Slow down the communication. Work at not taking offence.

Recall

Be present and receptive. Notice what it feels like to re-rehearse an argument in your head. Don't condemn yourself for it, but try to notice any defensive narrative and let it go by consciously distracting yourself, or challenging your thinking.

Be aware of inner narrative. Is what you are thinking helpful, does it get you anywhere? Have you thought about it enough now?

Decide what to do. If you are resenting somebody, you need to either let it go (and keep letting it go) or rehearse a creative strategy for communicating it and resolving it. Decide once and for all what you intend to do.

The mindful walk

Carry on with your daily walk as usual. Cultivate the four spheres of mindfulness and, at the same time, see if you can give more of your attention to the people around you. Make sure you stay in touch with the body as you do this.

Notice the people you don't usually notice or those you don't like. We tend to be aware of people we find attractive, but unaware of people we don't. So, as you walk, make an effort to notice the people you don't normally pay attention to, such as the elderly lady or the middle-aged businessman. Also give attention to people you feel averse to or are fearful of: teenagers in hooded tops or an alcoholic drinking on a park bench.

Appreciate diversity. Staying in contact with your body and feelings as you walk, notice all the different kinds of people. Notice all the different ethnicities and ages, and the activities people are engaged in. You could even try and tune in to their voices as they pass.

How are they? Without being too obvious about it, notice how people seem to feel. Do they look happy, relaxed, and cheerful? Are they stressed out, wound up, and worried? Just take in other people as you go on your mindful walk and notice their posture, how they move, how they look.

Cultivate loving-kindness. See if you can wish them well. Just as you want to have a pleasant day, so do they. Just as you want people to like you and be pleased to see you, so do they. So wish them well. Stay in touch with your body as before and, when you see someone, take them in and say to yourself, 'May you be well, may you be happy.'

The mindful moment

I suggest that you use the mindful moment to become more aware of the friend you have chosen to focus on this week. First of all, tune in to mindfulness of your body: notice weight and warmth, feel the sensation of your clothes on your skin. This kind of basic body awareness helps you stay rooted in present-tense awareness. See if you can let go of any tensions, remembering to pay attention to those habitually tight areas, such as the neck, the belly, or the shoulders. Then bring to mind your friend. You don't need to cultivate any particular feeling for them just now – we will come to that in the meditation – just see them in your mind's eye. You might remember a time when you were with them, or imagine what they are doing right now, or think about how they walk, the sound of their laugh, that old duffel coat they wear. Try to bring them to mind like this every day. You can do this whilst brushing your teeth or preparing to go to work – whatever activity you have chosen as your mindful moment. If you are finding it difficult to remember the mindful moment, you might try setting the alarm on your phone or on your computer. You might try changing your mindful moment to something that you will be more likely to remember: perhaps a more pleasurable activity, such as taking a shower.

This week's meditations

This week I suggest you emphasize cultivating positive emotion, especially towards the two people you are focusing on: the friend and the difficult person. You might like to have a look at Appendix 2 (page 320), where I describe the *Metta Bhavana* practice, which is the practice of cultivating loving-kindness in meditation. Or you could just follow the suggestions I give below. Before we move on to the meditations themselves, however, let's explore what cultivating positive emotion is all about.

Broadly speaking, there are four types of Buddhist meditation practices:

Concentrative	Dwelling one-pointedly on experience, such as the breath in the Mindfulness of Breathing practice.
Receptive	Being open to whatever is in our experience without trying to change it.
Generative	Cultivating as yet un-arisen positive mental states, or enhancing positive states that have already arisen.
Reflective	Fruitfully reflecting on experience, such as reflecting on the nature of reality.

Each kind of meditation is exemplified by particular practices: the Mindfulness of Breathing is a concentrative practice; the *Metta Bhavana* is a generative practice. But the distinction is really a matter of emphasis. Any meditation – whether you're observing the breath or cultivating loving-kindness – will have the four emphases within it. To take a simple example, I have occasionally suggested that you just sit in open awareness. Buddhists call this practice 'just sitting'. Obviously, it is primarily receptive, since the emphasis is on non-judgemental awareness and openness to what is. But, for the practice to have value, there will need to be some degree of reflection and concentration, as well as a desire to cultivate open and receptive states of mind. In the 'just sitting' practice, the receptive aspect leads, but the other three are present, at least in potential. They are ready if they are needed. In fact, this practice is most effective when you are already fairly concentrated.

Meditation alert

What helps deepen your meditation one week may not help the next. Decide on a particular approach for each practice: for in-stance, using the sentences, 'May I be well, may I be happy' in the *Metta Bhavana* meditation. Give the sentences time to work – don't chop and change all the time. But keep a lookout for your approach to meditation becoming stale and ineffective. Don't think you can just do the practice in the same old way, perhaps because it worked for you in the past. You need to keep it fresh. You need to keep finding new approaches and metaphors. So watch out for developing a habitual mindset in meditation. Try something out and keep checking that it is working for you.

I have known quite a few people who feel unable to generate loving-kindness when they sit to meditate. They often put this down to some wounding psychological cause or past trauma. Mostly, however, it's simply that they have not yet developed enough concentration. Feelings of well-wishing, empathy and connectedness are subtle, at least initially. You will not be able to feel them without receptivity, concentration, and relaxation. Assume that positive emotion is present. It's just that you are too strung out, tired, or distracted to tune in to it for the moment.

So, in this week's meditations, make sure that all four aspects of meditation are present. I shall emphasize one or another as we go along, but stop every now and then to check for yourself. As you go about cultivating loving-kindness, make sure you are still receptive to your experience overall by asking yourself the following questions:

- Are you trying to force something to happen?
- Are you trying to squeeze positive emotion out of yourself like toothpaste?
- Are you still sensitive to what is happening in your mind and body?
- Is there concentration present?
- Would it be worth stopping for a few minutes and focusing on your breath – especially if you find your mind is all over the place?
- Are you being reflective about your mental narratives, are you checking if they are true and useful?

And remember: if you've done any of the exercises I've suggested above (such as taking a small gift when you meet your friend), you have already developed positive emotion. If you have been aware of your friend in the mindful moment, that very awareness is an act of loving-kindness and generosity. And, of course, if you have got this far in the book, you will have worked on body awareness, mindfulness of *vedana*, *citta*, and *dhamma*. You will have started to feel more connected with nature and the environment. All of this will have had an effect on your relationships with other people. Even if you haven't managed to practise any of the above, you already have feelings of well-wishing and concern for others. You are not starting from scratch. We all carry the seeds of love and awareness within us. All we are doing in meditation is cultivating those seeds, giving them attention, and letting them grow.

So this is what I suggest you practise this week:

Day 1. *Cultivating sensitivity*. First of all, establish yourself in body awareness. See if you can find a fresh approach. You might, for instance, concentrate on becoming mindful of your hands and see if you can feel each finger and knuckle, the palm, the back of the hand, and the thumb. This will have an effect on your whole body. Then take your awareness into the chest area and belly. Leave your attention there. Wait. See if you can feel any sensations. Explore them gently without pushing or trying to make yourself feel something. Especially notice the sensations around your heart. How does it feel: tight or open, heavy or light? If you can't feel very much, don't worry. You already know that 'not being able to feel very much' is a neutral *vedana*. See if you can explore that. Try to become sensitive to the sensations in your chest and around your heart. Then rest in the body awareness once again.

Day 2. *Cultivating self-love*. Start the practice as above, exploring the *vedana* in your chest. Rest your attention in the heart area and let any feelings, sensations, images, or words arise. Then, leaving your attention in your heart area, say to yourself, 'May I be well. May I be happy. May I be free from suffering. May I make progress.' Don't try to make anything happen. Just say a sentence. Pause. Feel the sensations around your heart. Then say another sentence. See if you can feel any responsiveness in the heart, whatever that might be, even if it's a non-response, or a fear response. Try to mean the sentences. Keep your awareness down in the chest and heart area so the practice doesn't become too cerebral. Keep stopping and being receptive to any shimmer of response.

Day 3. *Enriching positive memories.* Once again, establish yourself in body awareness. Then explore the sensations, first in your belly: do you need to soften and release the belly? Then in your chest: is there any sense of tightness or soreness? Then in your heart area: how does that feel? Then bring to mind a time when you felt in a positive state of mind. You might choose a time when you felt in touch with your strengths and virtues: a difficult conversation in which you remained patient and helpful, an act of generosity, or the experience of learning, feeling warm towards someone. See if you can bring the memory vividly to mind: what were you saying, thinking, feeling, doing at the time? Can you remember what you were looking at? How did your body feel? Do this for a few minutes and then rest in receptivity. Alternate between bringing positive memories to mind and then resting in non-judgemental awareness.

Day 4. *Bringing your friend to mind.* Start by briefly scanning through your body and then rest your attention in the heart area. Develop sensitivity to the inner world of sensations and feelings, even if they are not very strongly felt. Then cultivate self-love either by using sentences or by enriching memories. You might like to experiment with finding sentences that express your own desire for authentic happiness. Then, after five minutes or so, bring your friend to mind (the one you are using to develop awareness). You already have lots of experience of your friend. You have been cultivating awareness of them in your mindful moment; you have been trying to be generous, to look and listen. So see if you could bring all that to mind just now. If you have cultivated awareness of your friend in day-to-day life, you will find yourself much more able to visualize them. Notice any tremor of response. Bringing the friend to mind like this can be enough to spark off positive emotion. Or you might like to reflect, 'Just as I want to be happy, just as I want to be free from suffering... so do they.' You might use sentences such as, 'May they be happy.' Or you might just repeat their name, turning it over in your heart. Remember to stop occasionally and rest, become receptive and aware of your body and *vedana*.

Day 5. *Dark and light*. Start with body awareness and then begin to tune in to your breath. If you are feeling speedy, pay special attention to your out-breath low down in the body. If you are tired, bring the attention to the tip of your nose and concentrate on the in-breath. In this way, you are cultivating concentration. Do this for five minutes or so, and then try to reflect. Keep some of your awareness on the breath so that you remain rooted in present-tense awareness. Then bring to mind some of the difficult aspects of your life, such as problems at work, or an upsetting phone call. Imagine breathing them into your heart. Breathing them in with kindness and understanding. Then, after a few breaths, bring to mind some of the things that give your life meaning, purpose, and satisfaction; anything that you find gratifying. And, again, breathe with this. You could breathe in difficulties and breathe out pleasures and values, or you could alternate between reflecting on difficult things and then on good things. In this way, you become more fully aware of the light and the dark side of your life without over-identifying with either.

And then do the same for your friend. Think of the difficulties that they have to face and then, after a few breaths, the positive things that are happening for them, their good qualities. Come back to dwelling in non-judgemental awareness at the end.

Day 6. *Awareness of someone we are finding difficult.* As usual, start with body awareness, then sensitivity, then spending time wishing yourself well or remembering satisfying experiences. Bring to mind your friend and wish them well. You might like to bring to mind a time when you were with them and felt the strength of the friendship between you (you'll have been on the lookout for this during the week). Again, make sure that concentration is present. Pause from time to time and sit in receptive awareness. Then bring to mind the person you are finding difficult. See if you can feel your response to them directly, without self-censorship. If there is hatred present, try to feel that in the body. Notice what happens in your belly, around your heart, in your face. Soften into any uncomfortable feelings. Consciously try to see the difficult person from another perspective – not just the aspect of their behaviour that you hook on to and feel averse to. Bring to mind the whole person, strengths and shortcomings, joys and sorrows, light and dark. You might reflect, 'Are there similarities between us? Do I sometimes behave in the ways that I criticize them for?' Try to understand them more deeply. See if you can forgive them if needs be. Consciously wish them well.

Day 7. *Going beyond our kindness to ten persons.* Once again start with body awareness, then awareness of the feelings (or lack of feelings) around your heart. Then see if you can expand your circle of concern. You might try using an image. Imagine that deep within your heart there is a red flower, which, as you become more aware of it, slowly opens. Try to imagine the petals unfolding. Dwell on

the warmth of the colour. Keep softening your eyes as you do this
– when we try to 'see' things in meditation, we often screw up our
eyes. Imagine the flower opening and rays of red light spreading out
in all directions. You could imagine that, every time the ray of light
touches someone's heart, it creates another flower. This flower opens
and sends forth its own rays of light.

Bring to mind all the people around you: your daughter downstairs;
people living opposite, or those going past on the bus, flying over
in planes, walking beneath your window. Imagine rays of red light
streaming out to all these people, engendering a red flower in their
heart, which in turn sends out beams of light. Then sit for a few
minutes without trying to do anything.

Week 7 Practice Review

1. Mindful walk

Were you able to remember to do the mindful walk?

	Day 1	Day 2	Day 3	Day 4	Day 5	Day 6	Day 7
Tick/yes Cross/no							

2. Mindful moment

Were you able to bring to mind your friend in the mindful moment?

	Day 1	Day 2	Day 3	Day 4	Day 5	Day 6	Day 7
Tick/yes Cross/no							

3. Developing mindfulness of the friend and the difficult person

Were you able to become more mindful of the friend and the difficult person during the week? Did you remember to try to learn something from the difficult person? Did you look at them, listen to them? Were you able to find a way of giving to them? What, if anything, have you learnt by becoming more mindful of the friend and difficult person?

Write your reflections here

Did you notice any of your strengths and virtues in your relationship with them, such as a willingness to listen, the desire to understand and empathize, an act of generosity?

Write your reflections here

4. Meditation

How did you get on with cultivating positive emotion? Did you manage to keep checking that receptivity and concentration were also present? Were you able to reflect? And what worked best for you: the sentences, memories, reflections, or imagination?

Write your reflections here

Your relationship with other people is the key to happiness. If you can listen to people, give to them, be kind to them, you will yourself become happier. You will be freed from corrosive self-absorption and you will avoid the danger of spiritualized selfishness. All genuinely spiritual practice is concerned with helping others. When we forgive people, when we put ourselves out for them, when we overcome our irritations and resentments concerning them, we transcend ourselves. Self-transcendence is the goal of Buddhism.

Earlier on in this chapter, I suggested you consider whether you want to move towards a transcendental attitude to life with full attention, or if you want to stay with a more psychological approach. Now it's time to decide. If you want to move towards self-transcendence, then turn to the next chapter where I explore insight into the nature of reality. If you are more concerned with psychological well-being, then you might prefer to skip the next chapter and fill in the end-of-course review (see page 313). It doesn't need to be a decision for all time. You might just feel you have gone as far as you want to just now, or that this is not the time for you to move onto a more transcendental approach. That's fine. You can come back to it later. If you are not sure whether you want to cultivate a more metaphysical approach to mindfulness, then you might like to read the next chapter but not put it into practice. Approaching mindfulness from a transcendental perspective is a Buddhist orientation that goes beyond psychology. So I would suggest you put this book down now and make a decision.

Insight

The nature of reality

Have there been moments in your life when a new kind of awareness seemed to dawn on you? It might have been triggered by the experience of beauty – looking down from a spectacular mountain range, or your first sight of the Taj Mahal. It might have been in the midst of everyday life; the ordinary becoming extraordinary. It might have been after the death of a loved one, when everything seemed invested with new significance. Or it might have been in the midst of pain, like Dennis Potter, dying of cancer and looking out at the, 'whitest, frothiest, blossomest blossom that there ever could be'. This new awareness, this other dimension, can be felt as profound calm, complete understanding, grace, or wordless beauty.

I remember a man telling me about his experience of transcendence during a walk in the Peak District in England. It had rained all day. By evening, he was cold and wet. His shoulders were aching from carry-

265

ing a heavy backpack. He had been standing on the brow of a hill feeling fed up and exhausted when, turning to go, he missed his footing and fell backwards into the mud. Powerless to free himself from the weight of his backpack, he slipped down a muddy bank into a ditch of freezing rainwater. In that moment, he told me, he realized that nothing could change his predicament. Resistance was useless. He just gave up and let go. And suddenly, he felt enormously happy. The world around him, hammered by rain and battered by wind, seemed indescribably beautiful. Everything was perfect and would always be perfect. It was this that brought him to the London Buddhist Centre.

Moments of transcendence can be experienced by anyone at any time. They are characterized by increased perspective, heightened significance, and a wordless sense of meaning. For some, they are the beginning of a spiritual quest. For others, they are gradually forgotten, or explained away. How we interpret them will depend on our background and views. If we consider ourselves to be a Christian, we might feel as though we have been touched by the hand of God; if we are more of a scientific rationalist, we might put such experiences down to peak moments of well-being. As a Buddhist, I think of them as glimpses of reality, a window opening – albeit briefly – onto the true nature of things.

Buddhism affirms the existence of a wholly new way of perceiving. It is completely different from our everyday mind. This 'new dimension', as I call it, is not me. It is not even me in a very good state of mind – it goes beyond me altogether. But it is not God, or union with the Absolute, or oneness with nature. It is something else – beyond the duality of science and religion.

This new dimension is commonly experienced as irrupting into consciousness from outside the self. After all, what we call 'ourselves' is mostly a habit: a 'habit of being me'. This habitual self goes very deep indeed. It is the deep patterning of our psyche. Who we are now is a result of everything we have done, said, felt, or thought in the past. But what happens if we have experiences, transcendental experiences, that don't fit in with that, that aren't part of the network of associations and experiences that we have come to identify with and habituate to? We experience them as coming from outside the self.

Transcendental experiences resolve contradictions and unify opposites. They feel both personal and supra-personal (nothing to do with the self at all). They are characterized by the feeling that language cannot describe them. Words can only say this or that, external or internal, self or other. What makes experiences transcendental is that they cannot be pinned down by words.

Buddhism distinguishes between two levels of transcendent awareness: glimpses of reality and insight into reality. We could call our glimpses 'vision experiences'. They are authentically spiritual and are not the result of wishful thinking, self-delusion, or hysteria. They can be faked, of course, but that is another matter. Vision experiences modify the person who has them: they can be a source of inspiration and a catalyst for change, or they can boost one's confidence that there is something worth striving for. But they can also be forgotten, undervalued, or overlooked. Some people go back to their habitual way of seeing life without giving their vision experiences much thought. Some never find anyone who can affirm what has happened to them. Some dismiss them as psychological. Unfortunately, vision experiences can also be unhelpful: they can be appropriated. Any good meditation teacher knows this. They can make the person who has had them feel self-important, which is spiritually disastrous. When this happens, vision experiences can hinder someone's spiritual growth so much that it would almost be better not to have had them. I stress 'almost'. Vision experiences are valuable. If we are fortunate enough to have had them, we need to cherish them and reflect on their meaning. They are too easily dismissed as irrational fantasies. At the same time, we need to remember that the most important thing is to transform our behaviour in accordance with them.

What we really need is insight. Insight into reality is more than just a glimpse; it is a shattering confrontation. And what is shattered is our fixed sense of self. If vision experiences modify the self, insight transforms it: we are never the same again. The difference between vision experiences and insight is a matter of degree – a question of how much we can allow the vision to transform us. With insight, a wholly new awareness comes into being. It is the awareness of how things really are, a seeing beyond the limitations of self into a new dimension of consciousness: we break the habit of being me. The emotional component to insight is joy and a feeling of complete freedom. It is said to be like suddenly finding your way out of jail, or putting down a heavy load. It is a feeling of relief, lightness, rightness, and liberation. But most importantly, it is a wholly new orientation: a decisive move away from self-orientation towards reality-orientation.

The path and the goal

Insight is talked about in different ways in different Buddhist traditions, but all traditions agree that there is a point in spiritual practice when you no longer fall back, when progress is assured. This is reassuring. It means that our progress before insight is always two steps forward and one step back. This is not a personal failing; it is how things are for those of us who have not gained insight. We need to build this understanding into our expectations of life with full attention. Each time we miss a meditation, lose our patience, our car keys – every time we lose our mindfulness – we need to remember that it is all part of cultivating life with full attention.

The fact that progress is guaranteed after insight, however, doesn't mean that effort isn't involved. It means we don't have to make an effort to make an effort. After insight, our desire to change and grow, our desire to be wise, kind, courageous, mindful, and creative comes naturally to us. These qualities are what we intrinsically want. After insight we don't have to work against recalcitrant aspects of ourselves – we don't have to tell ourselves it would be better to get up and meditate rather than lie in bed and snooze. The nature of the effort changes: it becomes playful, spontaneous, and responsive. The path of mindfulness, as I have described it in this book, can take us all the way to insight. After insight has been achieved, the path is no longer needed. We become the path.

Buddhist practice is aimed at insight. Vision experiences are a prefiguration of insight. They open us up to a whole new dimension of being. But they tend to close again; we fall back into day-to-day reality. And when I talk about 'day-to-day reality', what I mean is how we interpret reality in our mind – our everyday reactions of anxiety, greed, lack of perspective, irritation, or hopelessness. So the really important thing is not so much to have vision experiences – wonderful and uplifting though they may be – but to tread the path of mindfulness, to grow as a person. Vision experiences give us a taste of the goal but our real work, spiritually speaking, is treading the path. Some people have vision experiences, some don't, or at least not very often. That's not important. The real question is: how do we gain insight?

The Buddha tells us that the best thing to reflect on, if we want to gain insight, is the fact of impermanence. He says it is this reality – this fact of universal change – that we need to bring to mind, turn over in our heart, and dwell on. We can only do this effectively if we are emotionally positive, calm, and concentrated. If we reflect on impermanence in a negative state of mind, our mood will bias and therefore distort our reflections. The experience of insight is profoundly positive and life-changing. It is not stoic acceptance that one day we are going to die. It is not a life-denying wail of, 'We're all doomed!' It is a new species of consciousness.

Buddhism teaches impermanence pragmatically and metaphysically. Pragmatically, it is saying 'things end' – youth, beauty, health, life itself, ceases. This is Buddhism as a wake-up call. It is saying: time is short, wake up to the urgency of your situation; nothing is as certain as death, and nothing as uncertain as when it will happen. Only our love, our strengths and virtues, our moments of awareness have value in the face of death.

Metaphysically speaking, Buddhism is saying something incomparably more subtle and profound. It will take insight to comprehend it. It is alerting us that things change, that there is arising and ceasing. We often like newness and novelty, such as buying clothes, receiving an unexpected gift, or the first daffodils of spring. And we like it when painful things stop, whether it is the end of a toothache, or a pneumatic drill outside our window finally being switched off.

Then again, some things arise that we don't like – a credit card bill, a headache – and some things end painfully: a love affair, or a summer holiday. All of this – good things arising, bad things ceasing, good things ceasing, bad things arising – is impermanence at work. What happens is that we over-identify with one aspect of the arising-and-ceasing nature of things.

What we cannot grasp, what we need insight to understand, is that arising and ceasing are happening at the same time. We can think of the new daffodils poking their heads above the lawn as newly arising or, in the very same moment, already ceasing. This is true of everything. All things are impermanent; all things arise and cease. It is true of this book: from the moment you picked it up, the experience of reading it was both arising and ceasing. We can't help but attach to one aspect of reality. And this means we do not see things as they really are. In this way, our good and bad moods are metaphysical. We swing from one side of reality to the other – we feel happy because a pleasant thing is arising, then we feel sad because a pleasant thing is ceasing. Insight is standing back and seeing both. Insight is the widest possible perspective on life.

If we say we like change, what we mean is we like new events arising, such as a love affair or a holiday. If we say we don't like change, we are referring to the stress of having to move house, or being made redundant. Actually, we cannot say whether we like or dislike impermanence, because impermanence embraces the whole arising-and-ceasing nature of things. It's akin to never having tasted ice cream. If someone asked us if we wanted some, we wouldn't know whether to say yes or no. We'd have to have tasted it to know. Impermanence is like that. You have to taste it to know it. And you taste it with insight and with insight alone. I stress this because people so often

271

believe that Buddhism teaches that all things end, which is misleading. If we think that the law of impermanence is saying 'all things end', we are liable to misinterpret Buddhism as pessimistic, even nihilistic – which is not at all what the Buddha is getting at. Again and again, when I try to teach about insight, I notice that people focus on losing what they love, losing their health. They only see the ending, but this is only half the story.

One Buddhist text describes insight experience very simply: 'After careful examination, understand not to discriminate, to neither accept nor reject. As anything can happen, peace will arise from within.' If we see that all things are impermanent, if we can see that arising and ceasing are what life is all the time, we start to 'hang loose' to experience. We watch things come and go without attachment. When our experience is pervaded by insight, we stop pushing away painful experience and attaching to positive experience. We see both arising and ceasing, light and dark. We are not trying to make one pleasant experience happen and stop an unpleasant experience. We're not fighting life anymore. We let go and allow anything to happen. As a result, the transcendental peace of insight, 'will naturally arise from within'.

Avoiding pessimism

Strictly speaking, Buddhism is neither optimistic nor pessimistic. Optimism is being attached to good things arising/bad things ceasing; pessimism is over-identifying with good things ceasing/bad things arising. In practice, however, treading the Buddhist path will tend to cultivate a more optimistic attitude to life. Pragmatically speaking we need to avoid pessimism and cultivate optimism. This is true if we want to be happy, and even more so if we want to cultivate insight: pessimism is counterproductive. What happens with pessimistic behaviour is that we judge the causes of bad events as permanent: 'I'll never get a girlfriend', 'The boss hates me', 'I'm no good at study.' We are thinking of bad things in terms of 'always' and 'never'. Pessimistic people will tend to find universal explanations for painful experiences – a failure in one area of life is taken as a failure in all areas of life. Pessimism is the feeling of being a failure. It is the tendency to see painful events as catastrophes. By contrast, pessimistic people find temporary explanations for good events – 'It was my lucky day' – and specific explanations for good events: 'He was just being kind.' For optimists, the case is reversed: they find permanent explanations for good events – 'I'm popular, people like me' – and temporary and specific explanations for bad ones: 'My boss is under a lot of stress at the moment.'

If you tend to find pessimistic explanations for life events, you need to cultivate optimism, otherwise you will undermine your efforts to grow and develop. The key to doing this is acknowledging and then disputing your pessimistic thoughts. You need to treat your pessimistic thoughts as if they were spoken by someone else – someone whose mission it is to undermine you and make you feel bad. As the psychologist Martin Seligman points out, 'The most convincing way of disputing a negative belief is to show yourself that it is factually incorrect.'[50] So check whether your belief is true. Look out for distortions and exaggerations. Consciously find temporary and specific explanations for bad events, and enduring universal explanations for good ones. If pessimism is an issue for you, you need to concentrate on working with inner narratives as I have recommended in Week 4. And you need to be particularly careful not to over-focus on the 'good things ceasing/bad things arising' aspect of impermanence.

Cultivating insight

Specific factors need to be present for insight to arise. These factors are clarity; integration; sustained concentration/absorption; positive emotion; faith (or confidence-trust); and single-minded dedication. But remember, this is not a recipe: these factors do not guarantee insight. It is much more mysterious than that. The path of mindfulness does not lead to insight in the same way that a road leads to the supermarket. Insight is not just another step, even the last step, on the path. Insight isn't just a very mindful state of mind, however desirable that might be. There is a discontinuity. If the path of full attention is the map we have been following all these weeks, then insight is off the map. On the final phase of the journey, we go alone. All we can do is follow the map, tread the path of mindfulness. And we do this by cultivating the qualities I have listed below. Let's briefly look at each of them.

Clarity

First of all, there needs to be a developed sense of clarity about what spiritual life consists in. Even though the goal is said to be beyond words, we need to use words and concepts to approach it. We cannot hope to gain insight if we are confused about what insight is and how it might be cultivated. This may well mean studying Buddhist teachings, especially with the aid of someone who is more experienced than ourselves. Clarifying our thinking is an integral part of spiritual life. The capacity to reflect fruitfully, truthfully, and searchingly is indispensable. Part of this means exploring our views, assumptions and beliefs in the way I suggested in Week 4 (page 111). Intellectual clarity – which is poles apart from mere cleverness – is an essential part of life with full attention.

Integration

Clarity of thought is not possible without psychological integration. Thought needs to be complete: it needs to be a physical, emotional, and intuitive experience as much as a cognitive one. Without it, you are likely to end up with an alienated intellect, split off from emotion, sympathy, sensitivity, and nuance. Without full self-awareness, thinking will tend towards rationalisation or disguised autobiography. Psychological integration means becoming more and more rounded as a person. It entails coming to terms with oneself: strengths as well as weaknesses, light as well as dark. So often we are not really a self at all – we are a bundle of different selves competing for supremacy. We want opposing things, we often change our minds, or we don't know what we want. We need to become a whole person so we can attend to our experience in a complete way. This is psychological integration.

Sustained concentration/absorption

We can only become deeply concentrated if we are psychologically integrated. We need to be, a whole person wholly attending. Sustained awareness – the capacity to rest happily in calm and one-pointed concentration – is a necessary prerequisite to insight. We cannot attend to our experience if we are preoccupied by the future, worrying about the past, or, 'distracted from distraction by distraction'[51] as T.S. Eliot so memorably put it. I have already suggested that we live in an attention-deficit society. The modern urban environment is constantly competing for our attention, trying to manipulate it. This has the effect of forcing us to the surface of ourselves. We need to be able to remain aware of our experience without distraction if we are to gain insight. Deep experiences are primarily concentrated experiences. The royal road to concentration is meditation. An important way of sustaining our meditation is going away on retreats from time to time, to get away from the competing demands of the attention-deficit society. Even a weekend retreat can have a beneficial effect. It can provide new approaches to meditation and re-inspire our practice.

Positive emotion

Full absorption is not possible without positive emotion; psychological integration is not possible without positive emotion; and clarity of thought is not possible without positive emotion. We are aiming to live more and more fully and vividly, with ever-increasing positivity and awareness. If we try to reflect on impermanence in a bad state of mind, our reflections will be prejudiced by our negativity. Emotional negativity pushes us away from reality, just as it isolates us from other people. It is counterproductive. It blights our creativity, stifles our imagination, and poisons our perceptions. Without positive emotion, we will not be big enough to allow insight to change us; we will not be able to let it in. Insight is not possible without a very high degree of emotional receptivity. Negative emotion tends to be constrictive, fearful, and defensive. Positive emotions are broadening and expansive; they nurture receptivity and the willingness to learn and change. The key to developing positive emotion is cultivating our virtues and strengths, as we saw in Week 5.

Faith or confidence-trust

But we need something more: we need faith. The Sanskrit word for 'faith' is *sraddha*. We have no straightforward translation for this word in English. It is usually translated as 'faith', but for many people this has negative connotations of blind belief and superstition (both of which are inimical to Buddhism). Faith, or 'confidence-trust', is the capacity within the self to intuit what lies beyond the self. It acts like a mirror; it is within the contents of mind but it reflects something of what lies beyond the contents of mind. *Sraddha* is confidence-trust in the other dimension I talked about at the beginning of this chapter. In Buddhism, this quality – this intuitive sense of there being more to life beyond the everyday mind – is considered of the greatest possible importance. In all the different traditions of Buddhist psychology, it is enumerated first; and it is said to be present in any genuinely positive emotion.

We could think of faith as being similar to the aesthetic sense. When we organize a room, we instinctively arrange things in a pleasing fashion – we might put flowers on the mantelpiece and then decide they look better on the coffee table. We feel pleased and satisfied when the aesthetic feels right. But we would find it hard to explain what 'feeling right' means. Faith is like this. We have an instinct for what is morally good, meaningful and true, and we feel an intuitive sense of attraction towards those things. Faith, or *sraddha*, is the ability to perceive value and want to move towards it. Like the aesthetic sense, it can be developed, refined, and clarified.

Sraddha is also associated with respect and admiration for those who exemplify strengths and virtues. It is the capacity to look up to people. It is the willingness to be receptive, to emulate men and women who are more developed than we are. Traditionally, *sraddha* has three aspects:

A deep conviction of what is real. This is the conviction that Truth (with a capital T) exists, and that existence has meaning. It is a feeling of confidence. Compared with insight, our day-to-day, conventional way of seeing the world is less real. It is mirage-like, insubstantial, and painful. So this aspect of faith is about conviction – intellectual and emotional – that 'the other dimension' exists and that insight is attainable.

Lucidity as to what has value. This is a state of contentment, clarity, and serenity. Once we feel convinced about what is truly important in life, once we know what is real, we experience a special sort of calm. It is the calm that arises from knowing our priorities. In moments of faith, conflict and indecision fall away. We are left with a wonderful sense of certainty. Life becomes simpler.

Longing for what is possible. Because of our conviction in the truth of the teachings, because of our new sense of confidence – and the serenity that goes with that – we long to be united with what we value. This longing is an expression of our sense that spiritual experience is possible; that the path of full attention really does lead to meaning and transcendence, and that these things are intensely desirable. We feel that we can ourselves make progress.[52]

When I teach at the London Buddhist Centre, I find the quality most people lack is faith. It is as if we have become too sophisticated, sceptical, and rationalistic. Unfortunately, I cannot teach *sraddha*. It is not something anyone can learn, at least not in the sense in which you can learn history or geometry. You have to discover *sraddha* in the depths of your own heart, or catch it from those who embody it. Buddhist tradition highlights two main ways of catching *sraddha*. One is the study of Buddhism, and the other is taking part in Buddhist ritual, thereby cultivating a sense of devotion. I would add any experience that opens you up to the feeling that there is more to life, such as the arts at their best or the appreciation of nature.

Single-minded dedication

This is really an intensification of *sraddha*, which is an experience of being established in confidence-trust. It is the sum total of clarity, integration, concentration, emotional positivity, and faith. It is a clear sense of existential priorities, an emotional commitment to life with full attention. Most importantly, it is the desire to put spiritual practice right at the very centre of your life.

The law of impermanence applies to everything: from universes and planets to insects and atoms. But most importantly, it applies to ourselves. Insight into impermanence is fundamentally about letting go of our belief that we are a fixed and separate self. It is the letting go of our labels and roles, our predictions, assumptions, and expectations. It is seeing and recognizing that there is nothing fixed or permanent about us. To be able to let go in this way, we need faith that there is something to let go into. We need to have faith that we are not letting go into nothingness and annihilation. Insight is spiritual death. We die to our self-conceptualizations, to talking ourselves into being. There is no place to fix onto, nothing stable to grasp. On one side of insight, there is our constant attempt to create a fixed sense of self, pushing things away that threaten it, desiring things that seem to enhance it, and fearing to lose it. On the other side of insight, there is wordless freedom, fearlessness, openness, and compassion. We need to turn our attention to how we travel from one side of insight to the other.

Mind itself

Have you started to notice the difference between the contents of your experience and being aware/the awareness of it? When we are aware, we feel richer, calmer, and more alive than we do when we're just caught up in what's going on. Having tried to practise life with full attention, you will know by now how easy it is to get caught up in experience – how easy it is to be stuck in a 'sticky thought', and how hard it is to be aware. Part of the reason we get so caught up with what's happening is because our automatic pilot mode is useful for day-to-day living, but it is also because we habitually over-identify with the contents of our mind.

We habitually assume that the contents of experience –what we think about, imagine, remember, daydream, wish for, and feel – are who we are. Most of the time, we are locked into the contents of our mind. This will tend to mean that when we like the contents of our experience, we will think life is going well, and when we don't like them, we will think that things are going badly, or that our life is going wrong. And yet, if we look more closely at the contents of our experience, we notice that they are constantly changing; they are never fixed and secure. There is nothing we can call 'me'. In fact, much of the time, we have little or no control over thoughts, feelings, memories, and associations, they come of their own accord.

The Buddhist tradition is trying to get us to realize that, because the contents of experience are constantly changing, there can be no fixed and permanent self. What we are doing most of the time is becoming attached to roles and labels: we are a doctor or a mother, a talkative extrovert or a sympathetic listener. We might even think of ourselves as Buddhists. All of this, of course, is of practical usefulness and may even be valuable on the path of full attention, but it is provisional. We shouldn't over-identify with it or take our labels too seriously. They are not who we truly are. If we over-invest in our roles and labels, we will cause ourselves suffering. Modern psychology calls our self-labelling the 'conceptualized self'. We have fixed onto a concept: a mother, a doctor, a talkative person, and so on. But if we don't get caught up in the contents of our mind, there is still this sense of awareness, of attention. Awareness is not part of the contents of our mind. It is not a thought, a desire, or an attitude, but just awareness. Despite the fact that awareness is not part of the contents of experience, we can nevertheless rest in it. We can just watch the contents of our mind changing, shifting, and reforming. We can try to identify with this capacity to observe and be aware, rather than getting caught up in what we are aware of. We can start to identify with mind itself.

Eighth practice week

This week I will be asking you to reflect on impermanence in your day-to-day life, and to cultivate insight during meditation. Before I do this, however, I want to stress once again that I would not advise you to think in terms of cultivating insight unless you are fairly well established in positive emotion and happy concentration. If, during the week of reflection, you start to feel fearful or depressed, then you need to go back a stage. You need to cultivate the path, starting with body awareness. Insight practice assumes that you are a happy, healthy human, and that you are already emotionally robust, positive, and aware.

There is no shortcut to insight. Without the preceding factors of concentration and love, you will not be able to move towards reality effectively. What often happens, when people try to cultivate insight, is that they realize they have not yet developed enough awareness, faith, and receptivity. This is worth discovering. We need to embrace a more realistic view of ourselves, become less self-deceiving, and more honest. We need to go back to developing our strengths and virtues. After all, it is our strengths and virtues that really matter. The test of spiritual 'attainment' is in how we live our life and how we treat other people. If our day-to-day life has not yet been transformed, then we still have work to do – whatever experiences, transcendental or otherwise, we feel we have had. At the same time, a clear understanding that there is an attainable transcendental goal can be a way of accessing inspiration and the motivation to practise.

With all this in mind, let's turn to how we could usefully reflect on impermanence during our concluding week of life with full attention.

How to reflect

'Pay urgent attention to impermanence,'[53] is how one Buddhist text puts it. But how do we cultivate the life-changing feelings and attitudes that a real understanding of impermanence evokes? Unfortunately the idea of change, and even the phrase, 'all things are impermanent', can easily become a banality, an unthinking truism. It doesn't change our behaviour in any way. So the important question is: how do we give our reflections experiential and emotional bite?

Unfortunately, our capacity to manipulate ideas can be a hindrance. We can be very good with words and concepts. But this is not the same as reflection. When we reflect on the nature of reality, we are trying to cultivate wisdom, not intellectual sophistication. So the first thing we need to do is establish ourselves in the states of mind I have indicated above: clarity, psychological integration, concentration, positive emotion, faith, and dedication. Only then will our reflections take us to insight. Meanwhile, we have to be very wary of thinking we understand the law of impermanence. We need to make it an absolute rule to avoid banalities and spiritual platitudes. What we need is a state of mind that is deeply curious about the true nature of experience.

Usually we need to cultivate both the path and the goal: the four spheres of mindfulness and insight. We need a steady focus; we need calm and emotional positivity; but we also need to reflect on our human situation. After all, time is short; the moment of death is approaching. So let's look at ways in which we can integrate reflection into our day-to-day lives. I have included a range of suggestions; take up the two or three that strike you most. You can come back to the others once the course is finished. Here they are:

1. *Find a phrase that works for you.* For example, when you're looking after your new baby daughter, noticing an ugly scratch on your car, or visiting your elderly aunt, say to yourself, 'all things are impermanent', or, 'this, too, will change'. It's not a question of thinking about the phrase, just bring it to mind. Abraham Lincoln liked the saying, 'And this, too, shall pass away'. He said of it, 'How chastening in the hour of pride! How consoling in the depths of affliction.' So bring to mind, 'this, too, will pass away' in the moment of success or dejection, elation or pain. Let it be there like a musical refrain, coming back again and again to remind you of the true nature of things.

2. *Imagine it is already over.* For example, I practise something like this when I'm looking forward to something, whether it is going on holiday or settling down to a good book on a train. I tell myself it is already over. I imagine that I'm back at work, or that I have arrived at my destination. When we want something, we tend to cling to it and try to squeeze enjoyment out of it, as we have seen. If we think of it as changing, passing – already ceasing – we can hang loose to it, and appreciate it more in the moment.

3. *Or we could try to see that everything that happens to us is teaching the truth of impermanence.* This requires intensified mindfulness. We are trying to realize the truth of impermanence within the concrete specifics of the moment. This means marrying perception with reflection, catching the experience of change as it happens and letting its significance penetrate our awareness. It might be the first leaves of autumn, watching your daughter go off to live in her first home away from you, or being reunited with an old school friend. Mindfulness is noticing what's really going on, because what's really going on is change.

Of course, the most important teacher of impermanence is you: your face, skin, and hair. Nothing teaches the emotional reality of change quite like your own body. So notice your body ageing – your naked body in the bathroom mirror, the fact that you can no longer run up the four flights of stairs or climb over a fence. And notice other people's bodies – the first time you realize your mother is too old to walk very far, how your father gets out of breath when you go hill walking. All you need to do to gain insight is to notice change so deeply that you really notice: a broken cup, a child's exercise book, and a photograph of your glory days have the power to change your life, so long as you can give them your full attention.

4. *Notice how you tend to expect things not to change.* I taught this at a class I was leading one glorious August evening. Afterwards, when we came out, it was pouring with rain. Someone said, 'Well! I never expected it to rain.' We tend to assume that things will carry on being much the same as they are now.

Of course, the main thing we expect not to change is ourselves. I recently met a young woman who had struggled with depression since she was a teenager. She told me how, when she was feeling particularly low, she saw a group of girls eating in a restaurant, larking around, and generally having a good time. And she thought, 'I'm never going to be like that ever again.' For her, the thought of not changing was a nightmare. We can easily think that our dark moods will go on forever; our hard times will carry on unchanged. But the reverse is also true. We can believe that our run of luck will last; that our 'on top of the world' feeling is here to stay. And we feel crushed when we trip and fall. We expect our moods, our states of mind, not to change.

5. *See if you can keep a note in your journal of the times when you experience change as a good thing, and times when you experience it as bad.* The disappointment you feel when your lover walks out on you, when the car breaks down, and when the local shop runs out of fresh croissants arises because all things change. The excitement you feel as you set off on a skiing holiday, the frisson of pleasure you experience when pulling on a brand new jumper, or when test-driving a car is also because of change.

So, when you feel happy, elated, or excitable, see if change plays a part in that. It usually does. Perhaps something 'good' has come into being, or something 'bad' has gone out of being? When you feel low, disappointed, or unhappy; again see if it is to do with impermanence. See if you are reacting to the fact of change. After all, all we need to do to be unhappy is wish for something that goes against the nature of reality, such as wishing the past had been different, or that we had been different.

6. *Another way of doing this goes back to what I explored in Week 4 about prediction.* We often experience a background sense of existential insecurity because we know that nothing is permanent and secure. Because of this, reality threatens us and our sense of self. So we try to protect ourselves. We try to predict the future: the pleasure we might get, the irritation we might avoid. So see if you can notice when something that you feel should happen or will happen doesn't happen: you are overlooked for promotion; the Valentine card fails to drop onto your mat. Notice how upset you get when your positive predictions fail.

Then become aware of when your negative predictions turn out wrong. Perhaps you are going to meet a friend who has sent you a nasty email. How do you feel when they turn up with an apology and an embarrassed smile? Or those times when you get anxious about something that in the end turns out to be just fine. See what happens when something you think won't happen does happen: the delight of an unexpected gift, or the sun suddenly shining in the middle of a dreary February day. Isn't that just another experience of impermanence?

7. *See arising in ceasing, and ceasing in arising.* For example, Shelley's poem, 'Ode to the West Wind' ends with the famous line, 'O Wind, if Winter comes, can Spring be far behind?'[54] This is seeing arising in ceasing. Shelley's poem is set in autumn. Autumn can be seen as the end of summer or as the precursor to spring. Autumn is summer

ceasing and spring beginning. It is both at the same time.
So try to see arising in ceasing, and ceasing in arising. Nightfall is both today ceasing and tomorrow arising.

I have especially noticed this with my baby niece. How each new arising – starting to walk, being able to say new words – is also a kind of loss, a ceasing. So when she started to walk, walking was arising, but it was also the end of her motoring around on her knees (which she could do at great speed!) Her learning to talk was also the ceasing of her incredible babble – questions, exclamations, explanations – but in some utterly foreign toddler language. It is as though life is an arc from birth to death, and the nearer we are to one side of the arc – the very young and the very old – the more we notice the fact of change.

Death and rebirth

But what about death? Isn't death ceasing without arising? And isn't it the fact of death that makes us focus so exclusively on the ceasing dimension of impermanence?

I don't know what happens when we die. I know what the Buddhist tradition tells me, and I have some faith in that, but I do not know. And, what's more to the point, neither do you. No one knows. What we have are beliefs. Our current belief is that death marks the point of complete annihilation and extinction. The Buddha denied this. He thought it was narrow-minded, mistaken, and ugly. From the Buddha's point of view, the assumption that life is one headlong rush to death – our crude materialism – must have seemed particularly smug and complacent: a belief masquerading as a fact. But then he also denied any kind of eternal life. Nihilism (death as complete extinction)

287

and eternalism (belief in the afterlife, heaven, or hell) are usually presented as our only two options. The Buddha said there was a third: a middle way above and between the extremes of nihilism and eternalism. The Buddha taught rebirth, which is not the same thing as reincarnation. Reincarnation implies a self that is reincarnated, whereas Buddhism denies that there is any such thing as a really existent, non-changing self. From a Buddhist perspective, self is an 'epistemological error', a misreading of experience. All we have is constant change, with nothing to which we can attach the label 'me' or 'mine'. Reincarnation is a subtle form of eternalism: the belief that we go on forever, slipping ourselves into new bodies, like suits of clothes, with each new birth.

We can think of rebirth as being like waves rolling onto the shore. Each wave appears to travel across the sea and then crash onto the beach. But it is not like that. What we are seeing is oscillating molecules that give the appearance of a wave moving towards the shore. There is a causal connection between the wave on the sea and the ripple splashing around our ankles, but it is not the same water. This is what rebirth is saying: *there is continuance* but no thing continues. A traditional simile is of a fire lighting another fire. Just as one fire dies out, a spark flies off and lights another fire. It is a different fire, a different stack of wood, and yet there is some vital connection.

Until we have gained insight into impermanence, we will tend to believe in subtle forms of either nihilism or eternalism. The middle way is only accessible in the depths of profound contemplation. Meanwhile, all we can do is admit to our lack of knowledge and bow before the ineluctable mystery of death.

The significance of the pragmatic approach to impermanence – that things end – is in its shock value. The fact of death reminds us that we are alive now. At best, the awareness of death puts life into perspective. It makes us sit up and take notice. It makes us want to live deeply. It weans us off trivial chit-chat, bad television, and pointless arguments. We realize time is short and that it is absurd to waste it. So bring death to mind. Remember to watch your state of mind. If you start feeling fearful and anxious, then do not use this reflection.

I find this reflection useful when things go wrong, or when things around me are dreary or grim. It's a good reflection to bring to mind if you find yourself wanting something to end, or if you're bored. So if your train is delayed, you get a puncture on your way back from work, or if you're waiting for your bag to appear on the carousel in an airport terminal, these are all good times to remember that this moment is all you have, that you are alive now. So try to consciously find something to appreciate: bring your attention into your body; decide to live with full attention now by remembering that it will not last.

The mindful walk

You have been trying to cultivate mindfulness in your daily walk for seven weeks now. I imagine that you will have been through quite a few different phases in relationship to it. Perhaps you were keen at first and did it every day, but then your inspiration waned. Perhaps you stopped for a while, got bored or irritated, or skipped the parts of this book where I recommend ways of approaching it. Or maybe, occasionally, you really noticed the difference that practising mindfulness can make, and became inspired. In this concluding week, see whether you can resurrect the mindful walk if you have let it slip. If you only managed to do it once or twice a week, see if you can do it three or four times. If you have managed to keep up the mindful walk most days, then well done, keep at it!

Make sure the elements needed for insight to arise are present, or at least not glaringly absent. Check you have clarity about what you are trying to do and why. Look for an integrated approach, not just a 'bright idea' about mindfulness being good for you. See if concentration, positive emotion, and faith are present. Try to be mindful of what you need to cultivate in any particular practice. If you feel especially scattered, for instance, cultivate concentration (you might like to go back to using the counting technique, see page 67). Perhaps you feel doubtful about the value of the mindful walk. Perhaps you are in a bad mood. Once again, feel and recognize the state of mind you are in.

Start your walk by cultivating the path of mindfulness, then see if you can bring in a reflection on impermanence. You might try one of the reflections above, or you could try the following:

Arising and ceasing are both ways of thinking about experience. They can never adequately describe experience. They are both partial. The nature of reality is beyond conceptualization, beyond categorization. All experience, when it is lived with full attention, is beyond description.

Notice what arises externally: the sight of someone standing at an open window, the sound of a bird rustling in the undergrowth, or the sight of a child wearing a striped cardigan. You might say to yourself the word, 'arising'. Notice what arises internally: the memory of a pleasant chat with a friend, the panicky feeling of missing the bus. Notice what ceases externally: a cloud covering the sun and the street going dark, the child disappearing into the station with her mother. And internally: the angry thoughts you were having, which are finally quietening down. Again, you might say to yourself the word, 'ceasing'. Try to be open to arising and ceasing without attaching to either. 'As anything can happen, peace will arise from within.'

The mindful moment

All the phases of engagement and non-engagement will probably apply to the mindful moment as they did to the mindful walk. Perhaps you decided not to practise the mindful moment, or perhaps you decided to practise the breathing space instead. As I have said, it is easy to be mindful but difficult to remember to be mindful. Again, in this concluding week of the course, see if you can intensify your practice. Give it one last try.

But remember, just as with the mindful walk or the daily meditations, you can always come back to the mindful moment after you have finished the course. You don't need to think that you have missed anything. You can look at the end-of-week reviews and see what you didn't manage to do and come back to that, or you can mark the meditations you missed and try them out after the course ends. Mindfulness is a lifetime's practice; there are plenty of suggestions in this book that would be worth coming back to.

That said, see if you can use the mindful moment to establish the four spheres of mindfulness, then bring in one of the reflections on impermanence. For this last week, I would like to emphasize dropping back into *vedana* and bringing your reflections to mind in that context.

291

We tend to react to thoughts as if what we are thinking about is actually happening: a fact of experience rather than a fantasy about it. So, if we are having angry thoughts whilst we are having our daily shower, our mind and body will go into the same kind of state – physical tension, emotional aversion, mental irritation – as if the argument is actually happening in the here and now. One of the great values of mindfulness is noticing this and tuning in to what is actually going on, rather than being lost in a virtual world of thought and fantasy. See if you can notice this and can come back to actual experience: the warmth of the shower jet over your shoulders, the faraway rumble of a distant train. Bring your reflections on impermanence into that here-and-now context. And remember: in every aspect of your experience, what is really going on is change.

This week's meditations

You have been developing awareness throughout this course so that you can dwell whole-heartedly on direct experience. If you can sustain that awareness deeply enough, insight is more likely to arise. I stress 'more likely' because there is always a mysterious X factor. Insight is a mystical experience. It cannot be achieved through philosophical speculation or willpower. All we can do is create the conditions, external and internal, for insight to arise. 'The rest', as T. S. Eliot puts it, 'is not our business.'[55]

Essential to Buddhism, to life with full attention, is the fact that mind has depth. We easily forget this. We forget that words and concepts have a different value depending on how wholehearted and receptive we are. We might have experienced this reading poetry. In our best readings, the words become emotionally compelling and transformative. The same is true of meditation. If we can drop beneath our repetitive mental chatter, our planning and ruminating, the weight of our reflections changes. Meditation is the way to deepen our mind, to brighten our mind, and to integrate our energies. In concentrated meditation, our mind becomes richer and more coherent. Thought and emotion, which so often pull us in different directions, fuse and inform one another. Energy, usually tied up in internal conflict, is liberated. We feel alert and peaceful. In this state of mind, a new world of reality can be revealed.

As we have seen, we gain insight by reflecting on reality in our day-to-day life. We try to notice that what we are experiencing is impermanence. We consciously link the events that happen to us with that universal truth. Having reflected outside meditation, we try to gain insight inside meditation. To do this, we need to deepen the mind. We need a subtle and powerful 'tool' to experience a subtle and powerful reality. The mind needs to be concentrated, energized, relaxed, and emotionally positive.

Once we are established in this kind of positive and focused state, we try to cultivate what in Sanskrit is called the *animitta samadhi*. The word *samadhi* is sometimes translated as 'meditation', but it would be best to think of it as 'meditation proper'. *Samadhi* is the state of full absorption. It is a super-conscious mental state – in as much as it lies far beyond our usual range of positive experience. It is a more completely satisfying and fulfilling state of mind than we had ever dreamed possible. Compared to *samadhi*, our normal day-to-day mind is inflexible, distracted, and shot through with pain. *Samadhi* is the 'goal' of meditation. It is characterized by calm, one-pointed concentration, pleasure, and complete psychophysical integration; it is the whole person wholly attending.

293

The word *animitta* means, 'beyond characteristics, imageless, con-cept-free, direct'. It means seeing directly, unmediated by words and concepts. It is the nature of reality flashing upon us. *Animitta* is the true nature of things without our instinctive tendency to step back from experience, explain it to ourselves, and therefore fix and con-trol it. The *animitta samadhi* is supra-rational; it is not a jettisoning of reason – which is always regressive – but a going beyond reason. Words and thoughts can only ever talk about things, or fixed experi-ences. But there are no 'things' in experience. There is only change. There is not even something called change. Where is 'change' in our experience? Change is just another abstract universal concept.

You could think of the *animitta samadhi* as being like watching clouds. Imagine you are lying on your back on a warm afternoon, completely happy and relaxed. You play at giving the cloud-shapes names: a cat, a lizard, a ship, a face. But gradually, as you become more absorbed, you begin to notice that just as you name one shape, it changes into another. Gradually you stop seeing different shapes at all; you just see changing, shifting, reforming. You stop trying to fix things and name things. Nothing is stationary, so there is nothing that you can label. In the *animitta samadhi*, all concepts fall away. There is just wordless delight and unutterable freedom.

In your final week of meditation (at least as far as our course goes), I want to help guide you towards insight into the nature of reality. I suggest, if you possibly can, that you set aside a little more time to meditate. If you have been doing 15 minutes, then do 20. If you have managed 20, then try 30, and so on... My experience, especial-ly in the midst of my busy life in London, is that it takes me quite a while to settle down and change gear from doing mode to relishing mode. As we move towards the *animitta samadhi*, we can meaningfully talk of full attention. Full attention is the *animitta samadhi*, because change is all there is.

Day 1. *Getting closer to the true nature of experience.* Start, as usual, by scanning through your body. Then notice *vedana*: the general feeling tone of your experience. Move on to mindfulness of *citta*: are you aware of any internal narratives? What teaching (*dhamma*) do you need to bring to mind? Then, to develop concentration, count from one to ten at the end of each out-breath. If you find yourself beginning to feel more concentrated, let go of the counting and try to experience the breath more clearly and directly. The breath is not an idea or image, neither does it have any words attached to it like 'breath' or 'breathing'. Notice how much of you is talking about experience in your head, rather than actually experiencing it. We use the words 'in-breath' rather than feeling the unique sensations of this particular in-breath. See if you can let go of describing the experience in your mind and try to have a more direct experience of the changing sensations. If you find you start to become distracted, or if you are not feeling very happy or calm, go back to cultivating the path.

Day 2. *Suffuse yourself with loving-kindness.* Again, work your way through the spheres of mindfulness: body, *vedana* (feeling tone), *citta* (internal narratives), and *dhammas* (bringing the appropriate teaching to mind). Then bring your attention to the feelings around your heart. Notice the *vedana* in your heart area. Leave your attention in that area, wait, and feel. Then find a way of cultivating loving-kindness. You might say to yourself, 'May I be well, may I be happy...' Or you could use an image, perhaps a flower opening, petal by petal, in your heart. Or you could bring to mind people you feel grateful to, or five recent events that you have appreciated and valued. You will need to explore different approaches. See what works for you in this particular meditation. At the same time, give each approach you choose the chance to have an effect. Don't keep chopping and changing. See if you can find a way of kindling love and well-wishing. You will not be able to move towards insight without it.

Day 3. *Embracing the nature of experience.* Once again, establish yourself in body awareness. Then, without forcing, see if you can develop concentration. Use the counting technique and keep coming back to your breath in a gentle, relaxed, and non-judgemental way. With a concentrated mind, try to develop clarity about the real nature of breathing. The breath, like everything else in the universe, is constantly changing. There is no breath as abstract category; there is just each unique breathing moment. So, in this meditation, try to get closer and closer to the changing nature of the breath. Notice what is 'actual experience' and what is 'thoughts about experience', such as internal commentary, subtle sub-vocalization. See if you can let go of predicting the next in- or out-breath. Notice how, even on this micro-level, we want to predict experience, and how this tendency subtly controls what happens to us. See if you can let go of holding onto the breath, and see if you can feel the naked experience of what is actually happening in present-tense awareness. Let the breath blow through you like a breeze through leaves. Again, if you find that you are getting distracted, go back to cultivating concentration. If you are starting to over-focus, if you are getting tight and overly willed, relax and cultivate loving-kindness. You cannot push your way to insight. At the end of the practice, just sit quietly for a minute or two.

Day 4. *Loving and letting go.* Today, spend some time developing body awareness. Notice any tensions in the body and see if you can embrace them with kindly awareness. See if you can relax into discomfort. Then feel your breath in your body, see if you can relax around the breath more and more. Allow your body to become completely still. Then take your attention to the sensations around your heart, your chest, and your belly. With your awareness focused on the subtle *vedana* around those areas, say to yourself, 'May I be well, may I be happy.' Keeping your attention around your heart, bring a friend to mind and say to yourself, 'May they be happy...' Then direct your loving-kindness to someone you don't know very well, and to a person you're having difficulties with; then gradually include more and more people in your loving-kindness. Then, once again, relax. Let go. Just sit for five or 10 minutes without trying to do anything or not do anything.

Day 5. *The changing mind.* Once again, start with body awareness. After a while move on to *vedana* (how the body feels). Then to what state of mind you are in (*citta*). Find a way of responding creatively to whatever is happening in your mind (*dhamma*). Then turn your attention to the gentle massaging feeling of the breath. Pay special attention to what happens when you get distracted. Often, as I have said, we 'wake up into thought'. At one moment, we're attending to our breath; at the next, we wake up into some sort of narrative. Notice how these stories fascinate and obsess us, how we take them very seriously indeed. Especially notice how the mind sticks to them, how we give the stories we tell ourselves the status of permanent facts. We do this despite knowing that the mind is so very changeable, that soon enough we'll be stuck in some other distraction. Notice how we take our ephemeral worries, desires, angers, and wishes literally, as if they constitute our real identity. And try to notice that we can be completely absorbed in an internal narrative at one moment, and then have forgotten it the next. We are then left feeling that we've been somewhere else, but we can't remember where. Try to notice that we believe in each 'obsession' despite the fact that they are always changing. Thoughts are even more transitory than the body or the breath. At the end of the meditation, just sit in a state of pure receptivity.

Day 6. *Appreciating life as it happens.* Life is change. To appreciate life is to appreciate change. In this meditation, try to cultivate a warm and appreciative awareness. See if you can tune in to the changing nature of your experience, especially your breath. It is like looking at clouds in the sky, watching them change. The more you become absorbed in the experience, the less you can talk about it. Words fix things. In the same way, the closer you get to the experience of breathing, the more vividly you feel it, the less it is possible to label, predict, name, or describe it. If we get very concentrated, we will indeed find ourselves entering a wordless realm of pure flow, indescribable change, a world of pure appreciation. So you could think in terms of becoming more and more intimate with the breath. Describing our experience, though often very useful, means stepping back from it. Words and thoughts are abstractions, whereas all we actually experience are unique particulars. In this meditation, try to get closer and closer to what is actually happening, not to what you think is happening. Then, once again, sit completely still and receptive at the end.

Day 7. *Experiencing change.* In today's meditation, focus on an area of discomfort in the body. Be careful not to overdo this. If you find the feeling becomes too unpleasant, shift your attention to a more comfortable area. When you are easier again, gently bring your attention back to an uncomfortable physical sensation. Take your mind into the unpleasant sensation and see if you can feel it without describing it, or reacting to it with aversion. It might be helpful to try to feel your breath in that area. See if you can become aware of how the mind tightens around discomfort. Notice how we get caught in stories about it, such as, 'I don't like it, I wish it would go away.' Take a kindly attention into the discomfort. See if you can let go of the stories, if you can experience the bare sensations without even the idea of 'unpleasant'. Then see if you can notice how these bare sensations are constantly changing. See if you can feel change actually happening, not as an idea but as a lived experience. Then rest in broad body awareness before you conclude the meditation.

The Buddhist tradition talks of three great phases in spiritual life: ethics, meditation, and wisdom. Each phase needs to be fully established before the next one can arise. So, if we look at the path in these terms, we cultivate positive emotion first. We do this by exercising our strengths and virtues and by practising the five precepts and the four forces (see pages 164 and 169). Without establishing ourselves in positive emotion, we will have a troubled conscience, which will disrupt our meditation. Cultivating our virtues, channelling our energies into actions that are growthful, connecting, and spiritually fruitful is the foundation of meditation. It means that when we sit to meditate, we will have an energized and purified mind. There will be nothing pulling us away. We won't be anxious about a particular situation, wanting something, or feeling averse to something. Having established ourselves in positive emotion through ethical practice, we will be able to become fully absorbed in meditation. In the same way, once meditation (*samadhi*) is fully established, wisdom can dawn upon us.

Of course, this is an ideal picture of the spiritual path. It is probably never quite like this in practice. Most of us will need to cultivate all three stages at the same time. You can't really practise ethics for a few years and then begin sitting for meditation. Trying to meditate – learning how to relax, cultivating loving-kindness, developing a steady focus – is, in effect, working on the ethical aspect of the path. What the three phases do make clear is that, if we are having trouble with one phase, it means the previous phase has not been established and we need to go back to it. Many people, for instance, take up meditation only to realize that they have a lot of work to do in terms of becoming more emotionally positive and robust. They need to go back, so to speak, to cultivating strengths and virtues. Of course, we might find that our ethical life is far from perfect, in which case we go back to generosity. We can always give. The whole of the path of full attention can open up from there.

Week 8 Practice Review

1. Mindful walk

Were you able to remember to do the mindful walk?

	Day 1	Day 2	Day 3	Day 4	Day 5	Day 6	Day 7
Tick/yes Cross/no							

2. Mindful moment

Were you able to remember to practise the mindful moment?

	Day 1	Day 2	Day 3	Day 4	Day 5	Day 6	Day 7
Tick/yes Cross/no							

3: Reflection

Did you take up one or two of the reflections I suggested above? Which reflections did you use? What effect, if any, did they have?

Write your reflections here

4: Meditation

Were you able to cultivate insight in your meditations? If you found yourself insufficiently concentrated or not very emotionally positive, were you willing to go back to cultivating the path of mindfulness? If not, why not? Did cultivating insight in your meditation capture your interest? Did you find yourself more motivated? Or did it all feel rather abstract and cold?

Write about your meditation experience here

5: Thinking about what next

At the end of the next, concluding, chapter, I will be asking you to review how the course went, and I will be asking you to think about where you want to take your practice of mindfulness from here. So you might start thinking about that now. What have you gained from doing the course (or even from reading the book)? What could you do next?

Write your reflections here

When you practise insight reflection, you may well notice that the stage of meditation has not been fully established. You might notice that you are not sufficiently concentrated and emotionally positive. So you need to go back. You need to cultivate meditation. This means renouncing pride. Pride is one of the main obstacles on the path of human growth and fulfilment. Paradoxically, by admitting you need to go back to an earlier stage, by realizing that you still have a lot to learn, you are, in effect, becoming more genuinely mature. So you might decide to start going to a meditation class, or to try attending a longer retreat. Being overly concerned with insight as a goal is counter-productive. By doing so, we are making insight into something we can have – even something that makes us rather special – and this completely misses the point. As T.S. Eliot put it, 'The only wisdom we can hope to attain is the wisdom of humility: humility is endless.'[56]

Conclusion

For the sake of all beings

We want to be happy. Every thought, word, or deed expresses that desire. Even our destructive patterns and repetitive thoughts are distorted and counter-productive attempts to be happy. We need to educate ourselves in the fine art of happiness. We need to make the distinction between ephemeral pleasures – the taste of chocolate, the feeling of a hot bath, the thrill of riding a motorbike – and the deeper causes of joy. Psychologists make the distinction between pleasures and gratifications. Because we habituate to them so quickly, our pleasures are usually short-lived. We are trapped in the law of diminishing returns. Experiencing gratifications, by contrast, means exercising our strengths and virtues. This often requires us to develop a skill – such as meditation, or playing the piano – and involves facing and overcoming challenges. At best, when something gratifies us, it absorbs us completely: time seems to stop and the sense of self is temporarily suspended. Psychologists call this state 'flow'. When we are deeply absorbed (in, say, hill walking, meditating, or listening to a friend), it is as though we dissolve. Nothing is left over. We don't even feel emotion, even positive emotion. In 'flow-experiences' we have left self, and what we feel about self, behind.

Trying to become happy, however, can become self-defeating. It can lead to self-preoccupation on the one hand, and instrumentalism on the other. Self-preoccupation is essentially a negative state of mind, whatever excuses – spiritual or otherwise – we make for it. Authen-

tic happiness is authentic precisely because of its lack of self-preoccupation. When we are absorbed in meaningful activity, we don't
step back from the experience to think about whether it's making us
happy or not. I see this with my two year-old niece. If I ask her how
she feels when she's absorbed in playing with her Lego set, she might
say, 'fine' to get rid of me – my question is beside the point.

Then there is the problem of instrumentalism. If we focus too nar-
rowly on trying to be happy, whatever we do is done for the sake of
something else, not for its own sake. And of course, this changes
the value of our actions. There is a world of difference between
meditating because we find it intrinsically worthwhile, and meditating because it's good for us. If we are generous because we believe it
will help us to get into a better frame of mind, the spiritual value of
our generosity – its impact on giver and receiver – will be reduced.
Genuinely positive emotion is an end in itself. It is not instrumental.
If we are kind or forgiving in order to aid our self-development, we
are, in effect, being less than kind, and less than forgiving. It is still
worth doing. It will still have an effect, but we need to move beyond
this kind of self-orientation if our practice is to have lasting value.

A Buddhist motivation for life with full attention is expressed in the
beautiful phrase, 'for the benefit of all beings'. This is the true spirit
of mindfulness and the very core of all genuinely spiritual practice.
Personal happiness is the by-product of altruism, just as it is the by-
product of absorption in meaningful activity. The more we practise
mindfulness for the sake of others, the more the effects of our practice will change us. Doing it for ourselves – at least after the early
stages of the path – is counter-productive. From the Buddhist point
of view, we need to devote ourselves to the welfare of all beings. To
do this effectively, we need to be wise and mindful. We cannot help

others if we are in a bad mood, stressed out, anxious, or self-obsessed. We need to be on our best form: aware, happy, emotionally positive, creative, expansive, and playful. The culmination of the path of mindfulness is enlightened compassion for all beings. It is not a wonderful experience meant for ourselves alone!

Life with full attention – at a glance

Day-to-day mindfulness. Mindfulness of the 'small things' of everyday life that cause us so much frustration if we don't attend to them. We need to develop sustaining routines and reduce input. We need to cultivate mastery – the capacity to get things done, to rise to a challenge, to overcome obstacles, and to develop skills that is so foundational to positive emotion. (See page 27)

Mindfulness of the body and its movements. Drawing our attention into the body, using the body as an anchor for our awareness, and trying to live more fully from the body. Body awareness is an antidote to stress and toxic mind. (See page 47)

Vedana. We experience every sight, sound, feeling, physical sensation, thought, or memory as pleasant, unpleasant, or somewhere in between. We need to savour pleasant experiences, whilst resisting the urge to repeat them and thereby vitiate them. We need to embrace painful experiences, resisting the temptation to push them away, which makes them worse. Mindfulness of *vedana* creates the all-important gap between the raw sensations of experience and our actions. (See page 75)

Citta. We need to be much more mindful of our internal narratives – we need to question them, dispute negative predictions and assumptions, and notice whether we are mistaking a thought for a fact. In mindfulness of *citta*, we are trying to see how we often mistake our interpretations of experience for the facts of experience. (See page 111)

Dhammas – making wise choices. If we want to be happy, we need to cultivate positive emotion. We develop positive emotion about the past by valuing good memories and not overemphasizing bad ones, and by cultivating gratitude and forgiveness. We cultivate positive emotion about the future by examining and disputing pessimistic assumptions. And we create positive emotion in the present by practising mindfulness, and cultivating strengths and virtues. (See page 147)

Objects, art, and nature. We need to cultivate the appreciative mode of being, as opposed to the acquisitive mode. The more materialistic we are, the less happy we become. We need to cultivate a love of nature for its own sake; explore the arts as practice of wise attention; and become more mindful of the environment. (See page 189)

Mindfulness of others. We need to become mindful of our parents, partner, family, friends, people we don't like, and people we feel neutral about. Self-absorption is one of the major symptoms of depression. The antidote to self-preoccupation is other people. Focus on generosity. Develop trusting friendships. Happy people have more friends than unhappy people, they involve themselves in more group activities, and they are more altruistic. (See page 223)

Insight. Insight is the point of irreversibility on the spiritual path. The way to gain insight is two-fold: reflecting on impermanence in your day-to-day life, and direct awareness of reality through meditation. Insight is the culmination of the path. It requires intellectual clarity, integration, sustained concentration, positive emotion, faith, and single-minded dedication. In other words, to gain insight we need all the qualities we have developed on the path. (See page 265)

Final words

You have set off on a journey of discovery, but there is still much to learn. So spend some time thinking about what you have gained from doing the course. I have created an end-of-course review to guide you in your reflections (see page 313). Think about how you could continue cultivating mindfulness. What supports do you need? What lifestyle changes might you need to make? And remember: mindfulness is not something you learn and then unthinkingly do, like riding a bike. It is a lifetime's exploration. The end of this book is only the beginning...

As soon as you aspire to something, such as practising mindfulness, you open yourself up to failure. When we practise mindfulness, we are cultivating a sense of mastery (developing a skill, rising to a challenge, working through obstacles) – and failure, or at least the feeling of failure, is intrinsic to mastery. Failure is an important part of the learning process. There is no learning without it. So it's important to recognize its importance, and not to take it too seriously and therefore lose heart. Keep remembering that mindfulness is easy to practise, but that it is hard to remember to practise.

One last piece of advice: do something that confirms and strengthens your aspirations to continue cultivating life with full attention. You might buy a book on Buddhism, attend a meditation class, or book on a retreat. Best of all would be to go on a retreat. A retreat is a period of intensified mindfulness in good conditions, a quiet countryside environment where your efforts to be mindful are more likely to bear fruit. You can find out about retreats in the UK on www.goingonretreat.com. Do it now.

Closing ritual

To the degree that this book has resonated with your values (to the degree that you have put it into practice), to that degree you will be more aware, emotionally positive, and happier. In the Buddhist tradition, we call this 'merit', which is a kind of psychic bank account containing awareness and positivity. Having done this course (or read this book), you now have more in the bank. You need to give it away. From a Buddhist point of view, you need to share the merits you have gained with all beings.

So you might want to conclude this course by performing a simple ritual. First of all, fill in your end-of-course review (see page 313). Then spend some time flicking through the book. After reminding yourself of what you have been learning during the last few weeks, sit in front of your shrine and meditate. You might like to bring to mind how you have benefited from mindfulness. Then say these two simple verses, which come from an ancient Buddhist text and express the desire to share the merit you have gained with all beings:

Transference of merits

May the merit gained
In my acting thus
Go to the alleviation of the suffering of all beings.
My personality throughout my existences,
My possessions,
And my merit in all three ways,
I give up without regard to myself
For the benefit of all beings.

Just as the earth and other elements
Are serviceable in many ways
To the infinite number of beings
Inhabiting limitless space;
So may I become
That which maintains all beings
Situated throughout space,
So long as all have not attained
To peace.

End of course Review

Congratulations! You have finished this intensive course in full attention. However much you did, or didn't do – even if you only managed to read the book without putting much of it into practice – you should congratulate yourself. Considering all the other things you could have been doing with your time, spending time focusing on mindfulness and authentic happiness is very positive indeed. I am interested in hearing how you got on with the course. So if you have access to the internet, you can fill in this end-of-course review online at www.windhorsepublications.com/lwfa. A copy will be sent to me.

1: Reviewing your aims

You may remember that at the beginning of this book (page 24) I asked you to write down three aims for the course. Now it's time to look back at those aims and grade yourself on how well you feel you have done. Before you do that, however, remember that your aims might have changed during the course. Or you might feel that the aims you gave yourself were limited, or were not based on enough self-awareness. Were they realistic? Were they your real aims? Perhaps you have gained things from the course that you didn't expect? Write down how you feel about them now that you have come to the end of the book.

Write your reflections here

2: Reviewing the mindful walk

On a scale of one to ten, how often did you manage to practise the mindful walk? Ten means that you were able to do the mindful walk every day. One means you didn't do the mindful walk at all.

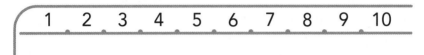

3: Reviewing the mindful moment

On a scale of one to ten, how often did you manage to practise the mindful moment? Ten means that you were able to practise the mindful moment every day. One means you didn't do the mindful moment at all.

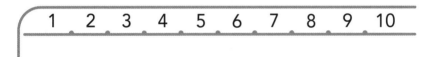

4: Reviewing the meditation

On a scale of one to ten, how often did you manage to meditate? Ten means every day. One means never.

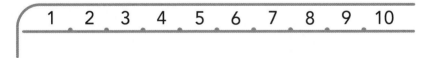

5: Five things you have learned

I hope you have found this book practical, thought-provoking, and inspiring. At the same time, I'm aware that you are bound to have forgotten much of it. There's nothing wrong with that. So see if you can jot down five things you have learned. They might be things that were new to you, that opened up a fresh perspective, or they might be things you learned about yourself. Alternatively, you could write down whatever felt emotionally significant in doing the course, what struck you as being valuable. Don't look back through your journal, or at your end-of-week reviews, just jot five things down now:

	What I have learnt	How I learnt it, or further comments
1		
2		
3		
4		
5		

6: What next?

Having evaluated your aims, reviewed the practices, and brought to mind five things you have learned, you can start to think about where you want to go from here. You might choose to make some resolutions – remembering that resolutions to do something tend to work better than resolutions not to do something. You might resolve to go on retreat, or go swimming twice a week, or become a vegetarian.

A good way of doing this is to write yourself a postcard. Find one that you respond to, if possible with an inspiring image that relates to your ideals. Write it to yourself. Remind yourself what you have learnt and how you intend to carry on practising mindfulness. Be specific: 'I am going to do an online meditation course' or, 'I am going to phone my mindfulness buddy every fortnight to check in about meditation.' Then give the postcard to a friend or family member. Ask them to put a note in their diary, and to post it to you sometime in the next two months (I suggest in no less than a month, and no more than two months). Ask them not to tell you when they plan to send it.

One day you will receive a postcard from yourself reminding you of what you have gained from reading this book, and how you hope to carry on developing life with full attention.

Appendix 1

Mindfulness of Breathing

Below is a very short introduction to the Mindfulness of Breathing meditation. This practice is taught at all Triratna centres. You can also learn it online at www.wildmind.org. For more information about Triratna centres, visit www.thebuddhistcentre.org.

Stage one: *Counting after each out-breath*

Breathe in, breathe out – silently count, 'one'.
Breathe in, breathe out – silently count, 'two'.
Breathe in, breathe out – silently count, 'three'...
and so on up to 10, then start again at one.

If you lose count, or if you go beyond the count – don't worry, that's what tends to happen – just start again at one. Even if you only get to three, if you get distracted, start again at one.

Stage two: *Counting before each in-breath*

Silently count, 'one' – breathe in, breathe out.
Silently count, 'two' – breathe in, breathe out.
Silently count, 'three' – breathe in, breathe out...
and so on up to 10, then start again at one.

If you lose count or go beyond the count, go back to one. You don't need to remember which number you got distracted at. Just notice that you have become distracted, then come back to one. Remember not to get frustrated if you lose count.

Stage three: *Drop the counting and watch the whole breathing process*

Feel the breath coming in and going out of the body. If you get distracted, gently and patiently come back to the experience of breathing.

Stage four: *Notice where the breath first enters and last leaves the body*

This is usually just inside the nostrils or on the top lip. Don't follow the whole breath anymore; just watch this particular, subtle sensation inside the nostrils. Again, if you get distracted, come back to the breath at this point in the body.

Try and let go of success and failure. When we do something – cook a meal or draw a picture – we can easily become overly concerned with success and failure. What we are trying to do is explore and learn. Being too concerned about success blocks progress.

Don't force the breath. You have been breathing quite naturally up to now. You don't need to breathe in a special 'spiritual' way. Just notice the breath you experience in the moment. If your breath is audible, you may well be forcing it.

Try to feel the breath. This practice is about feeling the breath. Breathing is a sensuous experience; it is not an idea or an image. Also try and keep the counting short, light, and crisp. We are cultivating mindfulness of breathing, not counting!

Appendix 2

Metta Bhavana

Below is a very short introduction to the Metta Bhavana meditation (cultivation of loving-kindness). This practice is taught at all Triratna centres. You can also learn it online at www.wildmind.org.

Stage one: *Self*

Start by cultivating feelings of loving-kindness towards yourself. You can do this by using an image or a memory, or by bringing to mind things you have appreciated. Or you can silently say to yourself, 'May I be well. May I be happy. May I be free from suffering. May I make progress.' Then, mindful of the sensations around your heart, see if you can feel any response. And don't worry if you can't!

Stage two: *Friend*

Bring to mind a close friend. Try to see them in your mind's eye. Then, in the ways I suggested above, wish them well.

The Buddhist tradition suggests you choose a friend who is:

- about the same age as you – i.e. not very much older or younger.

- not someone you feel sexually attracted to.

- someone who is still alive.

- someone of the same sex.

This keeps the practice simple. Again, say to yourself, 'May they be well. May they be happy', and so forth.

Stage three: *Neutral person*

Choose someone you neither like nor dislike, someone you feel neutral towards. The person you choose needs to be someone you see fairly often – perhaps at work – but for whom you don't have particularly strong feelings. In the same way, wish them well.

Stage four: *Difficult person*

This is someone you dislike, either at the moment or generally speaking. It could be someone you get irritated by, or someone you find annoying. Buddhist tradition suggests that you:

Don't choose someone you really loathe, as this would probably counteract any positive emotion you have developed;
choose someone you actually know, not a public figure you love to hate.

Try to let go of antipathy and wish them well.

Stage five: *All four people, then all beings*

Bring to mind all four people: yourself, your friend, the neutral person, and the difficult person. Imagine feeling loving-kindness equally for all four. Then cultivate loving-kindness for all beings. You might want to do this geographically, spreading out from where you are now, or in terms of different states of being – the old and the young; those being born, those who are dying; people who are happy, those who are unhappy. Then wish them well.

Appendix 3

Meditation Posture

Below is a short introduction to how to sit for meditation. It is better to learn about meditation posture from an experienced meditation teacher. You can find out about your nearest Triratna centre at www.thebuddhistcentre.org or learn more on www.wildmind.org.

When you sit for meditation you need to be:

• *Upright and relaxed* – not ramrod straight, but not slouching. Your head needs to be upright and balanced on top of your spine – not falling forward or tipping backward. Your hands need to be supported by a cushion or blanket.

• *Comfortable and stable*. It is much more important to be comfortable in meditation than to sit in a cross-legged posture. You also need to be stable. Your knees need to be firmly on the floor (if you sit on the floor) or flat on the floor if you sit in a chair. Many people use a blanket to keep warm while they meditate, as well as to support the hands.

Different postures you can try

Sitting in a chair
I recommend this posture if you are new to meditation. Find a good, hard-backed chair, not a floppy armchair. Your feet need to be flat on the floor. If your feet do not reach the floor you need to put something under your feet – such as a telephone directory or a cushion – to bring the floor up to your feet. You might try putting a paperback book under each back leg of the chair, as this will tip more of your weight forward – though this is not essential. A thin cushion should support your lower back, and your hands should rest in your lap on

a thin cushion or blanket. Again, your back should be straight and your head balanced on your spine. Many people are resistant to sitting on a chair because they don't think it looks 'spiritual' – however I know very experienced meditators who sit in a chair.

Sitting astride the cushions

To sit in this posture you really need special meditation cushions. You can find out where to buy these at the web addresses above. You will need to have a meditation mat or a blanket to sit on. You need enough cushions so you can easily sit upright without having to work the body – at least two or three cushions depending on your height and the size of the cushions. Sit astride the cushions with your knees firmly on the floor. If you find your feet or ankles are uncomfortable in this posture, make sure you have good thick mats or blankets to sit on and let your toes poke over the edge of them – this will take pressure off your ankles. A cushion or two should support your hands, so that you can completely let go of your arms. Your hands should rest together, one hand cupping the other. Don't interlock your fingers. Again your back should be upright and your head nicely balanced on the top of your spine.

Sitting cross-legged

I do not recommend this posture unless you do yoga and have very flexible hips. Most people I teach are not able to sit like this. If you sit in this posture incorrectly, you are likely to damage your back and knees. People often want to sit in this posture because they associate it with meditation, but you should only do so if an experienced teacher, who is willing to check whether you are sitting correctly, has taught you. You should sit with one ankle in front of the other (not crossed as we tend to in the west) and both knees should rest firmly on the floor. If your knees don't touch the floor, you can put a thin cushion underneath one of them. If you need a cushion under both knees, then you are not flexible enough to sit in this posture. A cushion must support your hands; otherwise you can damage your shoulders.

References

1. Potter, D., *Seeing the Blossom;* from *Two Interviews, a Lecture and a Story*; Faber, London 1994 p.5.
2. Kabat-Zinn, J., *Full Catastrophe Living,* Piakus, New York. 1990.
3. Beckett, S., *Worstward Ho,* Grove Press, New York, 1980.
4. Loy, D., *Consciouness Comodified : The Attention-Deficit Society* . See, *Money, Sex, War, Karma, Wisdom,* USA, 2008.
5. Dissanayake, E., *What is Art For?* University Washington Press, USA, 2002 p 172.
6. Fodor, J., (2007, May) *Headaches Have Themselves.* LRB, Vol 29, no 10.
7. www.breathworks-mindfulness.co.uk.
8. www.medicine.wisc.edu/mainweb.
9. www.guardian.co.uk/uk/2007/sep/06/lifeandhealth.health.
10. Segal, Williams & Teasdale. *Mindfulness-Based Cognitive Therapy for Depression,* The Guilford Press, New York, 2002, p 68 - 72.
11. Auden, W.H., Musée des Beaux-Arts' in *Selected Poems,* Faber, USA, 1979, p.79.
12. Auden, W.H., *The Sea and the Mirror, part III, Caliban to Audience,* Faber, USA, 1979, p.163.
13. Tsogyal, Y., 'Canto 38' in *Life and Liberation of Padmasambhava: The Advice and Admonition to the Revealers of the Treasures,* Cazadero, California, USA, Dharma Publishing, 1978, p, 239.
14. www.news.bbc.co.uk/1/hi/uk/3146781.stm.
    www.news.bbc.co.uk/1/hi/in_depth/uk/2001/trouble_in_the_air/1448843.stm.
    www.timesonline.co.uk/tol/news/uk/article396826.ece.addictions.co.uk.
15. Oliver, J., *Affluenza: How to Be Successful and Stay Sane,* Vermilion, Australia, 2007.
16. *The Depression Report,* LSE, London, 2006.
17. Stevens, W., *The Auroras of Autumn, Complete Poems,* Faber, USA, 2006, p.368.
18. Moore, M., *The Poems of Marianne Moore,* edited by Grace Schulman, Faber, London, 2003, p.258.
19. Lessing, D., *Nobel Prize speech* 2007.
20. As quoted by Andrew O'Hagan in *Living it,* London Review of Books January 24th 2008.
21. Segal, Williams & Teasdale, *Mindfulness-Based Cognitive Therapy for Depression,* The Guilford Press, New York, 2002.
22. Seligman, M.E.P., *Authentic Happiness,* Nicholas Brealey Publishing, UK, 2003, p.8.
23. *Ibid, p.39.*
24. *Dhammapada,* translated by Sangharakshita, Windhorse Publications, Birmingham, 2001, p.14.
25. This is 4th step of the 12 Step recovery programme of Alcoholics Anonymous (AA).
26. Seligman, M.E.P., *Authentic Happiness,* Nicholas Brealey Publishing, UK, 2003, p.226.
27. Segal, Williams & Teasdale, *Mindfulness-Based Cognitive Therapy for Depression,* The Guilford Press, New York, 2002, p.241.
28. Bishop, E., *Sandpiper* from *Complete Poems,* Chatto and Windus, UK, 2004, p.131.
29. Heaney, S., *The Redress of Poetry,* Faber, UK, 1995. p.176.

30. www.pet-educationresources.co.uk.
31. www.sixwise.com/newsletters/05/02/01/the_health_benefits_of_house_plants_including_the_top_nine_healthiest_plants.htm.
32. Kant, I., *Critique of Judgment*, sect. 29 as quoted by Will Durant in *The Story of Philosophy*, Simon & Schuster, New York, 1952, p.279.
33. Wordsworth, W., *Sonnet: The World is Too Much With Us*, The Collected Poems of William Wordsworth, Wordsworth Editions Limited, UK, 1994.
34. Heaney, S., *The Redress of Poetry*, Faber, UK, 1995.
35. *Udāna – Inspired Utterance of the Buddha:* 1.10, Bahiya, Buddhist Publication Society, Kandy, Sri Lanka, 1990.
36. Cohen, D., *Finding a Joyful Life in the Heart of Pain*; Shambala Publications, 2000.
37. www.climatecrisis.net.
38. Padel, R., *The Poem and the Journey: and Sixty Poems to Read Along the Way*, Chatto and Windus, London, 2007.
39. Barnes, S., *How to be a Bad Bird Watcher, Simon Barnes,* Short Books, USA, 2005 p. 132 -150.
40. *xxxix Samyutta Nikaya 45: Maggasamyutta,* in Bhikku Bodhi (trans), *The Connected Dicourses of the Buddha:* A translation of the *Samyutta Nikaya,* Wisdom Publications, Boston 2000, p.1524.
41. Seligman, M.E.P., *Authentic Happiness,* Nicholas Brealey Publishing, UK, 2003, page 70 - 75.
42. Burnside, J., *A Lie about My Father,* Jonathan Cape, London, 2006, p.252.
43. Sangharakshita, *Wisdom Beyond Words,* Windhorse Publications, Birmingham, 2000, p.83.
44. Aristotle, *Ethics*, Book Eight *The Kinds of Friendship,* Penguin Classics, London, 1976.
45. Sangharakshita, *A Stream of Stars*, Windhorse Publications, Birmingham, 1998, p.46.
46. Seligman, M.E.P., *Authentic Happiness,* Nicholas Brealey Publishing, UK, 2003, p.79 - 81.
47. Seligman, M.E.P., *Authentic Happiness,* Nicholas Brealey Publishing, UK, 2003, p.81
48. Freud, S., as quoted by Bryan Magee in *The Philosophy of Schopenhauer*, Oxford, Oxford University Press, 1983 p.217).
49. Heaney, S., *The Government of the Tongue*, Faber, London, 1998.
50. Seligman, M.E.P., *Authentic Happiness,* Nicholas Brealey Publishing, UK, 2003, p.95.
51. Eliot, T.S., *Four Quartets: Burnt Norton,* Faber, London, 1959, p.16.
52. Sangharakshita, *Know Your Mind*, Windhorse Publications, Birmingham, 1993, p.119.
53. Tsogyal, Y., 'Canto 103' in *Life and Liberation of Padmasambhava: The Advice and Admonition to the Revealers of the Treasures,* USA, Dharma Publishing, 1978, p. 688.
54. Shelley, P.B., *Selected Poetry,* Penguin Poetry Library, Penguin, London, 1956, p.160
55. Eliot, T.S., *Four Quartets: East Coker,* Faber, London, 1959, p.27.
56. *Ibid.*, p.23.

About Windhorse Publications

Windhorse Publications is a Buddhist charitable company based in the UK. We place great emphasis on producing books of high quality that are accessible and relevant to those interested in Buddhism at whatever level. We are the main publisher of the works of Sangharakshita, the founder of the Triratna Buddhist Order and Community. Our books draw on the whole range of the Buddhist tradition, including translations of traditional texts, commentaries, books that make links with contemporary culture and ways of life, biographies of Buddhists, and works on meditation.

As a not-for-profit enterprise, we ensure that all surplus income is invested in new books and improved production methods, to better communicate Buddhism in the 21st Century. We welcome donations to help us continue our work – to find out more, go to www.windhorsepublications.com.

The Windhorse is a mythical animal that flies over the earth carrying on its back three precious jewels, bringing these invaluable gifts to all humanity: the Buddha (the 'awakened one') his teaching, and the community of all his followers.

Windhorse Publications
169 Mill Road
Cambridge CB1 3AN
UK
info@windhorsepublications.com

Perseus Distribution
210 American Drive
Jackson TN 38301
USA

Windhorse Books
PO Box 574
Newtown NSW 2042
Australia

The Triratna Buddhist Community

Windhorse Publications is a part of the Triratna Buddhist Community, which has more than sixty centres on five continents. Through these centres, members of the Triratna Buddhist Order offer classes in meditation and Buddhism, from an introductory to deeper levels of commitment. Bodywork classes such as yoga, Tai chi, and massage are also taught at many Triratna centres. Members of the Triratna community run retreat centres around the world, and the Karuna Trust, a UK fundraising charity that supports social welfare projects in the slums and villages of South Asia.

Many Triratna centres have residential spiritual communities and ethical Right Livelihood businesses associated with them. Arts activities are encouraged too, as is the development of strong bonds of friendship between people who share the same ideals. In this way Triratna is developing a unique approach to Buddhism, not simply as a set of techniques, but as a creatively directed way of life for people living in the modern world.

If you would like more information about Triratna please visit www.thebuddhistcentre.com or write to:

London Buddhist Centre
51 Roman Road
London E2 0HU
UK

Aryaloka
14 Heartwood Circle
Newmarket NH 03857
USA

Sydney Buddhist Centre
24 Enmore Road
Sydney NSW 2042
Australia

Also available

Buddhism: Tools for Living Your Life

by Vajragupta

Listed as a top title in The Bookseller's Religion Preview 2007, *Buddhism: Tools for Living Your Life* is a guide for those seeking a meaningful spiritual path in busy – and often hectic – lives. An experienced teacher of Buddhism and meditation, Vajragupta provides clear explanations of the main Buddhist teachings, as well as a variety of exercises designed to help readers develop or deepen their practice.

"Appealing, readable, and practical...as directly relevant to modern life as it is comprehensive and rigorous." *Tricycle: The Buddhist Review*, 2007.

ISBN 9781 899579 74 7
£11.99 / $18.95 / €17.95
192 pages